STUDENT'S BOOK
A2

CITIZEN Z

Herbert Puchta,
Jeff Stranks, Peter Lewis-Jones

W0297018

CAMBRIDGE
UNIVERSITY PRESS

CONTENTS

LIFE SKILLS / LITERATURE	THINK	SKILLS	
Life skills: Empathy	**Values:** Taking care of yourself **Self-esteem:** Why it's good to have a hobby	**Reading** **Writing** **Listening**	Quiz: Do you take good care of yourself? Blog: So what do you do in your free time? Photostory: Olivia's new hobby Writing about routines Conversations about hobbies
Literature *Magic Jane* by Roz Warren	**Values:** Fashion and clothes **Train to Think:** Exploring numbers	**Reading** **Writing** **Listening**	Soap opera: Shopping Webchat: How not to spend money Culture: World markets An informal email to say what you're doing Shop dialogues
Life skills: Saying sorry	**Values:** Food and health **Self-esteem:** Being happy	**Reading** **Writing** **Listening**	Article: Food facts or food fiction? Blog: My brother's cooking Photostory: The picnic A paragraph about your favourite or least favourite meal Ordering food in a café
Literature *Holes* by Louis Sacher	**Values:** TV families **Train to Think:** Making inferences	**Reading** **Writing** **Listening**	Article: TV Families Article: The swimming pool heroes Culture: Around the world on Children's Day An invitation Why my family drive me mad
Life skills: Not making judgements	**Values:** Community spirit **Self-esteem:** Feeling safe	**Reading** **Writing** **Listening**	Article: The LEGO House Blog: Dad gets it right! (finally) Photostory: Hey, look at that guy! A blog post and a summary of a text What is home?
Literature *Great Expectations* by Charles Dickens	**Values:** Friendship and loyalty **Train to Think:** Making decisions	**Reading** **Writing** **Listening**	Article: Together Article: How we met Culture: Friendship myths An apology A story about Cristiano Ronaldo
Life skills: Solving problems	**Values:** Caring for people and the environment **Self-esteem:** Classroom rules	**Reading** **Writing** **Listening**	Article: Just because I didn't want to take a bath Website: Product reviews Photostory: The treasure hunt A paragraph about housework Radio programme – advice for young inventors
Literature *The Bone Cage* by Angie Abdou	**Values:** Trying, winning and losing **Train to Think:** Sequencing	**Reading** **Writing** **Listening**	Article: If you don't give up, you can't fail Web forum: Your favourite sports fails! Culture: The Olympic Games – the good and the not-so-good An article about a sporting event Teens talking about sport
Life skills: Helping our community	**Values:** Valuing our world **Self-esteem:** Being brave is ...	**Reading** **Writing** **Listening**	Article: An amazing place Article: Could you live there? Photostory: The competition An email about a place in the article Interview with a Kalahari bushman
Literature *The Phantom of the Opera* by Gaston Leroux	**Values:** Appreciating other cultures **Train to Think:** Problem solving	**Reading** **Writing** **Listening**	Blogs: Alice's world, The life of Brian Letters to a newspaper: Our town: what's wrong and what can we do about it? Culture: Ghost towns around the world An informal email A conversation between people arranging to go out
Life skills: Dealing with negative feelings	**Values:** Exercise and health **Self-esteem:** Getting help	**Reading** **Writing** **Listening**	Article: Changing bodies Webchats: Crazy things that parents say to their kids Photostory: The phone call A phone message Dialogues about physical problems
Literature *From a railway carriage* by Robert Louis Stevenson	**Values:** Travel broadens the mind **Train to Think:** Exploring differences	**Reading** **Writing** **Listening**	Blog: The non-stop traveller Interview: The taxi driver Culture: Hard journeys for schoolchildren An essay about someone you admire A traveller talking to children at his old school

Welcome

A ALL ABOUT ME

Personal information

1 🔊 **1.02** Rewrite the dialogue in the correct order. Listen and check.

ALEX: Hi. I'm Alex.
ALEX: I'm fourteen. How about you?
ALEX: The United States.
ALEX: Hello, Fabiola. Where are you from?
FABIOLA: Me? I'm fourteen, too.
FABIOLA: I'm from Italy. And you?
FABIOLA: Hi, Alex. My name's Fabiola.
FABIOLA: Cool! How old are you, Alex?

2 🔊 **1.03** Complete the dialogue with the phrases in the list. Listen and check.

are | meet | this | too

ALEX: Fabiola – ¹... is my friend Ravi.
RAVI: Hi, Fabiola. Nice to ²... you.
FABIOLA: Nice to meet you, ³... , Ravi. And this is my friend: her name's Patrizia.
FABIOLA: Hi, guys. How ⁴... you? I'm Patrizia. Patrizia Lambertucci.

3 Imagine you are a famous person. Work in pairs, then groups.

1 Tell your partner who you are.
2 Introduce your partner to others in the group.

Hi, I'm Ryan Gosling.

Hello, my name's Rihanna. And this is my friend, Barack Obama.

Nationalities and *be*

4 Complete the names of the countries. Rewrite and add the consonants.

1 ... ... a ... i ...

2 ... ... e a ... ... i ... a i ...

3 the ... e ... ... er- ... a ... ...

4 ... o ... o ... ... i a

5 I ... a ... ...

6 ... e ... i ... o

7 ... u ... ... i a

8 ... ... a i ...

9 ... u ... ... e ...

10 the U ... i ... e ... ... a ... e ...

11 A ... ... e ... ... i ... a

12 ... e ... ... i u ...

0 He's Brazilian.

1 She's …

2 …

3 …

4 …

5 …

6 …

7 …

8 …

9 …

5 What nationality are the people? Write the sentences.

6 **1.04** Complete the dialogue using the correct forms of the *verb* to *be*. Then listen and check.

FABIOLA: So, Ravi – where [0]are you from?

RAVI: Me? I [1]… from Britain. Alex here [2]… from the United States, but I [3]… British.

PATRIZIA: But, [4]… your name British?

RAVI: Oh, good question. Well, no it [5]… . My parents [6]… from India and so my name [7]… from India too. But my sister Anita and I were both born here, so we [8]… 100% British.

FABIOLA: That [9]… cool. I think your name [10]… really nice.

RAVI: Thank you! And you two, [11]… you both Italian?

PATRIZIA: That [12]… right. But we [13]… not from the same city. I [14]… from Milan and Fabiola [15]… from Bari. We [16]… students at the language school here.

Names and addresses

7 **1.05** Ravi phones for a taxi. Listen and complete the information.

COOPER'S TAXIS

Booking form

Taxi for	1
Going to	2
Pick up at	3 am/pm
From	4 Street
Number of passengers	5

8 **1.06** Now listen to a phone call. Correct each of these sentences.

0 Alex phones Patrizia.
No – Patrizia phones Alex.

1 They met last Wednesday.
2 There's a party at Patrizia's place next Friday.
3 The party starts at seven thirty.
4 Patrizia lives at 134 Markam Avenue.
5 Her phone number is 0788 224 234.

B WHAT'S THAT?

Things in the classroom

1 Look at the pictures. Match the item numbers to each word.

1 door

board | book | CD | chair | desk | floor
pen | pencil | ruler | window | door | notebook

Prepositions of place

2 Look at the pictures. Complete each sentence with a preposition from the list (you will use some words more than once).

on | between | in | under | in front of | behind

0 The notebook is on the chair.
1 The pencil is ... the floor.
2 The pencil is ... the chair.
3 The book is ... the desk.
4 The pen is ... the book.
5 The ruler is ... the notebook.
6 The board is ... the door and the window.
7 The book is ... the pen.

Classroom language

3 1.07 Complete each sentence with a word from the list. Listen and check.

ask | again | mean | hand | don't
page | me | say | spell | understand

1 Excuse ... .
2 Can I ... a question, please?
3 Can you say that ... , please?
4 How do you ... *cansado* in English?
5 Open your books at ... 21.
6 Put your ... up if you know the answer.
7 Sorry, I ... know.
8 Sorry, I don't ... .
9 What does this word ... ?
10 Excuse me. How do you ... that word? Is it T-I-R-E-D or T-Y-R-E-D?

4 1.08 Use one of the sentences in Exercise 3 to complete each mini-dialogue. Listen and check.

1 TEACHER: Good morning, everyone.
STUDENTS: Good morning.
TEACHER: OK. Let's start. ...

2 TEACHER: So, Michael, what's the answer?
MICHAEL: ...
TEACHER: That's OK. What about you, Susie?

3 STUDENT: ... , Mrs McFarlane. I've got a question.
TEACHER: Yes, what is it?
STUDENT: ... : 'fascinating'?
TEACHER: It means: 'very, very interesting'.

5 1.09 Put the lines in order to make a dialogue. Listen and check.

1 A How do you think you spell the word 'enough'?

A: E-N-O-U-G-H.
A: No, that's completely wrong!
A: How do you think you spell the word 'enough'?
A: No, that's really how you spell it.
B: OK, how do you spell it, then?
B: Oh. Let me think. Is it E-N-U-F-F?
B: You're kidding!

6 Work in pairs. Think of a word in English. Can your partner spell it?

How do you spell 'awful'?

A-W-F-U-L.

That's right.

Object pronouns

7 Complete each sentence with the correct pronoun.

0 She's a good teacher – we like *her* a lot.
1 My pens are under your desk. Can you get ... , please?
2 I've got a new book – I'm going to read ... this afternoon.
3 Sorry, can you speak more loudly? I can't hear ... .
4 I really can't do this homework – can you help ...
5 He doesn't understand so please help ... .
6 We like our teacher. She gives ... good marks!

this / that / these / those

8 Match the pictures and sentences.

1 What does this word mean?
2 What does that word mean?
3 These books are heavy.
4 Those books are heavy.

9 Complete the email with one word in each space.

Hi Shirley

I'm writing to you from Spain! My family and I [0] *are* on holiday here for two weeks. It's really nice here. Spanish people are very friendly but of course I don't speak Spanish so I don't [1]... when people talk to me. But a [2]... of people here speak good English, so it's all OK.

Our hotel is great. [3]... is a swimming pool downstairs and I swim there every day before breakfast. But of course I have breakfast late – usually nine o'clock! And it's always really good – the orange juice is delicious and I usually eat ham and eggs, too. Breakfast is my favourite meal – I love [4]... .

So, [5]... are you? I hope you are enjoying your holidays, too. I want to buy a present for you here in Spain. [6]... would you like? [7]... you like Spanish music? Write and tell [8]... , OK?

Have a good time and write soon.

Love

Howard

A

B

C

D

C MY THINGS

My possessions

1 Read Chloë's blog and choose the photos of the things she has got.

2 Work in pairs. How many things about Chloë can you write in each list?

personal possessions: TV , ...

pets: ... , ...

have got

3 Complete the table with *have*, *has*, *haven't* or *hasn't*.

Positive	Negative
I've (have) got a dog.	I haven't (have not) got a cat.
You [1]... (have) got a dog.	You [5]... (have not) got a cat.
He's (has) got a dog.	He hasn't (has not) got a cat.
She [2]... (has) got a dog.	She [6]... (has not) got a cat.
We [3]... (have) got a dog.	We [7]... (have not) got a cat.
They [4]... (have) got a dog.	They [8]... (have not) got a cat.

Questions	Short answers
Have I got a pet?	Yes, you have. / No, you haven't.
[9]... you got a pet?	Yes, I [13]... / No, I [14]...
Has he got a pet?	Yes, he has / No, he hasn't.
[10]... she got a pet?	Yes, she [15]... / No, she [16]...
[11]... we got a pet?	Yes, we [17]... / No, we [18]...
[12]... they got a pet?	Yes, they [19]... / No, they [20]...

4 Complete the sentences with *have*, *has*, *haven't* or *hasn't* so they are true for you.

1 I ... got a tablet.
2 My dad ... got a computer.
3 I ... got a dog.
4 My best friend ... got a brother.
5 I ... got a TV in my bedroom.
6 My mum ... got a car.

5 Walk around the classroom. Find someone who has got ...

1 a red bike
2 a cat and a dog
3 an English dictionary
4 an email address
5 two brothers or sisters
6 a smart phone
7 an unusual pet
8 a house with a garden

Have you got a bike?

Yes, I have.

What colour is it?

home about news contact

Welcome!

Hi, my name's Chloë,

I've got a bike – it's really my favourite thing!

I haven't got a pet but I'd love a cat or maybe something unusual like a lizard.

I haven't got a smart phone. I want one for my next birthday.

I've got an MP3 player and I've got a tablet. I haven't got a laptop. My dad's got one and I sometimes use that.

I've got a TV in my bedroom. And I've got a camera, a small one but it's nice.

I'm a very lucky girl.

I like and I'd like

6 Match the pictures and the sentences.

1 I like apples!
2 I'd like a hot shower!
3 I'd like six apples.
4 I like hot showers.

7 🔊 **1.10** Complete with *I like* or *I'd like*. Listen and check.

0 A What's your favourite food?
B I like curry best.
1 A Can I help you?
B Yes, ... a kilo of oranges.
2 A ... an ice cream, please.
B Chocolate or strawberry?
3 A What do you want to watch?
B Well, ... films, so can we watch a film, please?
4 A ... cycling. Do you?
B Not much. I think running's better.
5 A Do you want pizza or lasagne?
B Well, pizza's my favourite food – but today, ... lasagne, please!

8 Complete with the words in the list.

banana | orange juice | tuna | biscuit

Picnic Box
Sandwiches:
cheese or 1...
Desserts:
cake or 2...
Fruit:
apple or 3...
Drinks:
water or 4...

9 🔊 **1.11** Listen to the dialogue. What does Max choose for his lunch? Choose from the food.

10 🔊 **1.11** Complete the dialogue with the questions. Listen again and check.

What fruit would you like?
Have you got bananas?
What would you like for lunch today?
Would you like a tuna sandwich or a cheese sandwich?

DINNER LADY: Hi, Max. 1...
MAX: I'd like a picnic box, please.
DINNER LADY: 2...
MAX: A cheese sandwich, please.
DINNER LADY: 3...
MAX: 4...
DINNER LADY: Yes, we have.
MAX: A banana, please.

11 💬 Work in pairs. Make a picnic box for your partner. Ask and answer questions.

What would you like for ... ?

Would you like a ... or ... ?

D ABOUT TIME

Days and dates

1 🔊 **1.12** Listen and choose the correct information.

OLIVER: Hi, Shona. Why are you so happy today?
SHONA: Because it's the [1]*21st / 22nd / 23rd* February.
OLIVER: And what's special about that date?
SHONA: It's my birthday!
OLIVER: Really! Happy birthday, Shona.
SHONA: Thanks. I'm [2]*12 / 13 / 14* today.
OLIVER: Lucky you!
SHONA: When is your birthday, Oliver?
OLIVER: It's in [3]*August / September / October.*
SHONA: What date?
OLIVER: The [4]*11th / 12th / 13th.* I think it's on a [5]*Tuesday / Thursday / Friday* this year.

2 🔊 **1.13** Complete the names of the days and months. Listen and check.

Days

1 Monday
2 T_ _sd_ _
3 W_ _n_ _d_ _
4 _hu_ _ _ _y
5 F_ _ _ _ _
6 S_ _ _r_ _y
7 S_ _ _ _ _

Months

1 J_ _u_ _y
2 F_bru_ _ _
3 M_ _ _h
4 _p_ _l
5 M_ _
6 J_ _ _
7 J_ _y
8 A_ _u_ _
9 S_ _ _ _mber
10 O_ _ _ _er
11 _ _vem_ _ _
12 D_ _ _ _ _ _ _

3 Match the numbers and the words.

first 1st

first second third fourth fifth twelfth fifteenth twentieth twenty-second thirty-first

22nd 3rd 12th 4th 15th 2nd 5th 31st 1st 20th

4 🔊 **1.14** How do you say these numbers? Listen and check.

7th | 11th | 14th | 19th | 23rd | 28th | 30th

5 Walk around the classroom. Ask and answer questions. Whose birthday is close to your birthday?

When's your birthday?

It's on 17th March.

My day

6 Put the actions in the order you do them.

I go to school. | I get home. | I go to bed. | I have dinner. | I have breakfast. | I get up. | I do my homework. | I have lunch.

7 Copy the table. Look at the sentences in Exercise 6. Write them in the correct column for you.

Morning	Afternoon	Evening
I get up.		

8 Match the clocks and the times.

A 2

1 It's half past eight.
2 ~~It's quarter past three.~~
3 It's eleven o'clock.
4 It's six o'clock.
5 It's eight o'clock.
6 It's quarter to eight.
7 It's ten to one.
8 It's twenty past ten.

A
I get home.

B
I ...

C
I ...

D
I ...

E
I ...

F
I ...

G
I ...

H
I ...

Look!

midday to midnight = pm
midnight to midday = am
12 am = midnight
12 pm = midday
1 am = 1 o'clock in the early morning
1 pm = 1 o'clock in the afternoon

9 🔊 **1.15** Listen to Leah. Write sentences about her day in Exercise 7.

A – I get home.

10 Work in pairs. Talk about your day.

I get up at half past seven.

I have lunch at twelve o'clock.

1 HAVING FUN

LEARNING OUTCOMES

FUNCTIONS: talking about routines and everyday activities; expressing likes and dislikes; giving warnings and stating prohibition

GRAMMAR: present simple review; *like* + *-ing*; adverbs of frequency

VOCABULARY: hobbies; collocations with *have*

Work in pairs. Look at the photo. Discuss these questions:

1 Who is this boy and where is he?
2 Do you thing he is having fun?
3 What do you like doing to have fun?

READING

1 Match the activities in the list with the photos.

1 sleeping
2 doing homework
3 playing football
4 studying
5 reading
6 dancing
7 tidying up
8 singing

2 Are these activities fun? Write *always*, *sometimes* or *never*.

1 Sleeping is ... fun.
2 Doing homework is ... fun.
3 Playing football is ... fun.
4 Studying is ... fun.
5 Reading is ... fun.
6 Dancing is ... fun.
7 Tidying up is ... fun.
8 Singing is ... fun.

3 Work in groups of three and compare your ideas from Exercise 2.

I think dancing is always fun.

I think it's sometimes fun.

4 Think of more activities and say what you think.

Riding a bike is always fun.

Doing housework is never fun.

5 **1.16** Read and listen to the quiz. Match the pictures with the questions in the quiz.

1 D

GET IT *right!*

If we enjoyed a party we say
✓ *the party was* ***fun.***
not
✗ ~~*the party was funny.*~~

A

B

C

E

D

F

G

H

Do you take good care of *yourself*?

Does your teacher give you a lot of homework? Do your parents always want your bedroom tidy? School work, housework; life's not always easy. There are a lot of things to do and there isn't always time to do it all. But in your busy life it's important to think about yourself. It's important to do things you like, things that make you happy. Everyone needs fun.

So take our quiz and find out. Do you take good care of yourself?

A

B

C

1 Do you smile a lot?

a) Yes, I smile all the time.
b) I only smile when I'm happy.
c) My best friend says I don't smile very often.

2 How many hobbies do you have?

a) I've got lots of hobbies.
b) One or two.
c) I don't have any hobbies.

3 When do you relax?

a) In the morning, afternoon and in the evening.
b) I relax when I have time.
c) I never relax. I'm always busy.

F

D
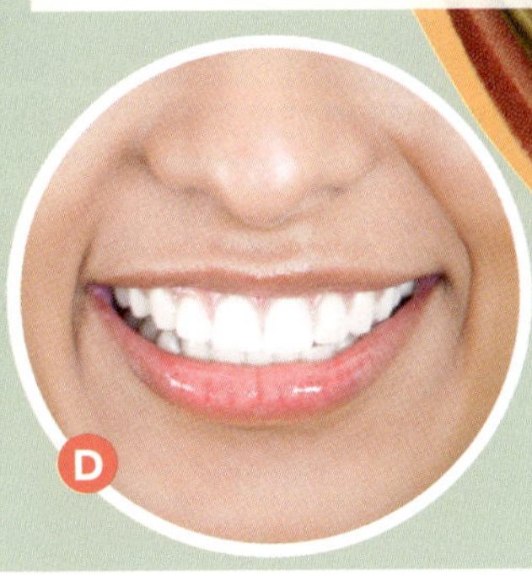

4 How many hours do you sleep a night?

a) nine to ten hours
b) about eight
c) less than eight

E

5 Do you like exercise?

a) Yes, exercise is fun.
b) It's OK.
c) No. It's really boring.

6 Do you like puzzles and crosswords?

a) I love them.
b) They're OK.
c) I don't really like them. They're boring.

G

7 Which of these things do you do most?

a) Talk with friends and family.
b) Meet friends online.
c) Watch TV and play computer games.

YOUR SCORE:

Mostly As: You take good care of yourself. You know how to have fun and enjoy life.

Mostly Bs: You take care of yourself OK, but can you do more? Try and find more time for yourself.

Mostly Cs: You don't take good care of yourself. Try and have more fun.

THINK *values*

Taking care of yourself

1 Which questions in the quiz tell us that these things are important for us?

a 7

a Being with people
b Enjoying exercise
c sleep
d Getting rest
e Giving your brain exercise
f Being positive
g Having interests

2 Compare your ideas with a partner.

Question 7 shows us that being with people is important.

GET IT *right!*

Which is the correct spelling: *excersise*, *exercise*, *exersise*?

GRAMMAR

Present simple review

1 Complete the sentences with the words in the list. Check your answers in the quiz on page 13.

~~relax~~ | do | does | don't | says

0 I never relax.
1 My best friend … I don't smile very often.
2 I … really like them.
3 … your teacher give you a lot of homework?
4 … you like exercise?

2 Look at the sentences in Exercise 1 and the table. Complete the rule with *do*, *does*, *don't* or *doesn't*.

Positive	Negative
I **like** milk.	I **don't like milk**.
You **like** milk.	You **don't like** milk.
He/She/It **likes** milk.	He/She/It **doesn't like** milk.
We **like** milk.	We **don't like** milk.
They **like** milk.	They **don't like** milk.

Questions	Short answers	
Do I **like** milk?	Yes, you **do**.	No, you **don't**.
Do you **like** milk?	Yes, I **do**.	No, I **don't**.
Does he/she/it **like** milk?	Yes, he/she/it **does**.	No, he/she/it **doesn't**.
Do we **like** milk?	Yes, we **do**.	No, we **don't**.
Do they **like** milk?	Yes, they **do**.	No, they **don't**.

RULE: Use the present simple for things that happen regularly or that are always true.

In positive sentences:

- with *I*, *you*, *we* and *they*, use the base form of the verb.
- with *he*, *she* and *it*, add *-s* (or *-es* with verbs that end *-s*, *-sh*, *-ch*, *-x*, or *-z*).

In negative sentences:

- with *I*, *you*, *we* and *they*, use [1]… .
- with *he*, *she* and *it*, use [2]… .

In questions:

- with *I*, *you*, *we* and *they*, use the auxiliary [3]… .
- with *he*, *she* and *it*, use the auxiliary [4]… .

3 Complete the sentences. Use the present simple of the verbs.

0 I don't like (not like) roller coasters. I get (get) really scared on them.
1 My dad … (not sleep) a lot. He only … (need) five or six hours.
2 A … you … (study) English?
B Yes, I … .
3 My dad … (cook) really well but he says he … (not enjoy) it.
4 A … your sister … (play) in the school football team?
B No, she … .
5 My grandparents … (not like) travelling. They … (prefer) to stay at home.
6 My brother … (watch) TV all day. He … (not do) anything else.

Workbook page 10

PRONUNCIATION
/s/, /z/, /ɪz/ sounds
Go to page 150.

VOCABULARY

Hobbies

1 Complete the phrases with the words in the list.

~~play~~ | write | keep | take | be | collect

0 to play an instrument
1 to … in a club
2 to … a blog
3 to … photos
4 to … a pet
5 to … things

2 Work in pairs. Ask questions about the hobbies in the pictures.

Do you play an instrument? *What do you play?*

Do you collect something? What …?

Workbook page 13

GET IT *right!*

We say

✓ *Let's **take** some photos.*

not

✗ *Let's ~~make~~ some photos.*

✗ *Let's ~~do~~ some photos.*

LISTENING

1 1.19 Listen to the conversations. Match each one with a picture.

2 1.19 Listen again. Complete the sentences with the names in the list.

~~Tom~~ | Carla | Lisa | Lisa's dad | James | James's mum

0 Tom has got a headache.
1 ... wants to join a football club.
2 ... doesn't have time to relax.
3 ... thinks music is good for relaxing.
4 ... wants to be a famous piano player.
5 ... thinks football is for boys.

THINK *self-esteem*

Why it's good to have a hobby

1 Choose the person from Listening Exercise 1.

I think it's good to have a hobby because ...

1 you can make new friends.
A Carla B Lisa C James

2 it helps you relax.
A Carla B Lisa C James

3 you can discover you have new talents.
A Carla B Lisa C James

2 Copy the diagram into your notebooks and complete it with the hobbies in the list.

playing the piano | joining a tennis club
collecting stamps | writing a blog
dancing | cooking | watching TV
playing online games | taking photos

3 Work in pairs. Compare diagrams with your partner.

Playing the piano is good. It helps you to relax.

4 What hobbies have you got? Think about why they are good for you. Make notes.

5 Tell your partner about your hobbies.

I dance. I'm not very good but it helps me to relax.

READING

1 Read the blog and answer the questions.

1 How many people like collecting things?
2 Who has got the strangest hobby?

So what do you do in your FREE TIME?

OK, we know you all like watching TV and playing computer games but we want to know some of the other things you do when you've got some free time. Write us a line or two and let us know.

Posted on January 22

NATHAN
I love collecting autographs of my friends and family. Now I want to get some from some famous people.

CHLOE
I enjoy lying on my back and looking at the clouds. I try to find different shapes in them. It's really relaxing and I occasionally fall asleep doing it.

IZZY
Once a week my granddad takes me out for a milkshake. I love listening to his stories. It's the best.

ADAM
I can't stand walking to school so I sometimes invent little games to help pass the time. For example I try to think of an animal, or football team or city for every letter of the alphabet.

LIZ
I like doing my homework as soon as I get home from school. Is there something wrong with me?

REBECCA
I really like going for a walk on my own in the forest near our house. There's always something interesting to see and I never get bored.

LEWIS
I collect bottle tops. I always take one home every time I go to a restaurant.

DYLAN
I like watching the news on TV. I watch it every day. My friends think I'm weird.

KUBA
I hate being on my own. So when I am by myself I usually start talking to my imaginary friends. But don't tell anyone!

JASMINE
I rarely get bored but if I do I just go to the library and get a book to learn about something new. It works every time.

DAISY
I like writing poems. I often write a poem when I've got nothing to do.

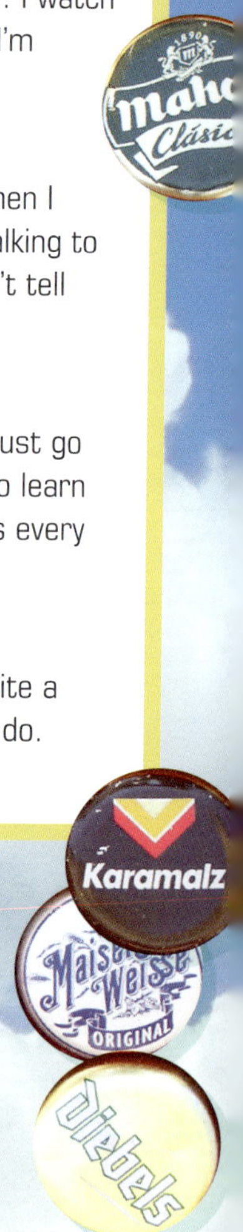

2 Read the sentences. Which of the people above do you think is saying each one?

0 A country that starts with R? Easy: Russia. — Adam
1 Have you got a book about birds? ...
2 Tell me more, please! ...
3 Can you write your name for me in my book? ...
4 Sorry, I can't come to the park now. I want to finish my maths. ...
5 Hey, that one looks just like a cow. ...

GRAMMAR

like + -ing

1 Look at the sentences from the blog on page 16. Match 🙂 or ☹️ to each one.

1 I love collecting autographs.
2 I can't stand walking to school.
3 I hate being on my own.
4 I like writing poems.

2 Use the sentences in Exercise 1 to complete the rule.

> **RULE:** Use the [1] … form of the verb after verbs which express likes and dislikes,
> e.g. *like, love, hate, enjoy, can't stand.*
> - To make this form add [2] … to the base verb.
> - If the verb ends in -e, drop the final *-e* (e.g. *live – living*).
> - If a short verb ends in a consonant + vowel + consonant, we usually double the final consonant before adding the *-ing* (e.g. *swim – swimming*).

3 Complete the sentences. Use the *-ing* form of the verbs in the list.

run | visit | swim | eat | ride | talk

0 I hate running to catch the bus to school.
1 My mum and dad enjoy … in nice restaurants.
2 My brother can't stand … on the telephone.
3 They quite like … in the sea when it's warm.
4 Donna really likes … her horse.
5 We love … new places on holiday.

4 What about you? Write two or three sentences about yourself.

Adverbs of frequency

5 Copy and complete the diagram with the words in the list.

always | occasionally | never | often

6 Complete the sentences so they are true for you.

1 I … do my homework when I get home.
2 I … write 'thank you' cards for my presents.
3 I am … late for school.
4 I … watch TV in the mornings.
5 Mum is … angry if I don't tidy my room.
6 I … turn off the lights when I leave the room.

7 Complete these sentences from the blog on page 16. Check your answers and complete the rule.

1 … / … / … my granddad takes me out for a milkshake.
2 I watch it (the TV news) … / … .

> **RULE:** Words like ***sometimes***, ***never***, ***always*** come [1]*before / after* the verb to be but [2]*before / after* other verbs.
> Phrases like ***every day*** or ***twice a week*** can come at the beginning or at the end of a sentence.

8 Write down things you do …

every day: I give my mum a kiss every day.
three times a week: …
once a year: …

9 Work in small groups. Compare your answers to Exercises 6 and 8.

How often do you go to the cinema?

I go once a month …

Workbook page 11

WRITING

Complete the sentences so they are true for you.

1 I rarely … at the weekend.
2 I can't stand … .
3 I … three times every day.
4 I love … in August.
5 I never … when I'm tired.
6 I … once a week.
7 I occasionally … .
8 I enjoy … after school.

Adverbs of frequency

0% ——————————————————————— 100%

[1] … | rarely | [2] … | sometimes | [3] … | usually | [4] …

PHOTOSTORY 1

OLIVIA'S NEW HOBBY

1 Look at the photos and answer the questions.

What do you think Olivia's hobby is?
Why does Ryan look worried?

2 1.20 Now read and listen to the photostory. Check your answers.

LUKE: Look. It's Olivia and Megan.

RYAN: What are they up to?

LUKE: I'm not sure what they're doing but they're definitely having a good time.

RYAN: Let's go and find out.

1

OLIVIA: Hi, Ryan. Hi, Luke.

RYAN: Hi, Olivia. So what are you two doing?

OLIVIA: It's my new hobby. I take photos of Megan reading a book in strange places.

LUKE: Cool! Can I video you on my phone?

OLIVIA: Of course you can. Come on.

2

LUKE: This is great. I think I've got a new hobby too – making videos.

RYAN: Be careful, Luke. Don't push too hard.

OLIVIA: That's right. Be careful.

MEGAN: Don't stop, Luke. I'm having fun.

3

OLIVIA: That's great, Megan.

MEGAN: Hurry up. My arms are tired. I need to have a rest.

OLIVIA: Just a few more.

RYAN: Look out, Olivia! You're very close to the water.

4

3 Work in pairs. Discuss what happens next in the story. Write down your ideas.

We think Olivia falls in the water.

4 EP1 Watch to find out how the story continues.

5 Choose the correct word in each sentence.

0 Ryan *tries* / ~~doesn't try~~ to warn Olivia.
1 Ryan and Luke *help* / *don't help* her out of the water.
2 Olivia *cries* / *doesn't cry* when she falls into the water.
3 Olivia *laughs* / *doesn't laugh* when she sees her camera.
4 Her camera *is* / *isn't* broken.
5 Luke *tells* / *doesn't tell* them what the surprise is.
6 Luke *gives* / *doesn't give* Olivia the money.

Phrases for fluency

1 Find the expressions 1–5 in the photostory. Who says them? Match them to the definitions a–f.

0 (What are they) up to? *Ryan e*
1 Cool! ...
2 Come on. ...
3 That's right. ...
4 Hurry up. ...
5 Look out! ...

a Be quick.
b Correct.
c Be careful.
d Let's start.
e Doing.
f Great.

2 Complete the conversation with the expressions in Exercise 1.

In the park

SARAH: Hi, Nicole. What are you [0]*up to*?
NICOLE: Not a lot. Just walking. Are you here for a walk too?
SARAH: [1] ... . I'm a bit bored at home.
NICOLE: Me too. We can walk together, if you want.
SARAH: [2] ... ! Oh no – [3] ... ! Mike Smith is coming. I don't like him!
NICOLE: [4] ... – let's walk over here.
SARAH: I don't want him to see me. [5] ... , Nicole!

VOCABULARY

Collocations with *have*

1 Match the sentence parts from the story.

1 e

1 I'm not sure what they're doing
2 Don't stop, Luke.
3 You're really dirty. You need to go home
4 My arms are tired.
5 Olivia, I think you *have a problem*.
6 We're just *having dinner*.

a I'm *having fun*.
b I think your camera's broken.
c It's pizza. Would you like some?
d I need to *have a rest*.
e but they're definitely *having a good time*.
f and *have a shower*.

2 Ask and answer the questions in pairs.

1 Who do you have the most fun with?
2 Do you have a good time at school?
3 What do you do when you have a problem?
4 What time do you have dinner?
5 Do you have a rest after school?
6 When do you have a shower?

Workbook page 13

FUNCTIONS

Giving warnings and stating prohibition

1 Put the words in order to make sentences.

1 Dan / Be / careful
2 out / Lucy / Look
3 do / that / Don't
4 push / Don't / hard / too

2 Match the sentences in Exercise 1 with the pictures A–D.

Life skills

Showing empathy

Empathy is understanding how other people feel. We need empathy to tell people we understand how they feel in bad situations. Sometimes, this is all people need when they feel bad. But empathy can help us decide what we can do to help.

1 Think about the photostory on page 18.

1 Imagine you are Olivia. Your camera is broken. How do you feel?

2 Imagine you are Olivia's friend. Olivia tells you her camera is broken. What do you say? What do you do?

2 Read this email from Michael to his friend, Jake. Does he like his new school?

Hi Jake,

How are you? Thanks for your email and the photos! I like the holiday pictures, but my favourite is the class photo. Say 'Hi' to everyone for me! Who is the new girl next to you in the photo?

I don't like my new school very much. The teachers are mostly OK, but I can't stand going to Maths now. Mr Allen, the teacher, always seems angry because I don't know things that rest of the class know from last year. I don't think I can pass the exam we have next week because I don't ask questions anymore.

Another thing is that I haven't got any friends. Everyone has got a small group of friends and isn't interested in talking to me – 'the new boy.' Luckily, I have a new mobile so can spend break playing games, but it's horrible when nobody wants to sit next to me in class, and the teacher moves someone to be my partner.

Are you free to Skype this weekend? Tell me when is a good time for you, OK?

Michael.

3 Work in pairs. Discuss the questions about Michael.

1 What are Michael's problems at his new school?

2 Imagine you are Michael. How do you feel?

3 When do your friends and family feel like this?

4 Do people like talking about these feelings?

4 Imagine you are Jake. Which of these sentences are good to say to Michael?

- I'm here for you.
- I've got some great friends!
- I'm sorry you feel this way.
- I hate Maths too.
- Talking about feelings is stupid.
- I understand how you feel.

5 Work in pairs. Discuss and think of more sentences you can say to Michael. What things can you do?

6 Write a short email to Michael. Use your ideas from Exercise 4 and 5 to help you. Don't forget to include a time for him to Skype at the weekend!

Tips for showing empathy

1 Listen to other people's problems. Don't always talk about your problems.

2 When someone is explaining their problems, don't say their problems aren't important, or be critical.

3 It's not always necessary to give advice. Sometimes just listening and understanding is enough.

2 MONEY AND HOW TO SPEND IT

LEARNING OUTCOMES

FUNCTIONS: buying things in a shop; talking about what people are doing at the moment

GRAMMAR: present continuous; verbs of perception; present simple vs. present continuous

VOCABULARY: shops; clothes

Work in pairs. Look at the photo and answer these questions.

1 Where are these people and what are doing?

2 How do they feel?

3 Do the clothes people wear demonstrate their personality?

READING

1 🔊 **1.21** Say these prices. Listen and check.

2 🔊 **1.22** What are these objects (A-F) here? Match them with the prices (1-6) in Exercise 1. Listen and check.

3 Work in pairs. Discuss the following questions. Then compare your ideas with other students.

Which of the things in Exercise 2 do you ...

1 think are cheap?
2 think are expensive?
3 think are fantastic?
4 dream about having?

4 Look at the picture on page 23. Answer these questions.

1 Who do you think the boy and girl are?
2 Do you think the girl likes the shirt?

5 🔊 **1.23** Read and listen to the script from a soap opera and check your ideas.

6 Mark the sentences T (true) or F (false). Correct the false ones.

0 It's six o'clock on Friday afternoon.
It's four o'clock on Friday afternoon.
1 Tom is deciding what to wear.
2 Maddy thinks yellow is a good idea.
3 Tom thinks he's good-looking.
4 Tom wants to buy expensive clothes.
5 Tom wants to be famous.

TOM: Hi, Maddy.
MADDY: Where are Mum and Dad?
TOM: They're out. At the supermarket, I think. They're doing some shopping or something.
MADDY: What are you doing?
TOM: Me? I'm looking for something.
MADDY: OK. What are you looking for?
TOM: A shirt. And some trousers. I'm going out. It's Friday and I have plans for tonight. So, I'm choosing my clothes.
MADDY: But it's only four o'clock.
TOM: I know. I need time to choose.
MADDY: Do you need any help? I can help you.
TOM: No. Well, maybe. OK, yes.
MADDY: Think about colours.
TOM: I'm thinking. I'm thinking about ... yellow.
MADDY: Not a good idea.
TOM: Why not?
MADDY: Because yellow just isn't interesting.
TOM: But I like yellow. Like this.
MADDY: I'm trying to help you, Tom. And I'm telling you – don't wear a yellow shirt.
TOM: You're laughing. Why are you laughing at me?
MADDY: I'm not laughing at you. I'm laughing at the shirt. It looks terrible.
TOM: I need some new ideas.
MADDY: You're right. Look at this. Here, in this magazine. See this guy? He's wearing beautiful clothes.
TOM: Yes, but he's good-looking. And rich too, probably. I'm not good-looking.
MADDY: Yes, you are! But of course, I'm only saying that because you're my brother. OK, have you got your money?
TOM: Yes. Why?
MADDY: I want to take you to town – to a clothes shop and maybe a shoe shop, too.
TOM: That sounds great. Nothing expensive though.
MADDY: Don't worry. Nice clothes aren't always expensive. Come on.
TOM: You know, I dream about being famous one day and about having fantastic clothes. Do you dream about that too?
MADDY: Tom, I'm nine years old. I dream about ice cream.
TOM: OK, we can get ice cream after we buy the clothes.

THINK *values*

Fashion and clothes

1 How important are these for you? Give each one a number from 0 to 5 (0 = not important, 5 = very, very important).

Clothes – my values:
I want to look cool.
I want to feel comfortable.
I always buy cheap clothes.
I like buying designer clothes.
I love wearing clean clothes.
I like wearing bright colours.
I always buy clothes in the same shops.

2 Work in pairs. Ask and answer questions.

How important is it for you to look cool?

Not very important. I have 3 points. What about you?

For me, it's very important. 5 points.

GRAMMAR

Present continuous

1 Look at the examples of the present continuous. Then complete the rule and the table.

1 They**'re doing** some shopping at the supermarket.
2 He**'s wearing** beautiful clothes.
3 Why **are** you **laughing** at me?
4 I**'m not laughing** at you, Tom.

> **RULE:** Use the present [1]... to talk about things that are happening at or around the time of speaking.
>
> Form the present continuous with the present simple of [2]... + the *-ing* form (e.g. *running / doing / wearing*, etc.) of the main verb.

Positive	Negative
I'm (= I am) working.	I'm not working.
you/we/they're ([1]...) working.	you/we/they aren't working.
he/she/it's (is) working.	he/she/it [2]... working.

Questions	Short answers
[3]... I working?	Yes, I am.
	No, I'm not.
[4]... you/we/they working?	Yes, you/we/they [6]... .
	No, you/we/they [7]... .
[5]... he/she/it working?	Yes, he/she/it [8]... .
	No, he/she/it [9]... .

2 Complete the sentences. Use the present continuous of the verbs.

0 Sorry, Jenny's not here. She 's doing (do) some shopping in town.
1 They're in the living room. They ... (play) computer games.
2 My brother's in the garage. He ... (clean) his bike.
3 Steven! You ... (not listen) to me!
4 I can't talk now. I ... (do) my homework.
5 It's 3–0! We ... (not play) very well, and we ... (lose)!
6 A ... you ... (watch) this programme?
B No, I ... . You can watch a different one if you want.
7 A What ... you ... (do)?
B I ... (try) to find some old photos on my computer.

Workbook page 18

VOCABULARY

Shops

1 Match the names of the shops to the photos.

bookshop – 1

newsagent's | chemist's | ~~bookshop~~
clothes shop | shoe shop | department store
supermarket | sports shop

1

2

3

4

5

6

7

8

> **GET IT *right!***
>
> Remember to say WHAT YOU BUY + shop so it's *clothes shop*, not ~~*shop of clothes*~~.
>
> In a similar way, we say *art class*, not ~~*class of art*~~.

2 Complete the sentences with the names of shops from Exercise 1. Then compare your ideas with other students.

1 In my town there's a very good ...
It's called ... It's good because ...
2 I often go there because ...
3 I never go into ... because they don't interest me.
I don't often go to ... because ...

In my town there's a very good clothes shop. It's good because the clothes aren't expensive.

Workbook page 21

GRAMMAR

Sense verbs

1 Look at the sentences from the script on page 23. Answer the questions.

1 *It looks terrible.* What is 'it'?

2 *That sounds great.* What is 'that'?

2 Match the verbs with the pictures. Then complete the rule.

1 look 2 sound 3 smell 4 taste

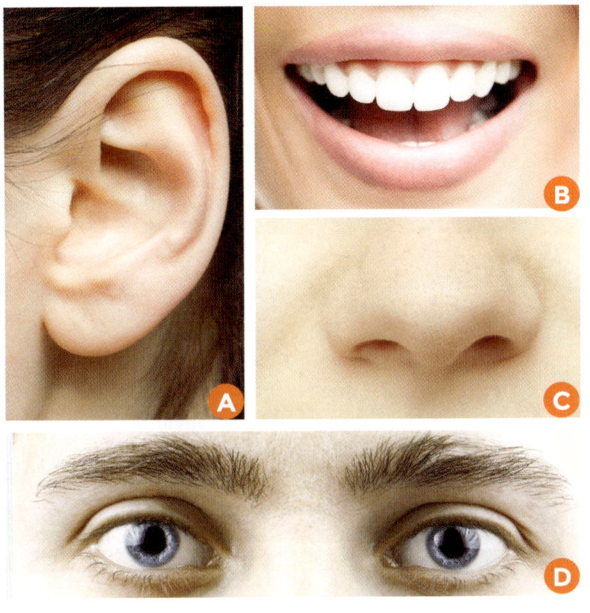

RULE: Sense verbs are used in the present [1]… when they are used to give an opinion.

The food ***tastes*** *great.* *That idea* ***sounds*** *good.*
That pizza ***smells*** *nice.* *His new shirt* ***looks*** *awful!*

The words after the sense verbs are [2]….

3 Match the responses (a-d) to the first parts of the conversations (1-4).

1 I'm going to the cinema.
2 My mother's making pizzas.
3 I'm wearing my new shoes.
4 Don't you like the juice?
a No. It tastes horrible!
b That sounds great.
c They smell fantastic.
d They look nice.

Workbook page 19

PRONUNCIATION
Contractions
Go to page 150.

LISTENING

1 1.24 Listen. What shop is each person in? Match a shop to each speaker.

1 … 2 … 3 … 4 …

bookshop | newsagent's | clothes shop | sports shop

2 1.24 Listen again. What does each person want to buy?

1 … 2 … 3 … 4 …

FUNCTIONS

Buying things in a shop

1 Read the sentences from the listening. Mark them C (customer) or A (assistant).

0 *Can I help you? – A*
1 Have you got … ?
2 What size do you take?
3 Can I try it/them on please?
4 How much is it/are they?
5 That's (twenty pounds) please.
6 Have you got it/them in (blue)?

2 1.25 Put the sentences in the correct order 1–9. Listen and check. Practise in pairs.

1 – A Hello. Can I help you?

a A It's £75.00.
b A Hello. Can I help you?
c A Great. So – that's £75, please!
d A Sorry, no. Only brown.
e A Yes, of course.
f B Can I try it on?
g B Very nice. I'll take it.
h B Yes, please. I like this jacket. Have you got it in black?
i B Oh, well, brown's OK. How much is it?

3 Work in pairs. Student A: Go to page 159. Student B: Go to page 160. Take two or three minutes to prepare. Then have two conversations.

train to THINK

Exploring numbers

1 You want to buy some new clothes. Here are some things you like. Answer the questions in pairs.

T-Shirt – £8.50 | shoes – £12.75 | jumper – £9.25
belt – £3 | jacket – £35

1 Choose three things. How much do they cost?
2 You've got £30.00. Name three things you can buy.
3 You've got £75.00. Can you buy all five things?

2 Compare your ideas with a partner.

VOCABULARY

Clothes

1 1.28 Copy and complete the names of the clothes. Listen and check.

0 belt	4 … … ai … e … …	8 … … o … … …
1 … … e … …	5 … oo … …	9 … … ou … e … …
2 … u … … e …	6 … a … … e …	
3 … … oe …	7 … … i … …	

2 Answer the questions.

1 What are you wearing now?
2 What do you usually wear at the weekends?
3 What do you never wear?
4 What clothes do you really like / dislike buying?

3 Work in pairs. Ask and answer the questions in Exercise 2. Then work with another partner.

I'm wearing a green shirt and jeans.

I never wear shorts.

GET IT right!

Trousers, *jeans* and *shorts* are always plural in English.

✓ *I'm getting some new **trousers/jeans**.*

not

✗ *I'm getting ~~a new trouser/jean~~.*

Workbook page 21

READING

1 Read the web chat. Answer the questions.

Who …

1 is interested in the sky?
2 is probably in the kitchen?
3 has a problem?
4 is in front of a TV?
5 is surprising her parents?

2 Think of three things you enjoy that don't need money. Write them down.

going for a walk   watching TV

3 Work in pairs. Tell your partner your ideas. Listen to what your partner says. Are his/her ideas really things that don't need money? Say what you think.

I like going for a walk. I also like watching TV.

I like baking cakes.

But you need money to buy ingredients!

How not to spend money

JollyMarie
5 June 2015

Wow! Problem. Not a lot of money right now and I don't want to spend it. I'm tired of spending money! So here I am at home and I'm thinking – what can I do that's free? (and fun lol)

LIKE COMMENT SHARE

goodgirl
an hour ago

I always go into town at the weekend – and I usually spend money! It's very easy to buy things if you go into a shopping mall or a street full of shops. So this weekend I'm staying at home. Right now I'm just reading a book – my parents can't believe it! lol

PeterJ
yesterday

I really like going to the cinema but it can be a bit expensive – especially because my friends and I often go for a pizza after the film. So tonight I'm watching a film on TV at home. I'm really enjoying it. And it's free! It's incredible how many good films there are on TV these days, too.

RonnieRaver
two days ago

It's funny, PeteJ – I'm just like you (going to the cinema, I mean). Right now, I'm not watching a film – I'm watching the stars! I've got a book about the sky and it's fantastic. I'm having a really good time here!

ellieParsons
two days ago

Oh JollyMarie, it's not such a problem. My friends and I often have a picnic on Sundays and I make the sandwiches the night before. So right now, it's Saturday night and I'm making sandwiches. hehehe

GRAMMAR

Present simple vs. present continuous

1 Look at the examples. Complete the rule.

present simple

I usually **watch** a film at the cinema.

I **make** the sandwiches the night before.

I always **go** into town.

present continuous

Right now, **I'm watching** a film.

It's Saturday night and **I'm making** sandwiches.

This weekend, **I'm staying** at home.

RULE: Use the ¹... to talk about habits, routines and things which are generally or always true.

Use the ²... to talk about temporary things which are happening around the moment of speaking.

2 Match the sentences with the pictures. Write 1–4 in the boxes.

1 She sings well. 3 He plays football.

2 She's singing well. 4 He's playing football.

A

B

C

D

Look!

These verbs are almost never used in the present continuous:

believe | know | understand | mean

remember | need | like | hate | want

*I **know** the answer.* (Not: *~~I'm knowing~~ the answer.*)

*I **understand** the problem.* (Not: *~~I am understanding~~ the problem.*)

3 Choose the correct options.

1 We *always wear* / *'re always wearing* a uniform to school.

2 Paula *wears* / *is wearing* black jeans today.

3 Come inside! It *rains* / *'s raining*.

4 It *rains* / *'s raining* a lot in February.

5 Dad *cooks* / *'s cooking* at the moment.

6 My mother *cooks* / *'s cooking* lunch every Sunday.

7 Steve's terrible! He *never listens* / *'s never listening* to the teacher!

8 Can you be quiet, please? I *listen* / *'m listening* to some music.

4 Complete the sentences. Use the present simple or present continuous form of the verbs.

0 Mandy usually goes (go) to school on her bike, but today she is walking (walk).

1 We ... (have) science lessons three times a week. This week we ... (learn) about trees.

2 Tom ... (do) some shopping this afternoon. He ... (want) to buy a new camera.

3 I ... (know) her face, but I ... (not remember) her name.

4 Alex ... (not watch) the game tonight because he ... (not like) football very much.

5 What ... this word ... (mean)? I ... (not understand) it.

Workbook page 19

SPEAKING

1 Look at these photos. Who are the people in each one?

2 Work in pairs. Discuss the questions.

For each person, say ...

- who they are.
- what they do.
- what they are doing.

It's Beyoncé. She's a ...
She's ...

Culture

1 Look at the photos. Name one or two things you can buy in each market.

Where can you see stalls?

Where can you see a canal?

2 🔊 **1.29** Read and listen to the article. Match the photos (A–E) with the places (1–5).

A

D

World markets

C

Wherever you go in the world, you find shops and stores – but you can find wonderful markets in most cities, too. Here's a selection from five different countries.

1 The **Spice Bazaar** in **Istanbul** is popular with both tourists and people from Istanbul. There are lots of shops and stalls and they all sell many different kinds of spices, sweets or nuts. You can buy spices from a lot of countries (like Iran, China, Russia and of course Turkey), and the smells and colours are amazing.

2 **Khlong Lat Phli** is a very unusual market about 80 kilometres south of **Bangkok**, Thailand. Early every morning, hundreds of local people sell fruit and vegetables from their boats on the canals. It's not the only boat market in the country but it's a very popular tourist one.

E

3 Do you like fish? Then the **Tsukiji Market** in **Tokyo** is the right place for you. It is the biggest seafood market in the world, and it never closes! It's very busy between the hours of 4.00 and 5.00 am, when people from the shops and restaurants in Tokyo buy the fresh fish that they need for the day. It is also very popular with tourists, but they can only visit the market later in the day, after the early morning buying and selling.

4 In **Madrid** there is a famous open-air market called **El Rastro**, which is open on Sunday mornings. There are over 1,000 stalls that sell many different things: books, CDs, paintings, antiques – beautiful old things. One of the streets sells only animals and birds. And of course visitors can stop to eat 'tapas' and get something to drink, and there are many street musicians with their guitars making music too.

B

5 **Portobello Road Market** in **London** is popular with tourists and with Londoners, too. You can find all kinds of bargains here. The market (in Notting Hill) has five different parts and you can buy new or second-hand things (like clothes) as well as fruit and vegetables, and antiques. It's very busy at the weekend.

3 There are eight highlighted words in the article. Match the words with these meanings.

0 stalls

0 big tables or small shops with an open front
1 not inside a building
2 fish and other things to eat from the sea
3 different or surprising
4 small man-made rivers
5 full of people
6 liked by a lot of people
7 things that you buy for a good, cheap price

4 Read the article again. Correct the information in these sentences.

0 All the spices at the Istanbul Spice Bazaar are from Turkey.
Not all the spices are from Turkey. You can buy spices from a lot of countries.
1 At Khlong Lat Phli, people sell spices from their boats.
2 The Tsukiji Market closes between four and five in the morning.
3 Tourists can go to the Tsukiji Market in the early morning.
4 You can't get food at El Rastro.
5 Portobello Road Market is very quiet on Saturdays.

SPEAKING

1 Make sentences about the markets that are true for you. Use adjectives from the list, or other adjectives if you want.

fantastic | interesting | fascinating
exciting | unusual | attractive

I think the ... market is fantastic / isn't very interesting because ...

2 Work in groups. Compare your sentences and ideas.

I think the Istanbul Spice market is fantastic because ...

WRITING

An email to say what you're doing

1 Read the email from Paul to his friend Lucy. Answer the questions.

1 Where is Paul and what is he doing?
2 Where are his father and sister?
3 What is Paul's family watching tonight?

2 How does Paul start his email? And how does he finish it? Complete the table with the words in the list.

Dear | Love | Hello | See you soon | Best wishes

starting an email	ending an email
Hi (Lucy), 1... (Mike) 2... (Mr Jones)	Hope you are OK. Bye 3... 4... 5...

3 Look at paragraphs 1 and 2 of Paul's email. Match the functions (a-d) with the paragraphs.

Paragraph 1: ... and ... .
Paragraph 2: ... and ... .

a saying what you are doing
b talking about your plans
c saying where you are
d a description of the place where you are

4 Choose the things Paul writes about in his email.

1 what he likes about the city
2 when he is coming home
3 his plans for tonight
4 where he is staying
5 what his mother/father/sister are doing
6 how Lucy is

5 Write an email to a friend (about 100–120 words). Imagine you are in a café or shop in a shopping centre. Use the example email and language above to help you.

GET IT right!

Remember that *Dear*, *Love*, *Hello*, *See you soon* and *Best wishes* all start with a capital letter. Only the first word starts with a capital letter, not ~~*See You Soon*~~.

Hi Lucy

(1) How are things with you? I'm in Madrid right now – we're here on holiday. Madrid is a really cool place. There are lots of great things to see and do here – shops, markets, and of course the football stadium! We're staying in a small hotel in the middle of Madrid, and it's really nice.

(2) I'm sitting in a café at the moment, in the middle of the city. I'm here with my mum and we're having a drink because it's really hot today! My father and my sister are at a market near here – they're looking for some shoes for my sister. Tonight we're watching a flamenco dancing show. I don't especially like dancing but all the family do, so ... !

(3) OK my father and sister are coming back so I'm going now. Write soon and tell me how you are.

Hope you're OK.

Paul

Literature

MAGIC JANE
BY ROZ WARREN

Jane's parents are divorced. Her father takes her to the bookshop every Saturday morning.

1 Read the text and answer the following question. What is new in Jane's life?

Before the divorce, her parents rarely bought Jane books. Instead, she and her mother went to the library each Saturday morning, where Jane chose ten books, which she'd always finish reading before their next visit.

Then Jane's dad moved out. Now each Saturday morning he picks her up and they go to the bookstore.

"How many can I buy?" Jane had asked him the first time.

He smiled and ruffled her hair. "As many as you want, cookie."

Each week, Jane browses the 'intermediate reader' shelves. When she's gathered as many books as she can carry, she'll sit on a quiet stretch of the carpeted floor with its happy pattern of puppies and clowns and dancing mice, and examine each book carefully. Although she can buy as many as she pleases, she only wants them if they're special, and not, as her mom would put it, mindless garbage. As she picks up each book, she removes the tiny plastic disk tucked into its pages. She's heard the bookstore staff call them 'chicklets' because they're small and white like the gum. When you buy a book, the register people remove the chicklet. If they forget and you leave the store with a chicklet still in your book, a loud alarm sounds and everyone stares. That happened to Jane once, so now she removes the chicklets herself, ahead of time, just to make sure.

She's deep in her tasks of reading and choosing when her father comes to find her.

"How's my little book worm?" he asks.

GLOSSARY

browses- looks at different things in the shop
stare – look at someone in a rude or shocked way
book worm – someone who likes reading a lot

2 How old do you think Jane is? Which details in the text help you guess her age?

3 Why do you think Jane's dad takes her to the bookshop?

4 Read lines 15–20. What does this tell you about Jane's personality? What other evidence can you find for this in the text?

5 What else do you learn about Jane's personality in this text?

6 How do you think the story continues? Do you think it has a sad ending or a happy one?

Cambridge English Corpus = GET IT right!

Units 1&2

Adverbs of frequency

Adverbs of frequency (*sometimes, never, always* etc.) come <u>between</u> the subject and the verb.

✓ *I **sometimes do** my homework on Saturday.*

✗ *I ~~do sometimes~~ my homework on Saturday.*

BUT these words come after the verb *to be*.

✓ *I **am often** late for school.*

✗ *I ~~often am~~ late for school.*

1 Find six mistakes in the text. Correct them.

Saturday- my favourite day!

I have always fun on Saturday! In the morning, I usually meet my friends in the park or they come sometimes to my house. In the afternoon, we go often swimming. I never do homework on Saturday. In the evening, we have always pizza. My mum usually cooks the pizza at home, but we go occasionally to a restaurant. I always am very tired on Sunday!

like + *-ing*

We use the *-ing* form of the verb after verbs expressing likes and dislikes.

✓ *He likes **watching** TV.* ✗ *He likes ~~watch~~ TV.*

2 Work in pairs. Find five mistakes in the conversation. Correct them.

LUCY: What do you like doing, Jim?

JIM: I love play with my dog, Spud.

LUCY: Does he enjoy swim?

JIM: No, he hates swim. But he likes go to the beach.

LUCY: I like play on the beach, too!

<u>Practise</u> the conversation with your partner. Then do it again- don't look at the book this time!

Sense verbs

We use the present simple with sense verbs (*look, taste, sound, smell, feel*) to talk about something that is true now. We don't use the present continuous.

✓ *His new jacket **looks** terrible!*

✗ *His new jacket is ~~looking~~ terrible!*

We use *look, taste, sound, smell, feel* + adjective, NOT *look, taste, sound, smell, feel* + *like* + adjective.

✓ *This pizza **tastes awful**!*

✗ *This pizza tastes ~~like~~ awful!*

3 <u>Choose</u> the correct sentence.

1 a The classroom smells bad!
  b The classroom is smelling bad!

2 a Yum! This chocolate tastes great!
  b Yum! This chocolate tastes like great!

3 a Look at that dog. He looks like happy.
  b Look at that dog. He looks happy.

4 a The music is sounding cool.
  b The music sounds cool.

Present continuous

Remember to use *am / is / are* with the present continuous.

✓ *I **am** looking at the sky.*

✗ *I ~~looking~~ at the sky.*

In present continuous questions, we put *am/is/are* <u>before</u> the person doing the action, NOT after.

✓ *Why **are you** looking at the sky?*

✗ *Why ~~you are~~ looking at the sky?*

4 Work in pairs. Put the correct form of *be* in the correct place in the sentences. Do it quickly!

1 What you looking at?
2 They going shopping today.
3 I looking for a new jacket.
4 She wearing a beautiful dress.
5 Why he laughing? It's not funny!
6 What you doing?

SAY IT right!

/z/, /s/, /IZ/ sounds

1 Work in pairs. Read the text. How many syllables are in the underlined words?

Clara [1] <u>lives</u> in Brighton now. She [2] <u>misses</u> her family in Madrid but she [3] <u>likes</u> living by the sea. Every day she [4] <u>finishes</u> school at four o'clock. In the evening, she [5] <u>watches</u> television in English and she [6] <u>loves</u> programmes about nature.

2 🔊 **1.30** Listen and check your answers. Then practise with your partner.

With verbs that end in the sounds /s/, /ʃ/ or /tʃ/ we add *-es* and add an extra syllable: /IZ/.
/s/ *misses* /ʃ/ *finishes* /tʃ/ *watches*

test yourself Units 1&2

VOCABULARY

1 Complete the sentences with the words in the list. There are two extra words.

newsagent's | take | dress | club | write | plays | collects
sports shop | supermarket | jumper | shoe shop | belt

1 I want to ... a blog about pop music.
2 If you're cold, why don't you put on a ...?
3 She ... the guitar and the piano. She's really good at both.
4 I need to go to the ... and buy some tennis balls.
5 My dad ... old toy cars. He's just a big child!
6 You need some new boots. Let's go to the ... .
7 I'm thinking about joining the golf ... but it's very expensive.
8 Your trousers are falling down. You need a ... .
9 Can you get some eggs and some milk when you go to the ... , please?
10 I always ... lots of photos when I travel.

GRAMMAR

2 Complete the sentences with the words in the list.

's working | 're writing | works | plays | 're playing | write

1 My dad's a cook. He ... at a restaurant in town.
2 I like poetry. I ... at least five poems every week.
3 Mum's in her office. She ... on something very important.
4 Paul's in a band. He ... the drums.
5 Ian and Dan are on the computer. They ... their blog.
6 Lucy and Rachel are in the garden. They ... football.

3 Find and correct the mistake in each sentence.

1 I can't stand to eat carrots.
2 We don't playing very well today.
3 They doesn't like playing video games.
4 That sandwich is tasting very good.
5 Does you speak French?
6 He goes always swimming at the weekend.

FUNCTIONAL LANGUAGE

4 Write the missing words.

1 A Be ... ! It looks very dangerous.
B Don't worry. I'm ... fun.
2 A How ... do you watch TV?
B ... day when I get home from school.
3 A Look ... ! There's a dog coming.
B And it ... look happy. Let's run!
4 A Please ... shout! The baby is asleep.
B Oh, OK. I'm ... .

CAMBRIDGE EXAMS
Review Units 1 & 2
Go to page 144.

MY SCORE

22–30
10–21
0–9

3 FOOD FOR LIFE

LEARNING OUTCOMES

FUNCTIONS: apologising; talking about food; ordering a meal

GRAMMAR: countable and uncountable nouns; *a/an, some, any; How much / many, a lot of / lots of ; too* and *(not) enough*

VOCABULARY: food and drink; adjectives to talk about food; expressions with *have got*

Work in pairs. Look at the photo and answer these questions.

1 What are these people doing?
2 What food shown in the photo do you know?
3 Do you like any unusual foods?

READING

1 What food and drink in the picture can you name? What food and drink do you know in English?

2 Make sentences that are true for you. Compare your ideas in class.

I	always often sometimes never	have ... for	breakfast. lunch. dinner.

3 Look at the photos on page 35. Ask your teacher for the words you don't know. Then answer the questions.

I go once a month ...

Can you think of a food that ...

- comes from another country?
- has got a lot of vitamins?
- is very healthy?
- is unusual?
- is good for your hair and skin?

4 1.32 Read and listen to the article. Match the parts of the sentences.

0 d

0 In Japan people think square watermelons
1 Bananas are a popular fruit because they
2 In Iceland people don't like
3 Honey is healthy and good
4 Avocado is a dessert in
5 Potato clocks are very popular in
6 Sugar is not only in sweets. It's also in

a 'normal' ice creams.
b Brazil.
c for our looks.
d West Africa.
e make very special presents.
f fruit.
g help us feel good.

5 Work in pairs. Three of the 'food facts' in Exercise 4 are not true. Which ones do you think they are?

I don't think that people give square watermelons as special presents in Japan.

I think it's true that ...

Yes, you're right. I think so too. / No, I think that's impossible.

What do you think about statement number ...?

I'm not sure. I think ... Do you agree?

Yes, I do. / No, I don't. I think ...

Food Facts or Food Fiction?

In Japan, square watermelons are very popular. People often buy them as presents. But these special fruits are of course very expensive. Round watermelons do not cost so much.

People all over the world love bananas. Food experts say that bananas contain a chemical that helps the body to produce serotonin. It's sometimes called the body's own 'happiness hormone'.

People in Iceland love eating unusual ice creams. There is pizza ice cream, sausage ice cream and even fish and chips ice cream, and they are all very popular. People eat them with a lot of ketchup. But you don't find any lemon or mango ice creams there. Icelanders just don't like them.

Honey is very healthy. It has got lots of vitamins. Some people say that honey makes us beautiful. They think it's good for the hair and the skin. Honey is also very special because it is the only food we eat that never goes off. We can eat 3,000- or 4,000-year-old honey!

The avocado is a fruit, not a vegetable. It comes from Central and South America originally, but now it also grows in other hot countries. Many people like avocados as a starter before their main meal. But how many people eat it as a dessert? Well, in Brazil, people eat avocado with ice cream and milk.

People in West Africa use a 'potato-clock' to tell the time. Every morning, they put exactly 7.5 kilos of potatoes in the clock. It looks like a big pot. They put it on the fire. They know that it takes two hours to cook the potatoes.

Everybody knows that fruit has got sugar in it. But how much sugar is there in a lemon? A lot. More than there is in a strawberry!

THINK values

Food and health

GET IT right!

Which is right *alot* or *a lot*?

1 Complete the five conversations. Choose the correct answer A, B or C.

1 Do you want some ice cream?
A No, thanks. Can I have an apple or a banana?
B She's not hungry.
C They're very good.

2 Have some water.
A I drink it.
B No, thanks, I'm not thirsty.
C Look at them.

3 Would you like more chocolate?
A It's over there.
B Yes, I do.
C I'd love some, but I'm trying not to eat too much.

4 Do you eat any vegetables?
A I hate apples.
B It's fast food.
C No, I don't. I don't like them.

5 Have some biscuits.
A Thanks, but one's enough for me.
B You can have a banana.
C I'm very healthy.

2 Work in pairs. Compare your answers. Do the people care about healthy food?

The person in number 1	doesn't want a … likes … never eats / drinks …	He/She asks for … He/She says … He/She wants …

I think he/she	cares about … doesn't care about …

VOCABULARY

Food and drink

1 1.33 Write the names of the food. Listen and check.

1 carrots

2 Work in pairs. Ask and answer questions to find out three things your partner likes and doesn't like.

Workbook page 31

GET IT right!

What is wrong with these sentences?

I like my phone because it has camera.

You have to bring pencil and rubber.

GRAMMAR

Countable and uncountable nouns

1 Read the sentences. Then choose the correct words in the rule.

1 Can I have a carrot? 2 I don't like rice.
3 I don't like peppers.

> **RULE:** Nouns that you can count (*one carrot, two carrots*, etc.) are [1]*countable / uncountable* nouns.
> Nouns you cannot count are [2]*countable / uncountable* nouns. They have no plural forms.

2 Look at the photos in Exercise 1. Which are countable and which are uncountable?

a/an, some, any

3 Complete the sentences with *a/an*, *some* and *any*. Then choose the correct words in the rule.

1 A Would you like ... water?
B No, thanks. I've got ... tea.
2 Can I have ... apple or ... banana?
3 Have ... biscuits.
4 Are there ... vegetables in the kitchen?
5 There isn't ... milk in the fridge.

> **RULE:** Use *a/an* with [1]*singular / plural* countable nouns.
> Use some with [2]*singular / plural countable* and *uncountable* nouns.
> Use *any* in questions and in [3]*positive / negative* sentences.
> Use *some* in questions when offering or requesting something.

4 Complete the sentences with *a/an*, *some* and *any*.

1 A Would you like ... vegetables?
B No, thanks. I don't like ...vegetables.
2 A I'd like ... strawberries, please.
B Strawberries? Yes, I think we have ... .
3 I'd like ... tomatoes.
4 I don't want ... coffee.
5 Can I have ... orange, please?
6 Do you want ... sugar in your tea?

(how) much / (how) many / a lot of / lots of

5 Look at the examples. Complete the rule.

How **much** sugar is there in a lemon?	How **many** people eat avocado as a dessert?
I don't eat **much** chocolate.	We haven't got **many** apples.
Bananas have got **a lot of** sugar.	**A lot of** people like avocados.
Watermelons have got **lots of** water.	Honey has got **lots of** vitamins.

RULE: We typically use *(How) much* and *(How) many* in questions and negative sentences.

Use *many* with plural [1]... nouns and *much* with [2]... nouns.

Use *a lot of* / *lots of* with both countable and uncountable [3]... .

6 Choose the correct words in questions 1–6. Then match them with the answers a–f.

1 – many b

1 How *much* / *many* apples do you want?
2 How *much* / *many* sugar is there in an avocado?
3 Are there *much* / *many* boys in your class?
4 How *much* / *many* peppers are there?
5 How *much* / *many* time have you got?
6 Have you got *many* / *a lot of* homework?

a I think there are about five.
b Just one, please.
c Only 10 minutes.
d No, I haven't got any.
e I have no idea. I don't think it's a lot.
f Yes, there are 12, and 5 girls.

Workbook page 28

LISTENING

1 1.34 Complete the menu with words from the list. Listen and check.

cheesecake | chips | tomato | onion rings
chicken | spinach and mushroom

BLUES CAFÉ MENU

OUR DELICIOUS STARTERS
[1]... soup
mushroom soup
[2]... omelette
ham and cheese omelette

LUNCH SPECIALS
steak
grilled [3]...
pasta with tomatoes

SIDE DISHES
[4]...
[5]...
mixed salad

DESSERTS
yoghurt and strawberries
vanilla and chocolate ice cream
[6]...

DRINKS
[7]... juices
mineral water
[8]...
tea
coffee

2 1.35 Jane and Sam are in the Blues Café. Listen and find out who eats more. Listen again and complete the sentences below.

1 Jane wants the ...
2 Sam orders ...
3 He doesn't want ...

3 1.35 Complete the sentences with *get*, *menu*, *drink*, *we'd*, *some* and *bill*. Then listen again and check.

Waiter:	Customer:
Can I help you?	[1] ... like something to eat.
Here's the [2]	Thanks.
What would you like to [3] ... ?	An orange juice for me, please.
I'll be right back.	And for me [4] ... mineral water, please
What can I [5] ... you?	I'd like the spinach and mushroom omelette.
Would you like a starter?	Yes, please. Can I have the ... , please? / No, thanks.
Of course. That's £	Can we have the [6] ... , please?
Thank you. Bye, bye / Thanks very much.	Here you are.
	Thank you. Bye.

4 Work in groups. One is the waiter, the others are customers. Order meals. Use the menu in Exercise 1 and the conversations in Exercise 3.

THINK *self-esteem*

Being happy

1 Read these statements. Which ones do you think are important for being happy. Which ones do you think are not so important.

1 There's no 'right' body shape or size. Healthy and happy people come in all shapes and sizes.
2 You can only find out what kind of person someone is if you get to know them better.
3 Never laugh about people for being too thin, too short, too tall or too fat.
4 Never laugh at other people's jokes about people's looks. That's unfair and it hurts.
5 Being thin is not the same as being healthy and happy.
6 Like yourself for who you are and for the things you are good at.

2 Work in pairs. Say what you think is important for being happy.

PRONUNCIATION
Vowel sounds: /ɪ/ and /iː/
Go to page 150.

READING

1 Look at Jenny's blog for not more than 15 seconds and answer the questions. Then read and check your answers.

1 How old is Jenny?
2 How is she feeling?
3 What's the problem?

2 Read the blog again. Answer the questions.

1 How do Jenny's parents react to Jeremy's cooking?
2 What does Jeremy sometimes do with the food his family don't eat?
3 Why does Jeremy sing when he serves his spaghetti?
4 What does Jenny like about the meals Jeremy serves?
5 Why does Jenny say that her mum and dad's dance class is 'unhealthy'?

WRITING

Your favourite meal

1 Put the sentences or phrases in order to make an email from Jenny to her friend.

1 i

a Actually this week it's not a surprise.
b My brother always cooks a surprise meal for us then.
c Best, Jenny
d Would you like to come and try this week's surprise?
e Are you free on Friday night?
f It's pear and bean omelette.
g Please say you can come.
h And for dessert it's some ice cream and strawberries.
i Dear Jimmy,
j Doesn't that sound good?

2 Write out the email in your notebooks.

3 Write a paragraph describing your favourite or least favourite meal.

Thirteenandsosmart.com

HOME ABOUT NEWS CONTACT

MY BLOG ABOUT MY DAY AND OTHER IMPORTANT THINGS

FRIDAY, 17TH MARCH

Not a good day. My older brother Jeremy is cooking tonight. 'What's the problem?' I can hear you saying. Well, the problem is that you don't know my brother. You don't know how he cooks. And you don't know that every Friday is a nightmare for me because my parents go to their dance class. When they come back we all sit down and Jeremy starts serving what he calls 'another surprise meal'. Jeremy isn't a bad cook. He's a catastrophe!

First of all he always cooks too many things, like fish, steak, boiled ham, roast chicken and sausages. All on one plate! That's too much food for a week! How can one person eat all that in one meal? Mum and Dad don't say a word, of course. They're too polite. And they don't want to give up their dance classes.

Spaghetti tonight. When Jeremy says 'spaghetti' he doesn't say it. He sings it (he loves cooking spaghetti, well, he loves cooking anything!). But that doesn't make a difference. It tastes terrible. There isn't enough tomato sauce on it. There's too much pasta. And there's too much salt. Yuck! Another one of my brother's favourites is vegetable soup. It's always too spicy, and there are never enough vegetables in it. And he puts in little pieces of fish, steak, ham, chicken and sausages. You can guess where they're from. It's the left-overs from the week before.

My brother's desserts aren't bad. He gets them at the supermarket. It's usually ice cream with strawberries or chocolate mousse with mango. But, of course, there are never enough strawberries and there's never enough ice cream. I want to talk to Mum and Dad today. I want them to give up dancing. It's not healthy. You know what I mean. It's unhealthy for me when they go dancing every Friday ...

GRAMMAR

too many / too much / (not) enough + noun

1 Complete the sentences with *much, many* and *enough* and then complete the rule.

1 He always cooks **too** ... **things**.
2 There's **too** ... **salt** in the spaghetti.
3 There's not ... **tomato** sauce on it.
4 There aren't ... **vegetables** in the soup.
5 There's not ... **sugar** in my coffee.

RULE: Use *too* [1]... with countable nouns, and *too* [2]... with uncountable nouns.
Use *(not) enough with* [3]... and [4]... *nouns*.

2 Complete with *too much, too many, not enough*.

1 There are ... mushrooms on this pizza. I hate them.
2 There's ... salt in this soup. I can't eat it.
3 There is ... sugar in my coffee. Can I have some more, please?
4 There are ... chairs. Can you stand?
5 There are ... cars on the road. It's dangerous to ride my bike.
6 We've got ... homework tonight. I want to watch TV.

too + adjective, (*not* +) adjective + enough

3 Use the example sentences to choose the correct options in the rule.

His vegetable soup is always **too spicy**.
This pizza is **not hot enough**.

RULE:
- We use *too* + adjective to say that something is [1]*more / less* than we like or want.
- We use *not* + adjective + *enough* to say that something is [2]*more / less* than we like or want.

4 Complete the sentences.

0 The test is too easy. It's not hard enough.
1 The film isn't exciting enough. It's ...
2 The T-shirt is too expensive. It's ...
3 It's not warm enough today. It's ...
4 Your bike's too small for me. It's ...
5 His car's not fast enough. It's ...

5 Complete with *not enough* or *too*.

My dad always says there's [1]... much rain in the UK in the summer, and that it's [2]... hot ... . He's right. And I feel that it's [3]... boring to spend holidays here. So I'm happy that we usually go to the south of Italy for our holidays. There are kilometres of beaches, and so there are never [4]... many tourists. I love the food there, that's why I often eat [5]... much.

Workbook page 29

VOCABULARY

Adjectives to talk about food

1 Match the adjectives to the photos.

roast | boiled | grilled | fried

2 Put the words in the list in order from 'very good' to 'very bad'.

nice | horrible | delicious | (a bit) boring

3 Work in pairs. Ask and answer questions. Use the words from Exercise 2.

boiled or roast beef? | grilled or fried chicken?
boiled or roast potatoes? | boiled or fried eggs?
grilled or fried fish?

What do you prefer, boiled or roast beef?

Roast beef. It's delicious.

4 How do you say these words in your language? Write two types of food next to each word.

sweet | spicy | savoury | fresh | tasty
yummy | fatty | disgusting | salty

sweet: chocolate, strawberries

Workbook page 31

GET IT *right!*

Correct the spelling mistakes in these food and drink words:
chiken, coffe, wather, tomatoe.

PHOTOSTORY 2

THE PICNIC

1 🔊 **1.38** Look at the photos and discuss the questions. Then listen and read and check your answers.

What food and drink have Megan and Luke got?

Why is Olivia unhappy?

MEGAN: A picnic. I love picnics. What a great idea, Ryan.

OLIVIA: Yes, Ryan. It was an awesome idea.

RYAN: Don't be so surprised. It's not my first one.

LUKE: Umm. Actually, I think it probably is.

1

OLIVIA: What drinks have you got, Megan?

MEGAN: Let me see. I've got orange juice, lemonade and apple juice. Oh, and some water as well.

OLIVIA: That's great. What about you, Ryan?

RYAN: I've got fruit: apples and bananas. Oh, and a couple of chocolate bars.

2

OLIVIA: Luke? What about the sandwiches?

LUKE: Well, I've got ham. I've got chicken, and tuna, and I've got a steak sandwich too.

OLIVIA: That's all? But what about me? I can't eat that.

LUKE: Why not?

OLIVIA: Because I've got a problem with eating meat. I'm a vegetarian, remember?

LUKE: So what? You can have the tuna sandwich, then.

3

RYAN: Oh, Luke! Olivia is really upset now.

LUKE: Is she upset with me? Why? Tell me. I've got no idea.

MEGAN: She's a vegetarian, Luke. She doesn't eat meat. It's important to her.

LUKE: Don't vegetarians eat fish?

MEGAN:Maybe some do, but not Olivia.

LUKE: Oh no!

4

2 Work in pairs. Discuss what happens next in the story. Write down your ideas.

We think Olivia eats a chicken sandwich.

3 EP1 Watch to find out how the story continues.

4 Mark the sentences T (True) or F (False).

1 Luke feels bad for not thinking about Olivia.
2 Ryan has got lots of biscuits.
3 Megan and Ryan play football against the other two.
4 Luke secretly makes a phone call.
5 They don't enjoy the football match.
6 The pizza man brings Olivia a pizza with no meat on it.

Phrases for fluency

1 Find the expressions 1–5 in the story. Who says them? Match them to the definitions a–f.

0 Luke – e

0 Actually, ...
1 ... as well.
2 ... a couple of ...
3 What about (me)?
4 So what?
5 upset with ...

a too
b unhappy with
c one or two (but not many)
d What is the situation (for me)?
e In fact, ...
f Why is that a problem?

2 Complete the conversations. Use the expressions in Exercise 1.

1 A Mum? John's got his sandwiches. But ... me?
B Well, I'm making ... cheese and tomato sandwiches for you right now.
A Cool! Can I have an apple ... ?

2 A I broke your watch. I'm sorry. Are you ... me?
B Don't worry about it. ... , it wasn't a very good watch.

3 A I can't go to the cinema. I've got homework.
B ... ? You can do it at the weekend.

VOCABULARY

Expressions with *have got*

1 Complete the things that Luke and Olivia say.

1 I've got a ... with eating meat.
2 I've got ... idea.
3 You go on. I've got ... to do first.

2 Complete with the expressions in the list.

a problem | an idea | a headache
time | something to do

0 A Dad! I've got *a problem* with my English homework.
B English? Sorry! I can't help you.

1 A Are you OK? Is something wrong?
B I've got ... . I want to go to bed.

2 A What can we do this afternoon?
B I don't know.
C Oh, I've got ... !

3 A Jan, can you help me, please?
B I'm really sorry, Tom. The lesson starts in two minutes! I haven't got ... .

4 A Let's go to town tomorrow.
B Tomorrow? Sorry, no, I've got ... tomorrow. It's a secret!

Workbook page 31

FUNCTIONS

Apologising

1 Who says these sentences? Mark them O (Olivia) or L (Luke).

1 I'm really sorry.
2 I feel bad.
3 Don't worry.
4 It's OK.

2 1.39 Complete the conversation. Listen and check. Then act it out in pairs.

MAN: Oh no. I'm really [1] ... .
WOMAN: [2] ... worry. It's not my favourite picture.
MAN: But it's broken. I [3] ... really bad.
WOMAN: [4] ... OK. Really. I don't really like it anyway.

3 Work in pairs. Write a short dialogue for the picture below. Act it out.

Life skills

Saying sorry

We all make mistakes. We say we're sorry so that the other person feels better, and understands that we care. Saying sorry is important, but sometimes we also need to show we are sorry by our actions.

1 Think about the photostory on page 40.

1. Imagine you are Olivia. Luke hasn't got any vegetarian sandwiches? How do you feel?
2. Imagine you are Luke. Olivia hasn't got any sandwiches to eat. How do you feel?

2 Read these situations. Who do you think needs to apologise and why?

Tom arrives late to school for the second time in a week. The teacher gives him a detention.

Abby's dad calls her lazy because she never tidies her bedroom.

Zoe forgets her friend's birthday. The next day, her friend doesn't speak to her.

Emily is wearing her new shoes. Amy says they look terrible. Emily is upset and tells her friends not to speak to Amy.

George orders a ham and cheese pizza. The waiter brings him a tuna and pepper pizza

3 Work in pairs. Compare your answers to Exercise 2. Do you agree?

4 Work in pairs. Discuss which of these things is a good idea for the people in Exercise 2? More than one answer is possible. Can you think of other ways of apologising?

- Say sorry immediately.
- I'm here for you.
- Change our future actions.
- Be quiet.
- Write a short apology letter or card.
- Tell a funny joke.
- Buy a present or flowers.
- Wait and say sorry later.
- Say 'I love you!' and smile.

5 Work in pairs. Write a situation similar to the ones in Exercise 2 where someone needs to apologise.

6 Read your situation to the rest of the class. Discuss these questions:

1. Who needs to apologise?
2. What is the best way to apologise?
3. What does the person apologising have to say? Do they need to do anything else?

Tips for saying sorry

1. Don't be afraid to recognise when you make a mistake.
2. Say sorry when you make a mistake. It shows that you respect others and care about them.
3. Saying sorry isn't always enough. Sometimes you also have to change your actions.

4 FAMILY TIES

LEARNING OUTCOMES

FUNCTIONS: asking for permission; talking about families

GRAMMAR: possessive adjectives and pronouns; *whose* and possessive *'s*; *was / were*

VOCABULARY: family members; feelings

Work in pairs. Look at the photo and answer these questions.

1 Describe the photo.
2 Do animals have families the same as people?
3 What makes a good and a bad family?

READING

1 Find the pairs of words.

daughter brother father
wife husband mother
son sister

2 Describe each person in the picture. Use two words from Exercise 1.

The girl is a daughter and a sister.

3 Work in pairs. Write down as many examples as you can of the following.

1 a TV brother and sister
2 a TV husband and wife

4 Compare your ideas with another pair.

5 1.40 Read and listen to the article on page 45. Do they mention any of the families you talked about?

6 Read the article again. Correct the information in these sentences.

1 Bart Simpson has got a cat called Santa's Little Helper.
2 Lisa Simpson has got one aunt.
3 Ben Tennyson is on holiday in Europe.
4 He can change into 12 different aliens.
5 Greg Heffley has got a little brother called Roderick.
6 His ideas are always successful.

tv families

Who is your favourite TV family? We want to know. It's not easy. There are so many great families to choose from. But to help you start thinking, here are some of ours.

Everyone knows *The Simpsons*; Bart, his mum and dad Marge and Homer, his sisters Lisa and Maggie. And then there's Granddad and those horrible aunts, Patty and Selma. And let's not forget Bart's dog, Santa's Little Helper. I love watching this family and their adventures around the town of Springfield. They get into all kinds of trouble but they never forget they are a family. And they always make me laugh. I love this show. Thanks, Dad, for introducing it to me.

When I was eight, *Ben 10* was my favourite TV programme. The story is crazy. Ten-year-old Ben Tennyson is spending his summer holiday with his Grandpa and his cousin Gwen. They are driving around the USA. One day Ben finds a strange watch and puts it on. Suddenly he is an alien. With this watch he can turn into ten different space creatures. But he needs these powers because some other evil alien wants Ben's new watch. So Ben spends the rest of the holiday fighting lots of monsters from outer space. But, of course, he still has time to fight with his cousin too.

The Heffley family are the stars of *Diary of a Wimpy Kid*, a really popular series of books and films centred around Greg, the middle son of the family. Greg lives with his mum and dad, his little brother Manny and his big brother Roderick. He's just a 'normal' kid who writes about his life in a journal. OK, so the Heffley family are not really a 'TV' family but they show the films on TV a lot so we think we can choose them. We want the Heffleys on our list because they are so funny. And we really love Greg and all the problems he has with his great ideas that never work out.

So these are three of our favourite TV families. Now write in and tell us about yours.

THINK *values*

TV families

1 Think about your favourite TV family. Write the things they do.

My favourite TV family is … .

- They help each other.
- They fight a lot.
- They laugh a lot.
- They spend a lot of time together.
- They talk about their problems.
- They are good friends.

2 Work in pairs. Tell your partner about your favourite TV family. Are they a good family?

The Simpsons are usually a good family because …

But sometimes they …

GRAMMAR

Possessive adjectives and pronouns

1 Complete the sentences with the words in the list. Look at the article on page 39 and check your answers.

our | ours | your | yours

1 Who are ... favourite TV family?
2 Here are some of ... .
3 These are three of ... favourite TV families.
4 Now write in and tell us about ... .

2 Complete the rule with pronouns and adjectives. Then complete the table.

> **RULE:** Possessive [1]... come before a noun to show who something belongs to: *It's* ***my*** *book.*
>
> Possessive [2]... can take the place of the possessive adjective and the noun: *The book* ***is mine.***

possessive adjectives	possessive pronouns
0 It's my book.	The book is mine
1 It's your book.	The book is ... .
2 It's ... book.	The book is hers.
3 It's ... book.	The book is his.
4 It's our book.	The book is ... .
5 It's ... book.	The book is theirs.

whose and possessive *'s*

3 Choose the correct words and complete the rule.

A [1]*Whose / Who* son is Bart?
B Bart is [2]*Homer's / Homers'* son.
A [3]*Whose / Who's* Lisa's mum?
B Marge.

> **RULE:** To ask about possession, use the question word [1]... .
>
> To talk about possession, add [2]... to the end of a name / noun.
>
> If the name / noun ends in an *-s*, add the apostrophe (') after the *-s*.

4 Choose the correct words.

1 A *Whose / Who* phone is this?
B Ask Jenny. I think it's *her / hers*.
2 Hey! That's *my / mine* sandwich not *your / yours*.
3 I'm sure that's *Kate's / Kates'* bike. It looks just like *her / hers*.
4 A *Whose / Who* do you sit next to in Maths?
B *Rashid / Rashid's*.
5 A Is that your *parent's / parents'* dog?
B Yes, I think it's *their / theirs*.

> **GET IT right!**
> Correct this sentence:
> *It is the wedding of my cousin.*

Workbook page 36

VOCABULARY

Family members

1 Read the text. Complete the spaces with the missing family words.

Here's a photo of my dad's side of the family. My dad's got a *big* brother called Bob. He's my *uncle* and he's great. He's so funny. His wife Jemma is my *aunt*, of course (and she's my dad's *sister-in-law*). She's also really nice. They've got two sons – Jimmy and his *little* brother Robin. They're my *cousins*. Jimmy is also my best friend.

Of course, my dad and Bob have the same mum and dad. They are my *grandparents*. I call them *Grandma Diana* and *Grandpa Roger*. They're really nice to me because I'm their only granddaughter.

2 Work in pairs. How many sentences can you make about the family in two minutes?

Diana is Roger's wife.   *Jimmy is Jemma's son.*

Workbook page 39

LISTENING

1 Read and match three of the sentences (1–6) with the pictures (A–C).

WHY MY FAMILY DRIVE ME MAD

1 My sister always wants to borrow my clothes. It drives me mad. (Lucy, 17)

2 My uncle tells really bad jokes. No one ever laughs – just him. (Howard, 15)

3 My dad never gives me any money. He's so mean. (Suzie, 16)

4 My grandpa just talks about the 'good-old days'. I'm not really interested. (Viv, 12)

5 I often fight with my parents about going out. They always want me to stay at home. (Tom, 14)

6 My brother plays games all day. He never lets me play. (Paul, 14)

2 **1.41** Listen to the conversations. What is the relationship between the speakers?

Conversation 1: ... Conversation 2: ...

3 **1.41** Listen again and answer the questions.

1 What does Lucy's sister Kathy want to borrow?
2 Why does she want to borrow it?
3 Does Lucy say yes or no?
4 Where does Tom want to go?
5 What does his mum say?
6 What does his dad say?

PRONUNCIATION
-er /ə/ at the end of words
Go to page 150.

FUNCTIONS

Asking for permission

1 Complete the sentences from the listening.

Asking for permission	Saying yes	Saying no
1 ... I borrow your yellow and black shirt? 2 ... I go out tonight?	Of course you can.	No, you 3... .

2 Write a short conversation for the picture.

3 Think of requests that you make to different members of your family. Write them down.

Can I borrow ... ? *Can I have ... ?*
Can I go ... ? *Can I play ... ?*

4 Read them to your partner. Can he/she guess who you say this to?

READING

1 Look at the photos. How do you think these girls were heroes? Read the article and find out.

2 Read the article again. Put the sentences in the correct order. There is one thing not mentioned in the article. Where do you think it goes?

a Miya goes under the water to help her dad.
b Tiffany phones for an ambulance.
c Their mother arrives home.
d David has a problem with his legs.
e David disappears under the water.
f Miya and Tiffany are swimming with their dad, David.

train to THINK

Making inferences

1 Work in pairs. Who says these sentences? Mark them M (Miya), T (Tiffany) or D (Dad).

1 'Help. I'm in trouble.'
2 'What's wrong, Dad?'
3 'Help him. Go under the water.'
4 'Call an ambulance.'
5 'My dad needs help.'
6 'My heroes.'

2 Work in pairs. Write one more thing to say to each person.

1 Miya
2 Tiffany
3 David
4 The ambulance driver
5 The girls' mother

3 Read your sentences to another pair for them to guess.

I think Miya says that.

That's probably Tiffany.

THE SWIMMING POOL HEROES

Miya Peyregne, aged nine, and her six-year-old sister Tiffany were in the swimming pool in the back garden of their house in Grandville, Michigan, USA. Their father David was with them. It was a lovely day. There wasn't a cloud in the sky.

Suddenly David shouted. He was in trouble. It was his legs. His legs weren't right. He was in pain.

Then he was under the water. The girls weren't scared but they were worried. Was it just a joke or was he really in trouble? Twenty seconds later he was still under the water. Now Miya was scared.

There was no time to wait. In seconds Miya was under the water with her father. He was heavy but with the help of the water she was able to pull him to one side of the pool. Now his head was out of the water. He was alive but he wasn't conscious.

There was a mobile phone in the house. Tiffany called the emergency services. Ten minutes later an ambulance was there. Soon their father was conscious again. The girls were relieved.

David still doesn't know what was wrong with his legs on that day. But he knows that his daughters were heroes and thanks them every day for saving his life. He is a very proud father.

GRAMMAR

was / were

1 Look at the examples from the article on page 48. Choose the correct words.

1 It *was / were* a lovely day. There *wasn't / weren't* a cloud in the sky.
2 The girls *were / weren't* scared but they *were / weren't* worried.
3 *Was / Were* he really in trouble?

2 Complete the table.

Positive	Negative
I/he/she/it [0]was	I/he/she/it [1]… (was not)
You/we/they [0]were	You/we/they [2]… (were not)
Questions	**Short answers**
[3]… I/he/she/it?	Yes, I/he/she/it [4]… . No, I/he/she/it [5]… .
[6]… you/we/they?	Yes, you/we/they [7]… . No, you/we/they [8]… .

3 Complete the questions and answers with *was*, *were*, *wasn't* or *weren't*.

1 A … you in bed at 9 pm last night?
B No, I … . I … in the kitchen with my mum and dad.
2 A … your teacher happy with your homework?
B Yes she … . She … very happy with it.
3 A … it hot yesterday?
B No, it … . It … really cold.
4 A … we at school yesterday?
B No, we … . It … Sunday!
5 A … your parents born in the UK?
B No, they… . They … born in India.

4 Work in pairs. Ask and answer the questions in Exercise 3.

Workbook page 37

VOCABULARY

Feelings

1 Match the sentences.

1 Our daughter was first in the race.
2 It was 9 pm and Mum wasn't home.
3 That wasn't a nice thing to say to Miriam.
4 That maths lesson was really difficult.
5 I wasn't expecting a big party.
6 The students were really noisy.
7 It was a really good horror film.
8 The test was really hard.
a She's really **upset** now.
b And the teacher was **angry**.
c I was very **surprised** to see so many people there.
d I'm really **confused** now.
e We are so **proud** of her.
f I was **relieved** when it was over.
g I was a bit **worried**. Where was she?
h I was really **scared** at the end of it.

GET IT *right!*

Remember that we spell *surprised* with an *R* before the *P*.

not

✗ ~~suprised~~.

2 Match the sentences in Exercise 1 with the pictures. Write the numbers 1–8.

Workbook page 39

Culture

1 Look at the photos. What can you see? What's the same in the two photos?

2 🔊 **1.44** Read and listen to the article. Which countries do the photos show?

3 Do people celebrate Children's Day in your country? If so how do they celebrate it?

Around the world on CHILDREN'S DAY

In 1954 there was the first Universal Children's Day on 20th November to **celebrate** and protect children all over the world. This was **International** Children's Day but now many countries around the world have their own day each year when they celebrate their children.

23rd April

TURKEY: This day is a **national** holiday in Turkey. On this day, Turkey invites groups of children from other countries to stay with Turkish families and celebrate with them.

30th April

MEXICO: Children's day is called *El Día Del Niño*. Some schools close for the day, other schools have a special day for the children when they play games. The children also bring in their favourite food to **share** with their friends.

5th May

JAPAN: The official children's day, called *kodomo no hi*, is on 5th May. But some people in Japan celebrate two children's days. One on 3rd March for girls and one on 5th May for boys. On 5th May they fly carp streamers (a type of wind sock in the shape of a fish).

1st June

BULGARIA: Parents do special things with their children and give them big **presents**. The day is like a second birthday for the children.

CHINA: This is a very special day in schools. They take the children on camping trips or trips to the cinema. Many children also get presents from their parents.

24th July

VANUATU: Children spend the morning at school where they celebrate and have fun. At midday, the children are free to go home and spend the rest of the day with their parents. Some parents buy their children a present but the most important thing is for children and parents to have some time to spend **together**.

GET IT *right!*

Remember that in British English we write *favourite* with a U.

not

✗ ~~*favorite*~~

This is American English.

14th November

INDIA: Indians chose this day to celebrate because it is the birthday of the country's first Prime Minister, Jawaharlal Nehru. Nehru was famous for his love of children. On this day, the children organise the celebrations at their school. Their teachers sing and dance for the students.

4 Read the article again. Answer the questions. Sometimes there is more than one correct answer.

In which country ...

1 do the children spend more time with their mum and dad?
2 do they have more than one Children's Day?
3 is Children's Day also a famous person's birthday?
4 do children get presents?
5 do children celebrate with children from other countries?
6 do children celebrate Children's Day at school?

5 Work in small groups. Talk about the perfect Children's Day.

All children get a big present.

School is closed for the whole day.

Mum and Dad do your homework.

6 There are six words in bold in the article. Match the words with these meanings. Write the words.

0 *celebrate*

0 to have fun, do something special, for example on a friend's birthday
1 with other people
2 to do with a whole country
3 to have something at the same time with other people
4 to do with two or more countries
5 something you give to a person on a special day

WRITING

An invitation

1 Read the emails. Answer the questions.

1 Who is Dana? 2 Can Liam go to the party?

Hi Liam,

Would you like to come to my house next Friday for a party at 7 pm? It's my cousin Dana's birthday.

My address is 32 Lime Street. Make a playlist please, I love your music.

Hope you can come. Let me know soon.

Tina

PS Don't tell Dana. It's a surprise.

Hi Tina,

I'd love to come to your party on Friday but I've got a small problem. I've got football training from 6 to 7.30 pm. Can I arrive a bit late? Is that OK?

No problem with the playlist. I've got some great new songs.

See you Friday.

Liam

2 Match the sentences with the same meaning.

1 *c*

1 Would you like to come to my party?
2 I'd love to come to your party.
3 I'm sorry I can't come to your party.
4 Make a playlist, please.
5 Don't tell Dana.

a I don't want Dana to know.
b Can you make a playlist?
c Can you come to my party?
d I'd love to come but I can't.
e I'd be very happy to accept your invitation.

3 Which pairs of sentences in Exercise 2 can you use to do these things?

1 give an order
2 accept an invitation
3 make a request
4 make an invitation
5 refuse an invitation

4 Read the invitation again. Answer the questions.

1 What is the invitation for?
2 What special requests does Tina make?

5 You want to invite a friend to your house. What information should you include? Choose the correct answers.

1 Your address.
2 How many brothers and sisters you've got.
3 The time you want them to come.
4 The reason.
5 Who your favourite singer is.
6 The day or date you want them to come.

6 Write an invitation (50 words). Choose one of these reasons. Include a special request or instruction.

- It's your birthday.
- You've got a great new DVD to watch.
- You've got a new computer game.

Literature

HOLES
BY LOUIS SACHAR

Stanley and Zero are prisoners in a work camp for teenage offenders. Stanley was sent there by mistake. They work very hard all day in the sun. People think Zero can't talk and is a bit stupid. Zero asks Stanley to teach him how to read and write.

1 Read the text and answer the question: Do you think Stanley is a good teacher?

Zero's A wasn't bad, just a little big. Stanley told him he needed to write smaller, or else they'd run out of paper real quick. Zero printed it smaller.

'Actually, there are two ways to write each letter,' Stanley said, as he realized this was going to be even harder than he thought. 'That's a capital A. But usually you'll see a small a. You only have capitals at the beginning of a word, and only if it's the start of a sentence, or if it's a proper noun, like a name.'

Zero nodded as if he understood, but Stanley knew he had made very little sense.

He printed a lowercase a, and Zero copied it.

'So there are fifty-two,' said Zero.

Stanley didn't know what he was talking about. 'Instead of twenty-six letters. There are really fifty-two.' Stanley looked at him, surprised. 'I guess that's right. How'd you figure that out?' he asked.

Zero said nothing.

'Did you add?'

Zero said nothing.

'Did you multiply?'

'That's just how many there are,' said Zero. Stanley raised and lowered one shoulder. He didn't even know how Zero knew there were twenty-six in the first place. Did he count them as he recited them?

He had Zero write a few more upper- and lowercase A's, and then he moved on to a capital B. This was going to take a long time, he realized.

'You can teach me ten letters a day,' suggested Zero. 'Five capitals and five smalls. After five days I'll know them all. Except on the last day I'll have to do twelve. Six capitals and six smalls.'

Again Stanley stared at him, amazed that he was able to figure all that out.

2 'Zero' is a nickname. Why do you think people call him 'Zero?'

3 Why does Zero nod to show he understands when he doesn't (line 6)?

4 Zero doesn't say very much. Why do you think this is?

5 What does Stanley realize about Zero and numbers as he teaches him to write the letters?

6 Why do you think Zero can't read? If he learns to read, how will this help him?

GET IT *right!*

Units 3&4

much and *many*

We use *many* with plural countable nouns and *much* with uncountable nouns.

✓ *How many sandwiches have you got?*

✗ *How ~~much~~ sandwiches have you got?*

✓ *We haven't got much cheesecake.*

✗ *We haven't got ~~many~~ cheesecake.*

1 Work in pairs. Read the conversation. Choose *much* or *many*.

SARAH: Hi, Julian, have we got everything we need for the party?

JULIAN: We've got some crisps, but we haven't got [1]*many / much* fruit.

SARAH: How [2]*many / much* apples did you buy?

JULIAN: We've got six apples, but we haven't got [3]*many / much* vegetables.

SARAH: I've got four tomatoes. How [4]*many / much* people are coming?

JULIAN: Everybody from our class is coming!

SARAH: Oh, have we got [5]*many / much* juice?

JULIAN: Yes, but we haven't got [6]*many / much* glasses.

SARAH: Oh dear! We've got a problem.

Practise the conversation with your partner.

too + adjective and *(not)* + adjective + *enough*

We never use *too much* + adjective.

✓ *The soup was too cold.*

✗ *The soup was too ~~much~~ cold.*

Remember to put enough after the adjective, NOT before.

✓ *The soup wasn't hot enough.*

✗ *The soup ~~wasn't enough hot~~.*

2 Find the correct sentence. Then correct the incorrect sentences.

1 We didn't go because the weather wasn't enough good.
2 The sausages were too spicy. And the pizza wasn't warm enough.
3 I didn't do my homework. I was too much tired.
4 The food he eats isn't enough healthy.
5 The room wasn't enough big and the price was too much expensive.

Possessive adjectives and pronouns and Possessive's

Don't use *she, he, her, him* or *his* for things. Use *it* or *its*.

✓ *I like the camera and its technology.*

✗ *I like the camera and ~~his~~ technology.*

3 Correct the sentences.

1 The pasta is fantastic and her sauce too!
2 The mobile is green and the best thing is that he has got a great camera.
3 This shirt is expensive but she is really nice.
4 My watch is new and I really love him!
5 I don't watch TV - she's boring.
6 I like his touchscreen and his functions.

SAY IT *right!*

Vowel sounds /I/ and /i:/

1 Work in pairs. Take turns to say the words in the list. You partner says if the word has the /ɪ/ or /i:/ sound.

cheese | meat | chips | beef | chicken | sing | jeans | sleep

2 Write the words in two lists: /I/ and /i:/, according to their pronunciation.

3 🔊 **1.45** Listen, check and repeat.

RULE: The letter *I* is never pronounced with the /i:/ sound. Spanish speakers often make the /ɪ/ sound too long and the /i:/ sound too short. So the two sound the same! Remember: They are two different sounds.

test yourself

Units 3&4

VOCABULARY

1 Complete the sentences with the words in the list. There are two extra words.

angry | big | boiled | grilled | relieved | scared
grandparents | carrots | confused | spicy | chicken | proud

1 I don't like many vegetables – just peppers and ... .
2 I was really worried about the exam so I was ... when it was over.
3 The curry is too ... . I can't eat it.
4 It was a really stupid thing to do. My parents were really ... with me.
5 To make ... potatoes you need to cook them in water for about 20 minutes.
6 There was a strange noise outside the house. We were a bit ... .
7 Nigel's a vegetarian. He doesn't eat ... .
8 I don't really understand this homework. I'm a bit ... .
9 Freddie's my ... brother. I'm 14 and he's 20.
10 My mum's mother and father are my ... .

GRAMMAR

2 Complete the sentences with the words in the list.

much | many | ours | our | was | were

1 How ... sugar do you want in your coffee?
2 It ... really cold yesterday.
3 That's not your dog, it's ... .
4 There are too ... socks on your bedroom floor!
5 ... dog's called Spike.
6 Where ... you last night?

3 Find and correct the mistake in each sentence.

1 This salad has got too much beans.
2 That's not your sandwich. It's my.
3 My parents was very proud of my school report.
4 I like Clara and I really like hers sister too.
5 How many water do you want?
6 I think this is Kevins' book.

FUNCTIONAL LANGUAGE

4 Write the missing words.

1 A I'm late. I'm really ... .
B Don't ... . We've still got lots of time.
2 A I ... this question is really difficult.
B I think ... too.
3 A ... I borrow your bike, Dad?
B Of ... you can.
4 A Can I go ... tonight?
B No, you ... .

CAMBRIDGE EXAMS
Review Units 3 & 4
Go to page 145.

MY SCORE

22–30

10–21

0–9

5 IT FEELS LIKE HOME

LEARNING OUTCOMES

FUNCTIONS: making suggestions; talking about events in the past

GRAMMAR: past simple (regular verbs); modifiers: *quite, very, really*

VOCABULARY: parts of a house and furniture; adjectives with *-ed* / *-ing*; phrasal verbs with *look*

Work in pairs. Look at the photo and answer these questions.

1 How do you think these bees feel in their house?

2 Do you feel relaxed when you are at home?

3 What is your favourite room in your house? Why?

READING

1 **2.02** Match the words in the list (1–6) with the photos (A–F). Then listen, check and repeat.

1 kitchen | 2 bedroom | 3 bathroom
4 living room | 5 dining room | 6 garden

2 Match the verbs in the list with the places in Exercise 1. (Some verbs go with more than one room.)

eat | sleep | cook | wash
watch TV | play football

3 Work in pairs. Have you got the same ideas? What other activities do you do in these rooms?

I talk to my dad in the kitchen.

I sing in the bathroom.

4 Look at the photos on page 57. What can you say about the house?

5 **2.03** Read and listen to the magazine article. Choose the correct option A, B or C.

1 The queue of people wanted to help James May to buy a house.
A Right B Wrong C Doesn't say

2 They finished building the house in one month.
A Right B Wrong C Doesn't say

3 The LEGO fridge worked.
A Right B Wrong C Doesn't say

4 James May liked the bed.
A Right B Wrong C Doesn't say

5 There were photos of the house on a Facebook page.
A Right B Wrong C Doesn't say

6 A charity for children has got the pieces of LEGO now.
A Right B Wrong C Doesn't say

The LEGO® House

A few years ago in August, there was a very long queue of people in the countryside near London, in England. Some people started queuing at 4.30 in the morning. Why were they there? They wanted to help James May, a TV presenter, to build a house.

But this was not an ordinary house. No, this was a LEGO house.

Together, 1,200 people used 3.3 million (yes, 3,300,000) LEGO toy bricks to make a real house.

It was part of a TV show called *Toy Stories*. In the programmes, James May used traditional toys to make 'real' things. Why LEGO? Well, because when he was young, James May loved LEGO and played with it all the time.

The people finished building the house on 17 September, almost seven weeks after they started. Everything was LEGO. All the walls, doors and windows were LEGO. There was a LEGO bedroom and a LEGO bed. There was a LEGO bathroom with a LEGO toilet and a shower – and they worked! In the kitchen there was a LEGO fridge (but no cooker) and there were LEGO tables and chairs. There was even a LEGO cat. James May stayed in the house one night and was surprised because the bed was quite comfortable.

At first, a theme park called Legoland planned to buy the house, but later they decided not to. James May tried to find another buyer. He started a Facebook page and asked other people to buy it, but nobody wanted it. So on 22 September, they started to take the house to pieces. A few days later, there wasn't a LEGO house any more.

James May was not happy about it as more than 1,000 people worked hard to build the house and everything inside it. Other people were not so sad. The television company donated the three million LEGO pieces to a charity for children.

THINK *values*

Community spirit

1 Read what people said about the LEGO house. Match the activities (a–d) with the comments (1–4).

a working together
b being creative
c having fun
d caring for others

1 *We really enjoyed this – we laughed a lot.*

2 *The idea of building a LEGO cat was really interesting.*

3 *I loved being with so many people, doing the same thing!*

4 *I think it's great that they donated the LEGO pieces to a charity for children.*

2 Put the activities a–d in Exercise 1 in order of importance for you. Compare your ideas with a partner.

I think working together is really important. It's my number 1.

Me too. It's my number 2.

What's your number 1?

Caring for others.

GRAMMAR

Past simple (regular verbs)

1 Find the past simple forms of these verbs in the article and write them down. Then complete the rules.

0 start *started*	5 stay ...
1 want ...	6 plan ...
2 use ...	7 decide ...
3 finish ...	8 try ...
4 work ...	9 ask ...

RULE: Use the past simple to talk about finished actions in the past.

With regular verbs:

- We usually add [1]... to the verb (e.g. *start – started / stay – stayed*).
- If the verb ends in *-e* (e.g. *use*), we add [2]... .
- If a short verb ends in consonant + vowel + consonant (e.g. *plan*), we double the [3]... and add *-ed*.
- We add *-ed* to verbs ending in vowel + *-y* (e.g. *stayed*).
- If the verb ends in consonant + *-y* (e.g. *try*), we change the *-y* to [4]... and add [5]... .

2 Complete the sentences. Use the past simple form of the verbs.

0 When my granddad was young, he *played* (play) with LEGO all the time.
1 We ... (start) to paint our house last month, and we ... (finish) yesterday.
2 She ... (decide) to change her bedroom, so she ... (paint) the walls pink.
3 We ... (try) to find another house last year because we ... (want) to move.
4 I ... (visit) my aunt and uncle because they ... (want) to show me their new flat.
5 My parents ... (study) lots of ideas for a new kitchen before they ... (order) it.
6 On my last holiday, I ... (stay) with my grandparents and ... (help) them tidy up the garden.
7 Last weekend Jack ... (plan) to organise his room but he ... (watch) television instead.

Workbook page 46

PRONUNCIATION
-ed endings /d/, /t/, /ɪd/
Go to page 150.

GET IT *right!*
Correct the spelling mistakes in these past tenses of regular verbs:
plaid, staid, enjoid.

VOCABULARY

Furniture

1 2.06 Match the words (1–12) with the photos (A–L). Then listen, check and repeat.

1 armchair | 2 carpet | 3 cooker | 4 curtains
5 desk | 6 lamp | 7 mirror | 8 shelves
9 shower | 10 sofa | 11 toilet | 12 wardrobe

2 Work in pairs. Where are these things in your house? Tell your partner.

There are mirrors in our bathroom, in my parents' bedroom and in our living room.

Workbook page 49

LISTENING

1 Work in pairs. Describe the pictures.

2 2.07 Listen to four people talking about 'home'. Match the names with the correct pictures.

Sophie | James | Mia | Daniel

3 2.07 Listen again. Copy and complete the table with the missing information.

	Where is home for you?	What I like doing there.
Sophie	Home is where I feel [1]... .	[2]...
James	Somewhere [3]... .	[4]...
Mia	The [5]... in our flat.	[6]...
Daniel	With [7]... in the garden.	[8]...

GRAMMAR

Modifiers: *quite, very, really*

1 Write the name of the person from Exercise 3 who says these things. Then underline the words before the adjectives and complete the rule.

1 I feel really happy there.
2 Our kitchen is quite small.
3 The armchair is very comfortable.

> **RULE:** Use words *very*, *really* and *quite* to say more about an adjective.
> The words *very* and [1]... are used to make an adjective stronger. The word [2]... usually means 'a little bit'.

2 Write true sentences about your home using the words.

0 kitchen – big / small
Our kitchen isn't very big / It's quite small.
1 bedroom – tidy / untidy
2 sofa – comfortable / uncomfortable
3 home – busy / quiet

Workbook page 47

THINK *self-esteem*

Feeling safe

1 Think about the questions and make notes.

1 Where do you feel 'at home'? Describe the place.
2 What's most important for you there? (furniture? things? colours? people?)
3 What does that place feel like for you? (relaxing? safe? comfortable?)

2 Write 2 or 3 sentences about where you feel at home. Read them out in groups.

I feel at home in my bedroom. My bed is quite small but it's very comfortable. I like lying on it and thinking about my life.

I feel at home when I'm with my family. My mum and dad are great and my brother is my best friend. I love doing things with them.

I feel at home in the living room. Our sofa is really comfortable. I love sitting there on my own reading a good book.

READING

1 Read Jenny's holiday blog and complete the sentences with a word or a number.

DAY 5 Dad gets it right! (*finally*)

Day five of the Italian adventure and we're in Naples. We arrived here early yesterday morning, but as usual we were only at the hotel for about five minutes before Dad wanted to take us somewhere. This time it was to the ancient city of Pompeii near Naples. I didn't really want to go. I wanted to go shopping for shoes.

We travelled there by train. The journey didn't take long – but long enough for Dad to tell us a bit about the history. Many years ago, Pompeii was a large Italian city near a volcano called Mount Vesuvius – then on 24 August 79 CE – the volcano erupted and completely covered the city in ash. It killed about 20,000 people. But the ash didn't destroy the buildings and now, 2,000 years later, you can walk around the city and see how people lived all those years ago.

2,000-year-old houses: thanks, Dad – really boring, I thought, but I was wrong! The houses were very interesting. Most of them were really big with lots of rooms (so lots of space to get away from annoying brothers and sisters!) There were paintings and mosaics all over the walls. I'd love a Roman mosaic of One Direction on my bedroom wall. Also, I was amazed at the bathrooms. I'd love a big bathroom in our house – ours is so small!

I got really interested in Pompeii. I wasn't bored at all. In fact, I've got lots of ideas for our house when we get home!

About [2]... people died here, all of them covered in ash.

The paintings and [3]... are really beautiful.

Mount Vesuvius – a real [1]... . (I hope it doesn't erupt!)

The houses in this ancient city are [4]... years old.

2 Answer the questions.

1. Where is Jenny's family staying at the moment?
2. How did they go to Pompeii?
3. What did Jenny's dad tell them about on the way there?
4. When did Vesuvius erupt?
5. What did Jenny like about the Pompeii houses?
6. What was Jenny's overall opinion of Pompeii?

WRITING

Use your answers in Exercise 2 to write a summary of the text in no more than 100 words.

Jenny didn't want to go to Pompeii and ...

GRAMMAR

Past simple negative

1 Compete the sentences from Jenny's blog and then complete the rule.

1 I ... really want to go.
2 The journey ... take long.
3 The ash ... destroy the buildings.

RULE: To make any verb negative in the past simple, use ... + the base form of the verb.

2 Here are some more things Jenny wrote about Pompeii. Make them negative.

0 We visited all of the houses.
We didn't visit all of the houses.
1 I wanted to go home.
2 The poor people lived in big houses.
3 Dad ordered a pizza for lunch.
4 It rained in the afternoon.

3 Work in pairs. Tell your partner two things that you did and two things that you didn't do last weekend. Choose from the verbs in the list.

work | climb | play | travel | clean
help | study | use | dance | walk

I didn't watch any TV. *I visited my friends.*

Workbook page 47

VOCABULARY

adjectives with *-ed / -ing*

1 How are the people feeling? Match the adjectives with the pictures.

annoyed | relaxed | bored | interested | amazed

2 What did Jenny say about Pompeii? Complete the sentences with interested or interesting.

1 I got really ... in Pompeii.
2 The houses were very ... .

3 Choose the correct words.

1 I get *annoyed / annoying* when people ignore me.
2 His painting was brilliant. I was *amazed / amazing*.
3 Bob talks about football all the time! He's really *bored / boring*.
4 A hot shower is always very *relaxed / relaxing*.
5 I think Maths is really *interested / interesting*.

4 Complete the sentences so that they are true for you.

1 I'm never bored when ... .
2 I find ... really annoying.
3 ... is the most amazing singer.
4 I'm really interested in ... .
5 I'm never relaxed when ... .

5 Work in pairs. Compare your answers.

Workbook page 49

WRITING

A blog post

1 Think about a real holiday that you went on or an invented holiday. Make notes about these questions.

1 Where did you go?
2 Who did you go with?
3 What did you do that was very special / different?
4 What did you like / not like about the holiday?
5 What was *boring / exciting / amazing / interesting / annoying* about the holiday?

2 Use your notes from Exercise 1 to write a blog post about your holiday. Write about 120–150 words. Write three paragraphs.

Paragraph 1 – your answers to 1 and 2
Paragraph 2 – your answer to 3
Paragraph 3 – your answers to 4 and 5

GET IT *right!*

Which is the correct way to spell these two words:
interesting or *intresting*; *exiting* or *exciting*?

Look!

We use *-ed* adjectives to say how we feel about something.
We use *-ing* adjectives to say what we think about something or to describe something.

PHOTOSTORY 3

HEY, LOOK AT THAT GUY!

1 Look at the photos and answer the questions.

What do you think the four friends are saying about the man?
What do they know about him?

2 🔊 **2.08** Now read and listen to the photostory. Check your answers.

RYAN: Stop looking at your satnav – we know how to get to school.
OLIVIA: Very funny. Hey, look at that guy!
RYAN: What about him?
MEGAN: I think he was here yesterday too. **1**

LUKE: So? A homeless guy. It's not a big deal.
RYAN: That's right.
OLIVIA: He's got problems. Don't you care?
RYAN: Well, to be honest – no, not very much. **2**

MEGAN: But it's really sad!
OLIVIA: I know what you mean. I watched a programme on TV a while ago about homeless people. Awful!
MEGAN: Can you imagine? No place to live. It must be horrible.
LUKE: Well, I'm sure that's true. But it's not really our problem. **3**

OLIVIA: Let's go and talk to him.
RYAN: Hang on! Do you think that's a good idea?
MEGAN: What do you mean? He's poor, but that doesn't mean he's dangerous.
LUKE: OK, maybe not dangerous. He's probably not very nice, though.
OLIVIA: Maybe he needs help. **4**

3 Work in pairs. Discuss what happens next in the story. Write down your ideas.

We think the boys go to school but Megan and Olivia talk to the man.

4 **EP3** Watch to find out how the story continues.

5 Put the sentences (a–h) in the correct order (1–8).

1–d

a The students decide to ask somebody from a charity for help.
b The girls are worried about the man.
c When they go back to the park, the man gives Olivia her necklace.
d The friends are on their way to school.
e Other students start laughing at her.
f Ryan tells the other students about the homeless person.
g In the park, they see a homeless person.
h The teacher notices that Olivia is not paying attention.

Phrases for fluency

1 Find these expressions in the story. Who says them?

1 ... not a big deal.
2 ..., to be honest, ...
3 I know what you mean.
4 it's not really our problem.
5 Hang on!
6 ..., though.

2 Use the expressions in Exercise 1 to complete the dialogues.

1 A She's usually a nice girl. She sometimes gets a bit angry, ...
B ... . Yesterday she really shouted at me!
2 A I need help. You've got to help me with my homework!
B ... ! It's your homework – so really, ...
3 A It's only a small test tomorrow. Ten questions. It's ... . Right?
B Well, ... , I'm a bit worried about it.

GET IT *right!*

Remember not to confuse *look at* with *see*. If it is a conscious action, we use *look at*, but if there is no choice, we use *see*.

VOCABULARY

Phrasal verbs with *look*

1 Look at these sentences from the story. Complete them with the words from the list.

after | up | for | at | into

1 Hey, look ... that guy!
2 The charity looks ... homeless people.
3 I'm just looking it ... on my phone.
4 We need to look ... why he's homeless.
5 Let's look ... him.

2 Choose the correct word in each dialogue.

1 A What's Janet doing?
B She's looking *after / like* the baby.
2 A Why are you looking *for / at* me like that?
B Because I'm angry with you.
3 A I can't find my pen.
B I'll help you look *after / for* it.
4 A Do the police know what happened?
B No, they are still looking *for / into* it.
5 A What does this word mean?
B I don't know. Let's look it *after / up* in the dictionary.

Workbook page 79

FUNCTIONS

Making suggestions

1 Complete the sentences from the story with words from the lists. Then write ✓ (agree), ✗ (disagree) or ? (uncertain).

A How | could | Let's | Why
B idea | do | great | sure

0 A *How* about asking our parents for money?
B I don't think that's a good *idea*.
1 A ... don't we try and help him?
B I'm not so ... .
2 A ... give him our school lunch.
B Let's ... that.
3 A We ... take him a bit of food after school.
B I think that's a ... idea.

2 Work in pairs. Student A: Go to page 159. Student B: Go to page 160. Take two or three minutes to prepare. Then have a conversation.

Life skills

Not making judgements

Sometimes it's easy to make judgements about people based on their appearance, but every individual person is different. Making judgements about people ignores these differences. Differences are good because they are what give people their characters.

1 Think about the photostory on page 62.

1 Imagine you are Luke and Ryan at the start of the story. Do you want to talk to the man? Why?

2 Imagine you are the homeless man. How do you feel when Olivia talks to you? Why?

2 Read and make a list of all the ideas Edna, Jack and Bill have about teenagers.

They have no respect

Edna

The problem with teenagers is that they haven't got any respect for other people. I was on the bus today, for example, and some teenagers were annoying everybody by listening to music on their mobile phones. I think it's good for teenagers to like music, but why don't they use headphones? We don't want to listen to their music. We like different music. They simply don't think about other people.

Jack

I think the problem is all the technology. Young people spend all day playing computer games on their own and not outside meeting people. Computer games are about killing people, not helping people or the local community, so young people aren't interested in those things. I understand that young people need technology these days but, reading and writing are also important. My grandson writes me messages saying 'R U OK?', which is terrible. I feel sorry for their teachers.

Bill

Parents have more problems with teenagers now than when we were teenagers. We did what our parents told us, but kids today do what they want. Food is a good example. My grandchildren are fantastic but they don't eat enough vegetables or fish, and they eat too many hamburgers, pizzas and chips. I like pizzas and chips, but they're not healthy. This is why most teenagers sit watching DVDs all day and don't like riding bicycles or playing sport. They don't eat the right food.

3 Work in pairs. Discuss these questions.

1 Are the items on your list true for all teenagers?

2 Do you think Edna, Jack and Bill are right to say all teenagers are like this?

3 Can you think of a teenager who isn't like this? Describe them.

4 Why is it a problem that these old people see teenagers like this?

4 Choose one of the following groups of people, and make a list about them like the one in Exercise 2.

Old people | Teachers | Girls | Boys

5 Work in pairs. Think about the group you chose in Exercise 4 and discuss these questions.

1 Is every item on your list true for all the people in your group?

2 Can you think of an old person/teacher/girl/boy who isn't like this? Describe them.

3 Do you think it's right to say all old people/teachers/girls/boys are like this?

4 Why is it a problem to have ideas about individual people you don't know?

Tips for not making judgements

1 **Don't judge people based on their appearance. Take time to know them better, then form an opinion.**

2 **Don't impose our own values on to others. Find out and try to understand other people's values.**

3 **Avoid generalising about groups of people. Remember groups are made up of individuals with their own personalities and beliefs.**

6 BEST FRIENDS

LEARNING OUTCOMES

FUNCTIONS: talking about past events; saying what you like doing alone and with others; talking about friends and friendships

GRAMMAR: past simple (irregular verbs); double genitive; past simple questions

VOCABULARY: past time expressions; personality adjectives

Work in pairs. Look at the photo. Discuss these questions:

1 Who are these people and where are they?
2 How do they feel?
3 What qualities make a best friend?

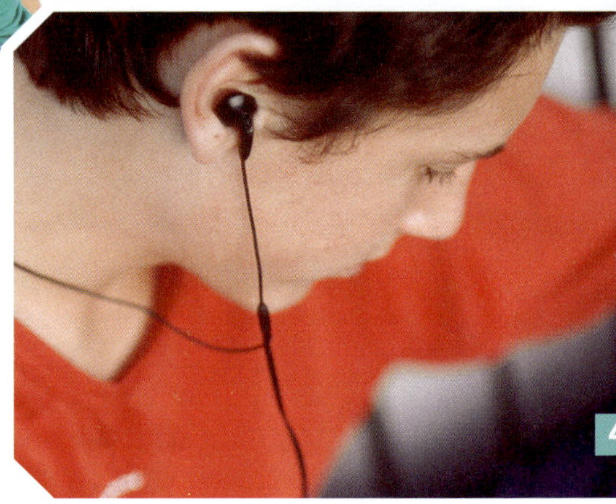

READING

1 Look at the photos. Say what the people are doing.

> *They're surfing the Internet.*

2 Match these words with the photos and compare with a partner. Some words go with more than one photo.

alone | together | happy | sad | bored | excited

> *In photo 1 they're together and they're excited.*

3 Work in pairs. Talk about things you like doing alone and other things you like doing together with other people. Here are some ideas to help you.

watch a film | walk | do homework
study | read | have breakfast | go shopping

> *I like going shopping with friends.*
> *I don't like going alone!*
> *I like doing homework alone.*

4 Look at the photos on page 67. What kind of television show is this? Who are the boy and the girl?

5 **2.09** Read and listen to the web article. Check your ideas.

6 Read the article again. Correct the information in these sentences.

1 Their parents had the idea of them singing together.
2 Jonathan thought that Charlotte didn't look right for the show.
3 Charlotte and Jonathan were the same age.
4 Everyone laughed when Charlotte and Jonathan came out.
5 Simon Cowell said that Jonathan needed to sing with another girl.
6 Jonathan told Simon Cowell that he wanted to go home.
7 Jonathan and Charlotte came first in the competition.
8 They recorded a song called *Together*.

Together

In a school in England, a few years ago, a teenage girl heard a boy singing in another room. She liked it, and found out that the boy's name was Jonathan Antoine. The girl – Charlotte Jaconelli – also liked singing. A little later, the music teach er at school suggested that they could sing together. They did, and they started singing together as a duo. They also became very good friends. They even sang together at the music teacher's wedding.

Around that time, there was a television programme called *Britain's Got Talent* – a show to find new singers and performers. Charlotte wanted to enter the show with Jonathan but he was worried about the way he looked. However, Charlotte persuaded him and they went on the show. Charlotte was 16 and Jonathan was 17.

They did the first audition in April 2012. When they came onto the stage, they were very nervous. The four judges didn't think they looked good. Some people in the audience laughed when they saw them. Then they began to sing and everyone was amazed. They sang incredibly well –especially Jonathan. When they finished, people stood up and clapped.

All the judges thought Charlotte and Jonathan were great, but one judge, Simon Cowell, suggested that Jonathan sing on his own without Charlotte because, although she was good, he was fantastic.

Jonathan didn't think for long. He looked at his friend, and then looked back at the judges, and said that he wanted to stay in the competition with Charlotte. They carried on together, but they didn't win the competition – they came second. (A dancing dog won!) However, they weren't disappointed.

A few weeks later, Simon Cowell gave them the chance to record a CD. They made the CD, and then they thought about a title for it.They chose the word: 'Together'.

GET IT *right!*

Which is right?

*They did the first **audition / casting** in April 2012.*

THINK *values*

Friendship and loyalty

1 Choose the best way to finish this sentence.

I think this story tells us that, in life, it is important ...

1 ... to look good.
2 ... to be good at what you do.
3 ... to come first.
4 ... to look after your friends.
5 ... to be nice to other people.
6 ... to have lots and lots of friends.

2 Compare your ideas with a partner.

3 Choose three of the values in Exercise 1. Put them in order of importance for you (1, 2, 3). Then compare with others.

I think the most important thing is to look after your friends.

That's my number 3. I think it's really important to be nice to other people.

GRAMMAR

Past simple (irregular verbs)

1 Read these sentences about the article on page 67. All the verbs are in the past simple. How are the verbs in 1 different from the verbs in 2?

1 She **liked** singing.
They **started** as a duo.
Some people **laughed**.

2 They **sang** together.
People **stood** up.
We **came** here as a duo.

2 Look back at the article on page 67. Write the past simple forms of these verbs.

0 find *found*
1 become
2 go
3 see
4 think
5 come
6 give
7 make

3 Find at least four more irregular past simple forms in the article on page 67. Write the verbs.

4 Correct these two sentences from the article. Make them negative.

1 Jonathan thought for a long time.
2 They won the competition.

5 Look at the pictures and the prompts and write the sentences in the past simple.

Workbook page 54

VOCABULARY

Past time expressions

1 Complete the lists with appropriate expressions.

When we talk about the past, we often use expressions like these:

- yesterday, yesterday [1] ... , yesterday afternoon
- last night, last week, last [2] ... , last December
- an hour ago, two weeks ago, a month ago, [3] ... ago

2 Complete the sentences with a time expression with *ago*.

0 Andy is twenty. He left school when he was sixteen.
Andy left school four years ago.
1 It's 8 o'clock. I had breakfast at 7 o'clock.
I had breakfast ...
2 It's 10.20. The film began at 10.00.
The film ...
3 It's December. Your holiday was in July.
My holiday ...

3 Complete the sentences with your own information. Use irregular verbs.

1 A year ago, I ...
2 Ten years ago, I ...
3 Last year, I ...
4 Yesterday morning, I ...
5 Last night, I...

Workbook page 57

GET IT right!

We say

✓ *yesterday morning / yesterday afternoon,*

not

✗ *~~yesterday in the morning~~ / ~~yesterday in the afternoon~~.*

LISTENING

1 Which sentences do you agree with?

1 Footballers are never friends with players from other teams.
2 Footballers never help other players.
3 Footballers only want to win cups.

2 2.10 Listen to a story about Cristiano Ronaldo. Choose the correct ending.

The two friends think the story is ...

- certainly true.
- possibly true.
- certainly not true.

3 2.10 Listen again and choose the right answer A, B or C.

1 What was the family name of Ronaldo's friend?
A Albert
B The boy doesn't remember.
C The boy didn't find the name.

2 How many places were there at the football school?
A one B two C three

3 Why did Albert pass the ball to Cristiano?
A Because Albert wanted a friend.
B Because Albert was tired.
C Because Cristiano was a better player.

4 What was the final score of the game?
A 1–1 B 2–0 C 3–0

5 What is Albert's job now?
A He's a footballer.
B We don't know.
C He drives cars.

6 What did Ronaldo give to his friend?
A A car. B A house. C A car and a house.

4 Work in pairs. Tell your partner about a great present someone gave you.

Last year my ... gave me a ... . I was really happy / excited because ... .

GRAMMAR

Double genitive

1 Read the sentence. Then choose the correct options to complete the rule.

Ronaldo was there, and there was a friend of his called Albert.

RULE: We form the 'double genitive' with noun + *of* + possessive [1]*pronoun / adjective* (*mine, yours, his, hers, ours, yours, theirs*).

We also form the 'double genitive' with noun + *of* + possessive adjective (*my, your, his, her, our, your, their*) + noun + possessive *'s*.

We use it to talk about [2]*one of many things / many things that we have.*

2 Choose the correct words.

0 She's a friend of *me* / *mine* .
1 Mr Smith is a teacher of my *sister / my sister's.*
2 She's a cousin of *John / John's.*
3 Mrs Jones is a neighbour of *ours / us.*

3 Rewrite the underlined parts of the sentences.

0 See that man? He's my father's friend.
He's a friend of my father's.
1 Steve is our friend.
Steve is ...
2 Mike borrowed my shirt.
Mike borrowed ...
3 I lost my mum's book.
I lost ...

Workbook page 55

train to THINK

Making decisions

1 Draw a mind map.

Copy the circles and put names of people who are close to you (friends, family) in the red circles.

What do these people like? Write your ideas next to the circles.

2 Work in groups. Imagine it's your friends' birthdays. Show your mind maps, make suggestions and decide on a present for each person.

READING

1 Read the magazine article quickly. Complete the sentences.

1 Richard and Sharon met for the first time on ...

2 The second time they met, they went ...

2 Read the article again. Put the events (a–g) in the order they happened (1–8).

1–g

a Richard and Sharon go to a show together.

b Richard has an accident.

c Richard gives Sharon a present.

d Sharon saves Richard's life.

e Richard goes to hospital.

f Sharon calls Richard.

g ~~Richard goes surfing.~~

h Richard sees Sharon for the first time.

3 Work in pairs. Tell the story. Use the ideas in Exercise 2. Put them into the past simple tense.

> Richard went surfing.
> He had an accident ...

Richard

Sharon

FUNCTIONS

Talking about past events

1 Think about a time when you made a new friend. Make notes.

- Who?
- When?
- Where?
- What happened?

2 In pairs tell your story.

> I met my friend Al five years ago. I was on holiday in France with my family. We were in a small hotel. Al's family were in the same hotel. We made friends on the first day and spent all the holiday together.

REAL LIFE

HOW WE MET

THIS WEEK LIFEGUARD SHARON EVANS AND STUDENT RICHARD LAMBERT TELL OUR REPORTER ABOUT THEIR FRIENDSHIP AND HOW THEY ALMOST NEVER MET.

So first of all, when and where did you meet?

RICHARD: We first met in 2012, one morning at about 10.30 am on Bondi Beach, in Sydney.

SHARON: Actually, we met in the water.

OK, so how did you meet?

RICHARD: I was out in the deep water on my surfboard when another board knocked me on the head. The next thing I knew, I was on the beach looking up at this face.

SHARON: I was on the beach that day. I saw what happened so I swam out and brought Richard back in. He was unconscious, but luckily I got him to start breathing again. But for a minute I thought he was dead.

RICHARD: And then they took me to hospital. I didn't have a chance to even say thanks to Sharon.

So what did you do?

RICHARD: There was a really big show the next week with a popular Belgian-Australian singer called Gotye. I bought two tickets for Sharon and left them at work for her a few days later. I thought she could take someone with her. I also left her a note to say thanks with my telephone number on it.

SHARON: He was really generous. They were expensive tickets.

Did you take a friend to the show?

SHARON: I didn't know who to take and then I had a great idea.

What was it?

RICHARD: Well, when I got home from work that day there was a voicemail on my phone. It was Sharon. She invited me to go with her. We had a great time. She was so cheerful and easy-going. We became really good friends right away.

GET IT right!

We say

✓ *Sharon saved **Richard's life**.*

not

✗ *Sharon saved ~~the life of Richard~~.*

GRAMMAR

Past simple questions

1 Put the words in order to make questions. Check your answers in the article on page 70.

1 do / did / what / you / ? 2 did / you / meet / how / ? 3 friend / show / take / you / a / to / did / the / ?

2 Complete the table.

Question	Answer
... I/you/he/she/we/they enjoy the show? What time ... I/you/he/she/we/they get home?	Yes, I/you/he/she/we/they ... No, I/you/he/she/we/they ... (did not). I/you/he/she/we/they ... home at midnight.

3 Match the questions and answers.

1 Did you have a good weekend?
2 Did you play computer games yesterday?
3 Where did you meet your best friend?
4 Who did you text yesterday?
5 What did you have for dinner last night?

a Yes, I did. I completed four levels.
b We met at school four years ago.
c We had chicken and chips.
d No, I didn't. It rained all the time.
e I texted my best friend.

GET IT right!

If someone asks us 'What did you do?', we say:

✓ *I **did** my homework.*

not

✗ *I ~~do~~ my homework.*

✗ *I ~~have done~~ my homework.*

4 Work in pairs. Ask the questions 1–5 and give your own answers.

Workbook page 55

VOCABULARY

Personality adjectives

Look at the pictures. Read the sentences and match the names to the people.

MY FRIENDS

- Nick is intelligent. He knows a lot about everything.
- Amelia is cheerful. She's always got a smile on her face.
- Kai is jealous. He's not happy when you talk to other friends.
- Ben is helpful. He's always ready to help you.
- Ruby is confident. She's not scared to talk in public.
- Liz is generous. She's always happy to share her things with you.
- Chloe is easy-going. She never gets angry about anything.
- Connor is funny. He always makes me laugh.

PRONUNCIATION

Stressed syllables in words

Go to page 150.

Workbook page 57

Culture

1 Look at the photos of friends. Who's having a good time? Who's having a bad time?

2 2.13 Read and listen to the web page. Five people commented on the different myths about friendship. Match the people to the myths.

Myth 1 ... Myth 2 ... Myth 3 ... Myth 4 ... Myth 5 ...

3 Which of the five people here do you agree with? Who do you disagree with? Compare with others in the class.

FRIENDSHIP MYTHS

Everyone wants to have friends, and friendships are important to teenagers all over the world. However, when people start a friendship, they sometimes expect too much from it. Here are five things about friendship that some people believe are true. But in fact they aren't – they are myths.

We spoke to teens from different countries. Read what they think.

1 Burcu, Istanbul, Turkey

Nobody's perfect, so why do we think friends can be perfect? We all make mistakes, so it's only normal that there are times when good friends make mistakes, too. Perhaps you think that a really good friend always knows what you need. That's wrong – be careful! Sometimes you need to say to your friends, 'Please do this' or 'Don't do that'. Don't forget that there are times when your friends are **stressed** or unhappy, too. Then they can't help you the way you would like them to.

2 Flávia, São Paulo, Brazil

There can be times in your life when you've got a lot of friends, and other times when you've only got one or two. Maybe you haven't got any friends **right now** because, for example, you're in a new city or school. When you haven't got any friends, it's important to wait and **be patient**. Make sure you're a friendly person – so other people want to **make friends** with you!

3 Luca, Florence, Italy

No, they don't! It takes time to build a good friendship. You don't want to tell your friend everything about yourself on the first day of your friendship. You and your friends want to share some things. But it's important to **remember** that there are other things that you don't want to share and that's fine! Don't feel bad about it.

4 Fernanda, Quito, Ecuador

You want to be a good friend, right? To build a good friendship, it's important to have fun together, to listen to your friends when they've got a problem, to help them when they need you, or just to go and watch a film together, or play some sport. And that takes time! That's why I think it's better to have one or two friends, and not a lot of friends.

5 Nikolay, St Petersburg, Russia

It's not a good idea to wait for others to make you happy. There are times when you're happy, and other times when you're sad. And when you're not happy, try to think, 'What can I do to stop this? How can I help myself?' Friendship is a place to share **happiness**, but there may be times when you and your friends aren't happy. And that's OK.

- **MYTH NO. 1:** Friends are there to make you happy.
- **MYTH NO. 2:** A real friend will never disappoint you.
- **MYTH NO. 3:** The more friends you have, the better.
- **MYTH NO. 4:** Friends share everything.
- **MYTH NO. 5:** If you've got no friends, something's wrong with you.

4 Read the web page again. Who says ...

1 you need to have a good time with your friends?
2 you won't make friends if you are an unfriendly person?
3 we need to remember that our friends have bad days too?
4 you don't have to tell your friends everything about you?
5 we won't always have the same number of friends in our life?
6 that it's not always a good thing to have a lot of friends?
7 we shouldn't expect our friends to always get everything right?
8 we shouldn't always expect friends to make us happy?
9 you can't always expect your friends to be happy?
10 you can't make a really good friend quickly?

5 There are eight words in bold in the web page. Match the words with these meanings. Write the words.

0 an idea that many people believe, but that is not true *myth*
1 the state of feeling happy
2 the relationships you have with friends
3 show that you are not in a hurry and have got time
4 worried, for example when you have too much work
5 get to know and like a person
6 keep in your mind
7 at this moment

SPEAKING

1 Choose the words that make the sentences true for you.

1 When I'm sad, I want my friends to *listen to me / tell me a joke / leave me alone.*
2 When I'm happy, I want to *watch a film / play a sport / listen to music / go shopping* with my friends.

2 Work with a partner. Read out your sentences and compare your answers.

WRITING

An apology

1 Read the message and answer the questions.

1 How does John feel and why?
2 What does he want to do about it?

Dear Alice,

I'm really sorry for forgetting your birthday. It was a terrible thing to do. I wanted to phone you but I forgot because I had a lot of work to do. I feel really bad. I'd like to see you soon to say sorry. I've also got something I want to give you.

Can we meet up on Thursday?

John

2 Read the messages. Which is the answer to John?

Thanks for your message.

Don't worry about it. I'm not upset. And yes, I'd love to see you on Thursday. I can't wait to see what you've got for me.

Thanks for the message.

I'm sorry I can't come to your birthday party on Thursday but I'm really busy. Have fun without me.

3 Put the words in the right order. Write the sentences.

1 birthday / your / really / sorry / for / I'm / forgetting
2 was / terrible / a / It / to / do / thing
3 really / I / bad / feel

4 Match the phrases with the photos.

eat the cake | break someone's tablet
not water the flowers

5 Write an apology for each photo. Include an explanation with each apology.

I'm really sorry. It was an accident.

6 Choose one of the situations from above and write a message to apologise. (60 words)

Literature

GREAT EXPECTATIONS
BY CHARLES DICKENS

Pip (a poor orphan) is invited to go to the house of a rich woman called Miss Havisham. Estella, a young girl, also lives in the house. Miss Havisham is her guardian. Miss Havisham never leaves the dark house.

1 Read the text. Is Estella friendly to Pip when they first meet?

'Who is it?' said the lady at the table.

'Pip, ma'am.'

'Pip?'

'Mr. Pumblechook's boy, ma'am. Come - to play.'

'Come nearer; let me look at you. Come close.'

It was when I stood before her, avoiding her eyes, that I took note of the surrounding objects in detail, and saw that her watch had stopped at twenty minutes to nine, and that a clock in the room had stopped at twenty minutes to nine.

'Look at me,' said Miss Havisham. 'You are not afraid of a woman who has never seen the sun since you were born?'

'No.' I lied.

'Do you know what I touch here?' she said, laying her hands, one upon the other, on her left side.

'Yes, ma'am.'

'What do I touch?'

'Your heart.'

'Broken!'

...'I sometimes have sick fancies,' she went on, 'and I have a sick fancy that I want to see some play..."

'Call Estella,' she said, flashing a look at me. 'You can do that. Call Estella.

"Estella"

She answered at last, and her light came along the dark passage like a star.

Miss Havisham beckoned her to come close. Let me see you play cards with this boy.'

'With this boy? Why, he is a common labouring-boy!'

I thought I overheard Miss Havisham answer - 'Well? You can break his heart.'

'What do you play, boy?' asked Estella.

GLOSSARY

ma'am - madam
take note of – to notice
sick fancy – something strange that you want
overhear – to hear something that is said to someone else

2 Pip notices some strange things in the house. What are they? Why are they strange?

3 Look at how the characters speak to Pip and how he answers. How do you think he feels about being in this situation?

4 The first time Pip sees Estella he says, "Her light came along the dark passage like a star". How is this description different from the rest of the text? Is the word *star* significant?

5 This is the first meeting between Pip and Estella. What kind of relationship do you think they will have in the future?

6 There are many stories about a poor person who meets a rich person. Do you know any? In your opinion, what makes "rich meets poor" an interesting story?

GET IT right!

Units 5&6

Modifiers: *quite, very, really*

Remember: we use modifier + adjective (+ noun). We don't use noun + modifier + adjective.

✓ *Pompeii has **a lot of very old buildings**.*

✗ *Pompeii has a lot of ~~buildings very old~~.*

✓ *The buildings are **very old**.*

Be careful when you write these words.

- **We write *quite* with the *e* after the *t*. Don't confuse *quite* with the adjective *quiet*.**
  ✓ *This chair is **quite** comfortable.*
  ✗ *This chair is ~~quiet~~ comfortable.*
- **We write *really* with two *ll*s.**
  ✓ *Pompeii is **really** interesting.*
  ✗ *Pompeii is ~~realy~~ interesting.*
- **We write *very* with one *r*.**
  ✓ *Their house is **very** big.*
  ✗ *Their house is ~~verry~~ big.*

1 Find seven mistakes. Correct them.

We went to see our new house on Sunday. My dad wants to live near his office. It's realy annoying for me because a lot of my friends live near my house now. I was very sad when we went into the house. But when I saw inside it, I was amazed really! It looked quiet small, but inside it was really big. It had a kitchen really big and the bedrooms were verry big too. But the best thing was the garden. It was beautiful really, with a swimming pool very big and lots of trees. I think my friends will like visiting my new house!

Past simple (regular and irregular verbs)

To make any verb negative in the past simple we use didn't + the base form of the verb. We don't use didn't + past simple. Remember to use the base form of regular and irregular verbs.

✓ *We **didn't visit** the LEGO house.*

✗ *We ~~didn't visited~~ the LEGO house.*

2 Circle the correct answer.

1 I'm sorry I didn't *come / came* to your party.
2 We didn't *went / go on* holiday last year.
3 I looked everywhere, but I didn't *found / find* my phone.
4 We visited the art gallery but we didn't *see / saw* anything interesting.
5 We didn't *spend / spent* a lot of time in Paris. It was too hot!
6 I didn't *knew / know* you liked One Direction.

Double genitive

We form the double genitive with noun + *of* + possessive pronoun *(mine, yours, his, hers, ours, yours, theirs)*. We don't use object pronouns *(me, you, him, her, our, your, their)* to form the double genitive.

✓ *She's a **friend of mine**.*

✗ *She's a friend ~~of me~~.*

We also form the double genitive with noun + *of* + possessive adjective (*my, your, his, her, our, your, their*) + noun + possessive *'s*.

✓ *She's a **friend of my sister's**.*

✗ *She's a friend ~~of my sister~~.*

3 Choose the correct answer.

1 Lisa is a good friend *of me / my / mine*.
2 Matt Damon is a favourite actor of my *sister / sister's*.
3 My brother went to the cinema with a friend of *him / he's / his*.
4 I met a cousin of *Rory's / Rory* at the party.
5 She brought a new classmate of *hers / her / she's* to the party.
6 Isn't that woman a teacher of *your / you / yours*?

SAY IT right!

Stress in compound words

1 Work in pairs. Copy the words and underline the stressed part. What is the rule?

homework	housework
dishwasher	bathroom
shoe shop	armchair
bedroom	clothes shop

2 🔊 **2.14** Listen, check and repeat.

RULE: In compound words the stress is usually on the first syllable. Spanish speakers often stress the second syllable or all the syllables.

test yourself

Units 5&6

VOCABULARY

1 Use the words in the list to complete the sentences. There are two extra words.

after | make | for | really | cheerful | do | annoying
shower | last | jealous | annoyed | cooker

1 She isn't happy when I see you. I think she's a bit ... of you.
2 I need a wash but Ian is still in the ... .
3 Mum died when I was 14 so I helped Dad look ... my little brothers.
4 My sister borrowed my shoes and she didn't ask me. I was really ... .
5 I moved school when I was eight and I found it really difficult to ... new friends.
6 I'm looking ... Anne. Do you know where she is?
7 He's a really ... boy. I really don't like him.
8 I had a great time ... night – thanks for everything.
9 It's a ... comfortable armchair. I just want to sit in it for hours.
10 Be careful – the ... is still hot.

GRAMMAR

2 Complete the sentences with the past form of the verbs in the list.

choose | find | go | think | like | see

1 I ... he was my friend but now I'm not so sure.
2 The present was very expensive. I hope she ... it.
3 I ... to a party last night and I only got home at 11 pm.
4 I liked the green T-shirt but eventually I ... the red one.
5 We ... a dog all alone in the street so we took it home.
6 No, not that film. I ... it last week.

3 Find and correct the mistake in each sentence.

1 I thinked you were at school.
2 Did you enjoyed your meal, Sir?
3 Paul wasn't go to school today. He stayed at home.
4 We were tired so we did go to bed early.
5 Where did you and Lucy met?
6 I wasn't hungry so I didn't ate anything.

FUNCTIONAL LANGUAGE

4 Write the missing words.

1 A How a... inviting Jake to our party?
B I don't think that's a good i... . Remember the last time he went to a party!
2 A We c... have pizza for lunch.
B Let's d... that. I love pizza!
3 A If you need some money, w... don't you get a Saturday job?
B I'm not so s... . I don't think my dad would like it.
4 A L... go to the park after school.
B That's a g... idea. We can play tennis.

MY SCORE

22–30
10–21
0–9

CAMBRIDGE EXAMS
Review Units 5 & 6
Go to page 146.

7 THE EASY LIFE

LEARNING OUTCOMES

FUNCTIONS: asking for repetition and clarification; giving advice; talking about obligation / lack of obligation

GRAMMAR: *have to / don't have to; should / shouldn't*; *mustn't* vs. *don't have to*

VOCABULARY: gadgets; housework; expressions with *like*

Work in pairs. Look at the photo. Discuss these questions:

1 When was the last time you used a public phone box?
2 Public phone boxes originally made life easier for people. Do they make life easier today?
3 What devices, apps, etc. do you use when you want to communicate with somebody?

AR

READING

1 2.16 What are the objects here? Match the words in the list with the photos. Listen, check and repeat.

1 e-reader | 2 digital camera | 3 flat screen TV
4 tablet | 5 laptop | 6 (desktop) computer

A

B

C

2 Work in pairs. Talk about the objects with a partner.

I've got a ...

I haven't got a ...

I think the (laptop) in the photo looks (cool / really new / quite old).

3 Imagine you could only have one of these things. Which would you choose?

I'd choose the ...
It's important for me because ...
What about you?

D

4 2.17 Read the sentences and guess the correct answer. Listen and check your answers.

1 A person who **invents** something *has got an idea and creates something new / has got enough money to buy something new.*
2 If you hear something that is **shocking** it makes you feel *happy and excited / surprised and upset.*
3 I **researched** the topic *on the camera / on the Internet.*
4 What is a **huge** problem for Africa? *There is not enough clean water / There is not enough space for people.*
5 You can get **trachoma** from *dirty water / bad food.*
6 Getting an **eye infection** can make people *deaf / blind.*
7 You buy **gel** in a *plastic bottle / paper bag.*

E

5 Work in pairs. Look at the title of the article and the photos on the next page. What do you think the article is about? Compare your ideas with other students.

6 2.18 Read and listen to the article about a young inventor. Are the sentences true (T) or false (F)? Correct the false ones.

0 Ludwick Marishane is from South Africa. T
1 Ludwick used his laptop to find out more about the world's water situation.
2 Millions of people get trachoma every year.
3 Trachoma is an illness that makes people blind.
4 Ludwick wanted to help people with trachoma.
5 Ludwick's dream was to help people find clean water.
6 'DryBath' is helping to save a lot of water all over the world.
7 DryBath is a success.
8 Ludwick wants to invent more things.

F

'... just because I didn't want to take a bath'

LUDWICK MARISHANE, a 17-year-old South African, was with his friends in Limpopo when they started talking about inventing something to put on your skin so you don't have to take a bath. Ludwick thought that this was a great idea. He used his mobile to do some research on the Internet, and he found some shocking facts.

Two point five billion people around the world haven't got clean water. This is a huge problem because dirty water can create terrible illnesses. One of them is trachoma: eight million people all over the world get trachoma every year. They wash their faces with dirty water, get an infection and become blind. To stop trachoma, people don't have to take expensive medication. They don't have to take pills. They don't have to have injections. They have to wash their faces with clean water. That's it.

Ludwick started thinking. He wanted to make something to help people in parts of the world where it's difficult to find clean water. He did more research on his mobile, and he did more thinking. Ludwick had a plan. He wanted to make a gel for people to put on their skin so they don't have to take a bath. He wrote the formula for the gel on his mobile phone. When he was at university, he never stopped thinking about his invention. He started to talk to other people about it, and three years later the dream came true. He made the gel and called it 'DryBath'.

Ludwick Marishane is the winner of lots of prizes. People call him 'one of the brightest young men in the world'. He is very happy about his success. DryBath is helping people to be healthy. And DryBath also helps to save water. That's important in many parts of the world where it's difficult to find clean water. Now he wants to invent other things, and he wants to help other young people to become inventors too.

GET IT *right!*

Which is right

People doesn't / don't have to take expensive medication

THINK *values*

Caring for people and the environment

1 Match the values in the list (a–d) with the sentences in the speech bubbles.

a caring about the environment
b caring about the quality of your work
c caring about your appearance
d caring about other people

1 The water in a lot of rivers and lakes is not clean.

2 I need to wash my hair. It's dirty.

3 Are you feeling cold? I can give you my jumper.

4 Can you switch off the radio, please? I'm doing my homework.

2 Work in pairs. Ask and answer questions about Ludwick Marishane. Try and find as many answers as possible.

Does he care about the environment?
his appearance?
the quality of his work?
other people?

Yes, because DryBath helps to save water.

GRAMMAR

have to / don't have to

1 Complete the sentences from the article on page 79 with *have to* and *don't have to*.

1 They ... wash their faces with clean water.
2 To stop trachoma people ... take expensive medication.

2 Complete the rule and the table.

RULE: Use 1... to say 'this is necessary'.
Use 2... to say 'this isn't necessary'.

Positive	**Negative**
I/you/we/they 0 have to help	I/you/we/they don't have to help
he/she/it 1... help	he/she/it 2... help
Questions	**Short answers**
3... I/you/we/they have to help?	Yes, I/you/we/they do. No, I/you/we/they don't.
4... he/she/it have to help?	Yes, he/she/it 5... . No, he/she/it 6... .

3 Match the sentences with the pictures.

1 The bus leaves in 20 minutes. He has to hurry.
2 The bus leaves in 20 minutes. He doesn't have to hurry.

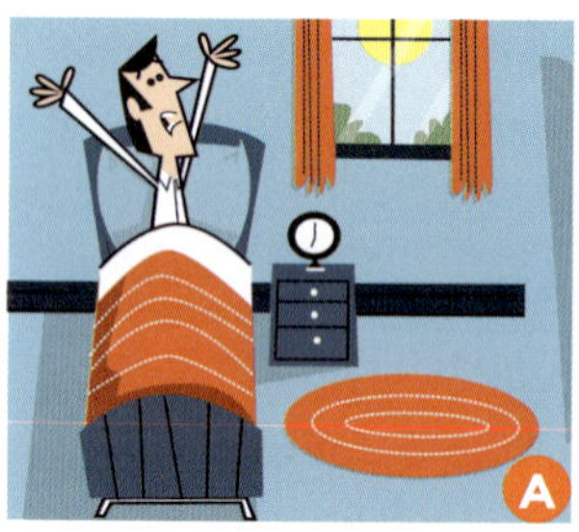

4 Complete the sentences with *have to / has to* or *don't / doesn't have to*.

1 Our teacher doesn't like mobile phones. We ... switch them off during lessons.
2 I know that I ... work hard for this test! You ... tell me!
3 My sister is ill. She ... stay in bed.
4 Your room is terrible! You ... tidy it up.
5 Mario's English is perfect. He ... study for the tests.
6 I can hear you very well. You ... shout!

Workbook page 64

VOCABULARY

Gadgets

1 2.19 Match the words (1–10) with the photos (A-J). Then listen, check and repeat.

1 satnav | 2 MP3 player | 3 torch
4 games console | 5 remote control
6 coffee machine | 7 calculator | 8 docking station
9 hair dryer | 10 headphones |

2 How important are these gadgets for you? Make a list from 1 to 10 (1 = most important, 10 = not important at all).

3 Work in pairs. Compare your ideas and tell your partner how often you use these gadgets.

I often use ...
I use my ... almost every day.
What about you?
I rarely use ...

Workbook page 67

LISTENING

1 Look at the pictures (A–D) of different inventions. Match them with the phrases (1–4). Then make sentences to explain what the inventions are. Compare your ideas in class.

1 not tidy up room / have got robot
2 machine help / ride bike up a hill
3 invention help homework / more time for friends
4 machine can get places around the world / 10 seconds

The girl in picture A has got a cool machine. It helps her to ride her bike up a hill.

2 **2.20** Martin and Anna want to become inventors. Try and match the sentence parts to find out what their situation is. Then listen and check.

1 Martin has got an idea for an invention,
2 He's got a job,
3 Anna has got a lot of ideas,
4 She's thirteen,
a and wants to be an inventor.
b but doesn't want to say what it is.
c but doesn't know where to start.
d and hasn't got enough time to work on it.

3 **2.20** Complete the expert's answers with *should* or *shouldn't*. Listen again and check.

1 You ... start thinking 'What idea can I have to make a million pounds?'
2 You ... start with a little idea.
3 You ... think 'What can I invent that makes one little thing in my life easier'?
4 You ... give up your job.
5 You ... work on your best idea first.
6 You ... forget about your other ideas.

GRAMMAR

should / shouldn't

1 Look at the sentences in Exercise 3 of the listening. Match the sentence parts in the rule.

RULE:

1 Use should to say a 'It's not a good idea.'
2 Use shouldn't to say b 'It's a good idea.'

GET IT right!

We say
✓ *You **should do** that.*
not
✗ *You should ~~to~~ do that.*

2 Use *should / shouldn't* and a word from each list to give advice to these people.

~~take~~ | go to | eat | drink | read
~~aspirin~~ | book any more | bed | any more cake | water

0 I've got a headache. *You should take an aspirin.*
1 I'm really thirsty. ...
2 My eyes are tired. ...
3 I'm tired. ...
4 I feel sick. ...

Workbook page 64

SPEAKING

Read the sentences. Decide whether you agree or disagree. Then work in pairs. Tell your partner.

1 Students shouldn't take phones into their lessons.
2 Students should use computers in all lessons.
3 There should only be six students in a classroom.
4 Students shouldn't wear school uniforms.

I disagree with number 2. Students should use computers in most subjects, but not in all of them. That would be boring.

READING

1 Work in pairs. Look at the pictures and think about what the machines do. Then choose one of the two machines and talk about it.

I think it's called ... *It helps with ...*
It's a cool machine because ...
It gets angry when ...

2 Read these product reviews on a website from the year 2066. What do the robots do?

I bought the Sunny Star robot two weeks ago. It does everything for me in the morning. I don't have to do anything. It wakes me up with a nice song. I don't have to get out of bed myself. It helps me to get out of bed and carries me to the shower. Then it washes my face and brushes my teeth. It makes my bed and packs my bags for school. But you should be careful! You mustn't use it on rainy days. Sunny Star gets very angry when it rains. Then it only turns the cold water on when it puts you in the shower!

Do you like visiting other countries? Yes?

Then this invention is perfect for you. You don't have to have a lot of money. And you don't have to get up in the morning. It looks like a bed. It's got a computer. You only have to type the name of a city, and it flies you there. You can stay in bed, and you can have breakfast too. But don't tell your teachers! They would take it away from you! Oh, and there's one more thing you should know. You mustn't forget to switch Travel Plus off at night. Do you know why? Because it wants to travel day and night. It waits until you're sleeping and then it starts travelling. Then you might wake up at the North Pole or in the middle of the ocean!

3 Read the reviews again and answer the questions.

1 What's the first thing that Sunny Star does for you in the morning?
2 When does Sunny Star create problems?
3 What does Sunny Star do when it's angry?
4 What don't you have to do when you use Travel Plus?
5 Why don't you have to get up in the morning?
6 What mustn't you forget when you use Travel Plus?

GRAMMAR

mustn't / don't have to

1 Complete the sentences from the reviews. Then complete the rule with *mustn't* or *don't have to*.

1 You ... do anything. Sunny Star does all the work for you.
2 You ... forget to switch Travel Plus off at night.

RULE: Use ¹... to say 'it's not necessary'.
Use ²... to say 'don't do it! I'm telling you not to!'

2 Match sentences 1–2 with a–b.

1 You don't have to go swimming.
2 You mustn't go swimming.
a There are sharks.
b You can do something else if you prefer.

3 Complete the sentences with *mustn't* or *don't have to*.

1 A Dad, I don't want to go to the park with you.
  B No problem, Mike. You ... be there.
2 A I'm so thirsty.
  B Stop! You ... drink that!
3 A I'm sorry I can't join you.
  B That's fine. You ... come.
4 A Sorry, I can't stay. I'm in a hurry.
  B Oh, no problem. You ... wait for me.
5 A I don't like swimming.
  B We ... go swimming. We can go to the park.
6 A The neighbour's dog is in the street. You ... go out.
  B Thanks for telling me. I'm scared of that dog.

Workbook page 65

PRONUNCIATION
Vowel sounds: /ʊ/ and /uː/
Go to page 151.

VOCABULARY

Housework

2.23 Match the words (1–10) with the photos (A–J). Listen and check. Then listen again and repeat.

1 vacuum the floor | 2 tidy up | 3 do the ironing
4 do the shopping | 5 set / clear the table
6 do the washing-up (wash up) | 7 make the beds
8 do the cooking | 9 do the washing
10 load / empty the dishwasher

Workbook page 67

GET IT *right!*

Remember we write
✓ *Shopping.*
not
✗ ~~*Shoping*~~.

SPEAKING

1 Read the questions. Make notes.

1 What do you have to do at home: tidying, shopping, cooking, etc.?
2 What don't you have to do?
3 What should parents / children do at home?

2 Plan what you are going to say. Use these phrases.

I have to … I think / don't think that's fair.

I don't have to … I'm quite happy about that.
But it would be OK for me to do that.

I think … should do the same amount of work.
It's not fair that …
Mothers / Fathers should do more work because …

3 Work in pairs or small groups. Compare your ideas about housework.

WRITING

A paragraph about housework

Ask your partner these questions and make notes. Then write a paragraph.

1 What do you have to do at home?
2 What don't you have to do at home?
3 When do you have to do housework?
4 What do you feel about this housework?

Kate hates clearing the table, but she has to do it every evening. She also has to vacuum her bedroom floor once a week. She doesn't have to do …

THINK *self-esteem*

Classroom rules

1 Write sentences about things students *have to*, *should(n't)* or *mustn't* do.

Students have to study for their tests.
Students should speak English as much as possible.
Students mustn't leave rubbish on their desks.

2 Compare your sentences in class. Say what you think.

I think it's a good idea / fair / not fair that …

I think students / teachers / we all should(n't) …

3 Carry out a vote to agree on the rules for your class. Make a poster, sign it and put it on the wall.

PHOTOSTORY 4

THE TREASURE HUNT

1 2.24 Read and listen to the photostory and answer the questions.

Why can't Ryan come to Luke's house after school?

What's a GPS treasure hunt?

LUKE: Come to my house after school.

RYAN: Sorry, no chance. I have things to do.

LUKE: Oh, yeah? Like what, Ryan?

RYAN: Oh, homework and stuff. And I promised to help my dad with the garden. Sorry.

LUKE: OK. Never mind.

1

RYAN: Hey, come here, Luke. I've found something. It looks like a box. It IS a box!

LUKE: What's in it? Gold coins? Diamonds? 'Ladies and gentlemen. We are now talking live to the two lucky boys who found the treasure in the park.'

RYAN: You think you're really funny, Luke.

LUKE: Absolutely! Come on, open the box!

2

RYAN: What do we do now?

LUKE: Eat it?

RYAN: That sounds like a good idea. But hurry up.

LUKE: What do you mean?

RYAN: Look. Olivia and Megan are coming. I don't want to share it with them.

3

LUKE: Hi, you two.

RYAN: So, what are you up to? Using the GPS on your phone to find your way home?

MEGAN: No. We're on a treasure hunt.

RYAN: Sorry?

MEGAN: We're trying to find some treasure. Here in the park. Using the GPS on my phone. It's such good fun!

LUKE: Treasure? You mean, like a box with a little surprise in it?

OLIVIA: Exactly! Now, can we keep looking?

4

2 Work in pairs. Discuss what happens next in the story. Write down your ideas.

We think Olivia and Megan find the box. They find … there.

3 EP4 Watch to find out how the story continues.

4 Answer the questions.

1 What is Luke worried about?
2 Where does Ryan think Luke is going?
3 What's the problem with the mobile?
4 What does Olivia do to solve the problem?
5 What's the problem for Luke and Ryan?
6 What do the girls find in the box?

Phrases for fluency

1 Find the expressions 1–5 in the story. Who says them? How do you say them in your language?

0 no chance *Ryan*
1 … and stuff. …
2 Never mind. …
3 Absolutely. …
4 So, … ? …
5 … such good fun …

2 Complete the dialogue with the expressions in Exercise 1.

A Do you want to come round tonight? We can play computer games ¹… .
B Sure. I love computer games, they're ²… .
A Of course. And can you bring your new laptop?
B ³… . It's my brother's, too. I can't take it.
A ⁴… . We can use mine. ⁵… , is seven o'clock OK?
B ⁶… ! See you at seven!

VOCABULARY

Expressions with *like*

1 Complete the sentences from the story with the phrases in the list.

like | looks like | sounds like | Like what

1 Oh, yeah? … , Ryan?
2 It … a box. It IS a box.
3 That … a good idea.
4 Treasure? You mean, … a box with a little surprise in it?

2 Match the sentences.

1 This chicken isn't very good.
2 Someone's talking. Who is it?
3 Let's buy her a present.
4 He's a really nice guy.
5 What's that animal?

a Like what? A poster perhaps?
b Yes, he's just like his sister, she's nice too.
c I'm not sure. It looks like a dog, but it isn't.
d That's right. It tastes like fish!
e It sounds like Jim.

3 Complete the dialogues using a phrase with *like*.

1 A I really hate tomatoes.
B I'm … you. I hate them, too.
2 A Here's a photo of my sister.
B Wow. She really … you!
3 A We should do some exercise.
B …? Go for a walk?
4 A Let's go to the cinema.
B That … a great idea.

Workbook page 67

FUNCTIONS

Asking for repetition and clarification

1 Complete the extracts from the conversations with the words from the list.

you mean | Sorry? | Like what

LUKE: Come to my house after school.
RYAN: Sorry, no chance. I have things to do.
LUKE: ¹… , Ryan?
RYAN: OK, that sounds like a good idea. But hurry up!
LUKE: What do ²… ?
MEGAN: We're on a treasure hunt.
RYAN: ³…
MEGAN: A GPS treasure hunt.

2 Match the expressions in Exercise 1 with their definitions.

a Say that again.
b What are you trying to say?
c Give me an example.

3 Work in pairs. Student A: Go to page 159. Student B: Go to page 160. Take two or three minutes to prepare. Then have a conversation.

Life skills

Solving problems

Everybody has problems to solve. Sometimes the problems are big, and sometimes they are small, but it's always a good idea to think of all the possibilities before we decide what to do.

1 Think about the photostory on page 84.

1 Imagine you are Ryan and Luke. What is the problem when you eat the chocolate?

2 How many possible solutions can you think of?

3 Did you chose the right solution?

2 Read the conversation. What is Ben's problem?

Andy: Hey Ben. What are you doing?

Ben: Hello Andy. I'm thinking about how to go to school next week.

Andy: Why?

Ben: My mum's car is broken so we have to find another way. One idea is getting the bus.

Andy: Good idea. The bus is fast so you can get to school early. So, can we go out now?

Ben: Hang on! I can see here that the bus goes at 7:10, so I have to get up at… 6. No chance! Also, I need to take my little sister to her school and I don't want to be at school an hour early.

Andy: So why don't you walk? You can take Annie to school, walk from there to my house and then we can go to school together.

Ben: Sounds good, but I'm not so sure. Annie's school is a long way from your house. And I don't want to arrive at school late, but I can't leave Annie at her school at 8am. It's not open until 8:15.

Andy: OK, so the bus is a no, and walking a no too? How about going on your bikes? You can cycle with Annie to her school at 8:15 and have time to get to school about 10 minutes early.

Ben: Good idea! The only problem is Annie doesn't have a bike…

3 Ben and Andy think of three solutions. What are they? What are the positives and the negatives about each solution?

4 Work in pairs. Think of one more solution for Ben. Choose the best one.

5 With your partner, choose one of the problems below and:

1 think of at least three solutions;

2 think of positives and negatives for each solution;

3 choose one of the solutions.

What to wear to a party

When to do your homework

What to buy a friend for their birthday

How to save money

6 Explain to the rest of the class which solution you decided to use and why you chose it. Do the other students agree with you?

Tips for solving problems

1. When you have a problem, spend some time trying to think of all the possible solutions.
2. When you have all the possible solutions, think about the positives and negatives for each solution.
3. After listing the positives and negatives, choose what you think is the best solution.
4. Remember sometimes there is no good solution, and you have to choose one that is least bad.

8 SPORTING MOMENTS

LEARNING OUTCOMES

FUNCTIONS: talking about feelings; talking about sports

GRAMMAR: past continuous; past continuous vs. past simple; *when* and *while*

VOCABULARY: sports and sports verbs; adverbs of sequence

Work in pairs. Look at the photo and answer these questions.

1 This woman is rock-climbing. Why do you think she wants to do something difficult and dangerous?

2 What physical and mental abilities do you think she has?

3 Is this something you would like to do? Why / why not?

READING

1 Match the words (1–6) in the list with the photos (A–F).

1 basketball | 2 horse racing | 3 mountaineering
4 athletics | 5 swimming | 6 tennis

2 Which sport(s) in Exercise 1 has these things?

a ball | a race | a track | water
rope | a net | a match | a rider

3 Name other sports in English.

4 Which sports are popular in your country? Which ones do you like? In your notebook write P (popular) and/or L (like) for each photo.

5 Compare your ideas with a partner.

Basketball is popular here but I don't like it very much.

I like tennis and it's very popular here.

6 Look at the photos on page 89. Answer these questions.

1 Which sports are the stories about?
2 There is something that connects both stories. What is it, do you think?

7 2.25 Read and listen to the article and check your answers.

8 Read the article again. Correct the information in these sentences.

1 The weather in Barcelona was bad.
2 Derek Redmond ran in the 200-metre race.
3 The race organisers tried to help Derek.
4 Derek was running when he crossed the finish line.
5 In 2010, Gerlinde Kaltenbrunner had already tried to climb K2 three times before.
6 Gerlinde was alone on the mountain.
7 The accident happened in the evening.
8 Gerlinde's dream of climbing all of the mountains in the world that are 8,000 metres or higher, is still incomplete.

If you don't give up, YOU CAN'T FAIL

There are many stories of brave people in sport who didn't give up. Here are two of our favourites.

Derek Redmond

It was the Olympic Games in Barcelona in 1992; the semi-final of the 400 metres. The sun was shining and the crowd were ready for a great race. The British athlete Derek Redmond was a top runner: he had a very good chance of winning a medal.

The race began. At first, Derek was running well. Then, after about 150 metres, he felt a pain in his leg. He fell down on one knee. He had a bad injury and couldn't carry on. The other runners went past him and finished the race.

After about five seconds, Derek got up and started to run again, on one leg only. Some organisers tried to stop him but he kept going. The crowd stood up and started to clap. Then another man came onto the track – Derek's father, Jim. His father put his arm around him and said, 'Derek, you don't have to do this.' Derek replied, 'Yes I do. I have to finish.' And so together they walked the last 50 metres and crossed the line.

When he finally crossed the line, Derek was crying and 60,000 people were cheering him.

Gerlinde Kaltenbrunner

In the summer of 2010, mountaineer Gerlinde Kaltenbrunner was almost at the top of a mountain called K2 in Pakistan. She was trying to climb the 8,611-metre mountain for the fifth time, and this time she was climbing with her friend Fredrik Ericsson.

It was about 7 o'clock in the morning and it was snowing a little. The two climbers were getting ready to go up the last 400 metres. Fredrik was trying to tie some rope but he slipped and fell past Gerlinde. He fell 1,000 metres and was killed.

Gerlinde went back to base-camp. K2 was now a very sad place for her, and she thought perhaps she would never climb the mountain.

But there was something very important that she wanted to do: K2 is one of 14 mountains in the world that are 8,000 metres or higher, and her dream was to climb them all.

So in August 2011 she went back to Pakistan and K2, and tried again. This time, she got to the top. Her dream was complete.

THINK values

Trying, winning and losing

1 Think about these sentences. Which one do you think is the most important?

The two stories tell us that ...

1 it's important to try to win a race.
2 you shouldn't start a race if you think you can't win.
3 when you start something, you should try to finish.
4 if things go wrong, you should try to keep going.
5 if you try to climb a mountain but don't get to the top, you fail.

2 Work in pairs. Compare your ideas with a partner.

I think number 1 is the most important. What about you?

GET IT right!

Which is right?

fifth or *fith*

slipped or *sliped*

GRAMMAR

Past continuous

1 Complete the sentences from the article on page 89 with the words in the list. Then choose the correct words to complete the rule.

run | try | climb | shine

1 The sun ... in Barcelona.
2 At first, Derek ... well.
3 Gerlinde ... with her friend Fredrik Ericsson.
4 Fredrik ... to tie some rope.

RULE: Use the past continuous to talk about *completed actions / actions in progress* at a certain time in the past.

2 Find more examples of the past continuous in the article on page 89. Then complete the table.

Positive	Negative	Questions	Short answers
I/he/she/it [1] ... working	I/he/she/it [3] ... (was not) working	[4] ... I/he/she/it working?	Yes, I/he/she/ it [6] ... . No, I/he/she/it [7] ... (was not).
you/we/they [2] ... working	you/we/they weren't (were not) working	[5] ... you/we/ they working?	Yes, you/we/they/ [8] ... . No, you/we/they [9] ... (were not).

PRONUNCIATION
Strong and weak forms of *was* and *were*
Go to page 151.

3 Yesterday the sports teacher was late. What were the students doing when he got there? Complete the sentences with the correct form of the verbs in brackets.

0 Lucy *was talking* (talk) on her phone.
1 Daniel and Sophie ... (play) basketball.
2 Samuel ... (read) a book.
3 Ken ... (climb) up a rope.
4 Lisa ... (dream) about a day on the beach.
5 Andy ... (look) at his photos on his tablet.

4 Complete the dialogues with the past continuous form of the verbs.

1 A What ... (you/do) yesterday when we phoned you?
B I ... (wait) for my mother in town. And it was horrible because it ... (rain)!
2 A Why didn't you answer when I phoned you?
B I ... (cook) my lunch.
3 A Was it a good game yesterday?
B Well, the beginning was fine. We ... (play) well and we ... (win). But then they scored four goals!
4 A ... (you/watch) TV when I called last night?
B No, I wasn't. I ... (read) a magazine.

Workbook page 72

GET IT *right!*
Which is right?
we all were waiting or *we were all waiting*

VOCABULARY

Sports and sports verbs

1 Match the words in the list (1–10) with the photos (A–J).

1 sailing | 2 diving | 3 golf | 4 gymnastics
5 rock-climbing | 6 rugby | 7 snowboarding
8 skiing | 9 volleyball | 10 windsurfing

A

B

C

D

E

F

2 Answer the questions.

1 Two of the sports in Exercise 1 have *players* and a *team*. Which ones are they?
2 Seven of the sports in Exercise 1 add *-er* or *-or* for the people who do them. Which ones are they?
3 What do we call someone who does gymnastics?

3 We use different verbs for different kinds of sports. Read the rule and then copy and complete the table with the sports in Exercise 1.

RULE:
play + game (e.g. football)
go + *-ing* (e.g. running)
do + activity (e.g. athletics)

play	*go*	*do*
football	running	athletics

4 Work in groups. Answer the questions about the sports in Exercise 1.

Which sports …
1 are team sports?
2 are dangerous?
3 are water sports?
4 are in the Winter Olympics?
5 are expensive?
6 are difficult to play or do?

Workbook page 75

G

H

I

J

LISTENING

1 2.28 Five teenagers were asked the question: 'How do you feel about sport?' Copy the table listen and tick (✓) the sport(s) that each one mentions.

	Gemma	Andy	Tracey	Paul	Ryan
football					
swimming					
running					
skateboarding					
gymnastics					
skiing					
tennis					

GET IT *right!*

Talk about the activity, we say
✓ ***running*** or ***jogging***
✗ ~~***footing***~~ (because it is not a word in English)

2 2.28 Listen again. Who expresses these ideas?

1 I practise a lot.
2 I am not competitive.
3 I like doing things alone.
4 I'm learning another sport.
5 I can't do my sport at school.

3 Work in pairs. Which of the five teenagers are you like? Tell your partner.

I'm like Gemma because I don't really like sport.

I really like running, so I'm like Andy.

FUNCTIONS

Talking about feelings

1 You are going to answer the question: 'How do you feel about sport?' List some sports you want to talk about.

running, football, swimming, surfing

2 What do you want to say about each sport? Mark them ✓ for positive comments; and ✗ for negative ones.

running ✗ football ✗ swimming ✓ surfing ✓

3 Think about why you put ✓ or ✗. Look at the words and ideas in Vocabulary, Exercise 4. Use these words and / or other words you know.

running ✗ boring football ✗ team sport
swimming ✓ fun surfing ✓ difficult and fun

4 Work in pairs. Ask each other: 'How do you feel about sport?'

Well I don't like running because it's boring. But I love surfing because it's fun and it's difficult to do.

A

B

C

D

Your favourite sports FAILS!

1 ALAN Today 4 pm

I saw a really funny thing on YouTube the other day. It was a tennis match. Four people were playing – it was in a big competition. One of the players was hitting the ball when a bird flew in – and the ball hit the bird and it fell to the ground. The players stopped and one of them picked the bird up – they thought it was dead. But suddenly the bird flew away again and they all laughed!

2 JILLY Today 1 pm

I was watching an American football game, a long time ago. There were some girls who were standing at the side of the ground. One player threw the ball really hard – and very badly! One of the girls was looking the other way when the ball hit her. She just didn't see it – and it knocked her over. Everyone was worried; the player went to see if she was OK – then she stood up and laughed and the player gave her a big hug.

3 MARK Today 10 am

I love sumo wrestling – you know, the big Japanese men who wrestle in a small ring. I was watching some on TV, and one wrestler started pushing the other one. He was pushing and pushing and they started to fall over, and the little referee was there behind them – he was trying to get out of the way but then the two men fell on him and he fell out of the ring!

4 PAULA Today 9 am

I went to watch a cycling race the other day. I was standing at the finishing line, and I saw the first cyclist come round the corner to finish the race. At first, he was very happy because he was winning – but he wasn't at the finishing line yet! While he was still cycling, he put his arms up in the air to celebrate. After two seconds, he lost control of the bike. And finally he fell off! He got back on the bike but another cyclist went past him, so in the end he came second. Poor guy – but it was his fault!

READING

1 Look at the pictures. What do you think is happening in each one?

2 Read the stories (1–4) and match them with the pictures (A–D).

3 Read the stories again. Answer the questions.
   1 Why does Alan think the story about the bird is funny?
   2 Why didn't the girl see the ball coming at her?
   3 What happened to the referee?
   4 Why did the cyclist lose control of the bike?

4 How funny do you think these stories are? Give each one a number from 0–5 (0 = not funny at all, 5 = very, very funny). Compare your ideas with a partner.

train to THINK

Sequencing

1 Look at the lists. Put them in a logical order.
   1 morning – night – afternoon – evening
   2 tomorrow – today – next week – yesterday
   3 Saturday – Wednesday – Monday – Friday
   4 have lunch – come home – go to school – wake up
   5 baby – adult – child – teenager
   6 first half – kick-off – half-time – second half

2 Compare your ideas with other students. Are they the same or different?

GRAMMAR

Past continuous vs. past simple

1 In your notebook, copy these sentences from the stories on page 92. Underline the past continuous verb and circle the past simple forms.

1 One of the players was hitting the ball when a bird flew in.

2 One girl was looking the other way when the ball hit her.

3 He was trying to get out of the way but the two men fell on him.

4 While he was still cycling, he put his arms up in the air.

2 Look at the diagram. Which part of the sentence tells us the background action? Which part of the sentence tells us what happened at one moment? Complete the rule.

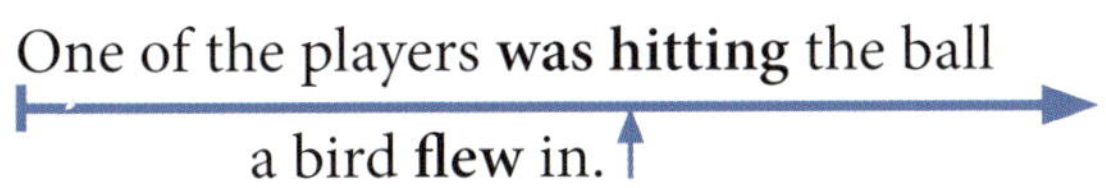

RULE: Use the [1]... to talk about background actions in the past, and the [2]... for actions which happened at one moment (and sometimes interrupted the background action).

3 Complete the sentences. Use the past continuous or past simple form of the verbs.

0 He *was running* (run) and he suddenly *felt* (feel) a pain in his leg.

1 The ball ... (hit) me while I ... (watch) a bird.

2 Jenny ... (sail) with her father when she ... (see) some dolphins.

3 He ... (chase) the ball and he ... (fall) over.

4 When I ... (look) out of the window, it ... (snow).

5 The electricity ... (go) off while we ... (watch) a match on TV.

4 Complete the text with the correct form of the verbs.

A few years ago, in a football match in England between Chelsea and Liverpool, a strange thing happened. Chelsea [1]... (win) the match 2–1 and there were about twenty minutes left. Two players – Luis Suárez and Branislav Ivanović – [2]... (run) after the ball. While they [3]... (try) to get to the ball, Suárez suddenly [4]... (take) Ivanović's arm and [5]... (bite) it! The referee [6]... (not see) it happen so Suárez [7]... (continue) playing.

when and *while*

5 Look at the sentences in Exercises 3 and 4. Complete the rule.

RULE: We often use *when* before the past [1]... and *while* before the past [2]... .

6 Complete the sentences. Use the past continuous for the longer activity and the past simple for the shorter one.

0 I *was writing* (write) an email. My phone *rang* (ring).

1 Alex and Sue ... (watch) a film on DVD. Their friends ... (arrive).

2 Marco ... (have) breakfast. He ... (have) a great idea.

3 Cristina ... (talk) on the phone. Her father ... (go) out.

4 They ... (walk) in the mountains. They ... (see) strange bird.

7 Join the sentences in Exercise 6 in two different ways. Use ***when*** and ***while***.

I was writing an email when my phone rang.
While I was writing an email, my phone rang.

Workbook page 73

VOCABULARY

Adverbs of sequence

1 Match the parts of the sentences.

1 At first,	a two seconds, he lost control of the bike.
2 Then	b he was very happy.
3 After	c he fell off.
4 Finally,	d he put his arms up to celebrate.

2 Complete the story with the words in Exercise 1.

[1] ... , I was very nervous.
[2] ... the starter fired the gun.

[3] ... ten seconds, I crossed the finish line and won! I was the Olympic champion!

[4] ... the photographers took photos of me. [5] ... an hour, they gave me the gold medal.

[6] ... , I woke up.

Workbook page 74

Culture

1 Look at the pictures and answer the questions. Then say what you think the article is about.
Where can you see the following things?
- a marathon race
- an athlete
- spectators
- the finishing line

2 2.29 Read and listen to the article. Match the pictures with the correct Olympic Games.

3 Which Olympic moment do you like most? Which do you not like? Compare your ideas with others in the class.

THE OLYMPIC GAMES – the good and the not-so-good

The Olympic Games takes place every four years and usually there is something special that people never forget. Here are some of those moments from the past – some good, some not so good.

1908 London – the marathon
At the end of the marathon, the man who was winning – Dorando Pietri, from Italy – was very tired and fell down four times. People picked him up and he crossed the line – so of course he didn't win the gold medal because people helped him. But he became very famous.

1960 Rome – a winner with no shoes
The winner of the marathon in Rome was Abebe Bikila from Ethiopia. A lot of other runners (and some of the spectators – the people in the stadium) laughed when they first saw him – he had no shoes. They weren't laughing at the end when Bikila won the gold medal. (He won in 1964 in Tokyo too – but wearing shoes.)

1968 Mexico – a big jump
Mexico City is very high and the air is thin – which was a good thing for some athletes, not so good for others. One special moment was the long jump – Bob Beamon of the USA jumped 8.9 metres. Beamon's jump was the World Record for 23 years.

1996 Atlanta – a bomb
During the 1996 Olympic Games, something very sad happened. A bomb exploded in a park near the Olympic stadium. One person was killed, and 111 people were taken to hospital.

2000 Sydney – the Green Games
The Sydney Olympic Games were called 'The Green Games' because all the buildings (the stadium, the houses for the athletes, etc.) were built to be as friendly as possible to the environment. Many people thought these Olympic Games were the best ever.

2004 Athens – another marathon story
In the men's marathon, after about 35 kilometres, Brazilian Vanderlei de Lima was running very fast. He was first, and the second runner was 40 seconds behind him. But then an Irishman ran out from the crowd and pushed him. Other people in the crowd stopped the Irishman. Then de Lima started to run again. He was smiling when he finished the marathon third – he won the bronze medal.

2012 London – a bottle-thrower
It was the final of the men's 100 metres. All the athletes were ready to start the race. Suddenly a man in the crowd threw a plastic bottle at the athletes. But they were lucky. The bottle didn't hit any of them. The race started. A Dutch woman was sitting next to the man. She grabbed him so he couldn't run away. The woman, Edith Bosch, was a bronze-medal winner in judo at the Games.

A

B

C

4 Read the article again and answer the questions.

Who ...

1 had help to finish the race?
2 raced barefoot?
3 was stopped in the middle of his race?
4 caught a criminal?
5 won gold in two different Olympics?
6 came 3rd in an event at the London Olympics?
7 finished first but didn't get a medal?
8 broke an Olympic record?
9 won a marathon bronze medal?

5 There are eight highlighted words in the article. Match the words with these meanings.

0 took quickly in their hands *grabbed*
1 the prize given to the athletes that come third in a race at the Olympics
2 a 42.2 km race
3 happens
4 the prize given to the winners at the Olympic games
5 a competition where athletes run to see who is the fastest
6 people who watch a race or game
7 went from one side to the other side

WRITING

An article about a sporting event

1 Read Max's article in a school magazine about going to an important tennis match. Answer the questions.

1 Who did Max go with?
2 Who did Max think would win?
3 Who won?
4 What did Max do after the match?

2 Find these words in the article. What does each word describe? Why does Max use them?

0 lucky *my family*
1 full
2 excited
3 unhappy
4 great
5 fantastic

3 Look at the three paragraphs of Max's article. Match the paragraphs with the contents.

Paragraph 1 a after the event
Paragraph 2 b introduction to the event
Paragraph 3 c details of the event (the match itself)

4 Think of a sports event that you went to or would like to go to. Answer the questions.

1 When is / was the event?
2 Where is / was it?
3 What is / was the atmosphere like (the crowd and the noise, etc.)?
4 What happens / happened at the event? (players / goals / winners, etc.)
5 How did / would you feel after the event? (happy? tired? excited? unhappy?)

5 Write an article for a school magazine (about 120–150 words) about the sports event. Use Max's article and the language above to help you.

SPORTS NEWS

(1) Last Saturday was the final of the women's singles at the Wimbledon Tennis Championships, played (of course) at the Wimbledon Tennis Club. My family were lucky enough to get tickets. When we got there, we went to the court and found our seats. Of course the stadium was full and everyone was very excited. It was brilliant!

(2) At ten to two, the players came out: Marion Bartoli from France and Sabine Lisicki from Germany. At first, I was sure Lisicki was going to win but when the match started, it was clear that I was wrong. Bartoli played really well and after thirty minutes, the first set ended: 6–1 to Bartoli. And twenty-five minutes later, the second set was 5–1 to Bartoli. Lisicki was very unhappy but she started to play better, and soon it was 5–4. Could Lisicki come back? No. Bartoli hit great shots and won the second set 6–4. The crowd stood and clapped and cheered. And then Bartoli got the trophy.

(3) When the match ended, we looked around a bit and then went home. We had a great time. Maybe the match wasn't the most exciting ever, but it was fantastic to see a big sports event 'live'.

Literature

THE BONE CAGE
BY ANGIE ABDOU

Sadie wants to compete in the Olympic Games but at 26 she is near the end of her swimming career. Does she have the strength and determination to make her dreams a reality?

1 Read the text below and answer the following question. Is Sadie enjoying herself?

Sadie belongs to the water. Only here, her body performs as trained. Heat tingles her neck, mingling with the cold fluid enveloping her. She's near the end, should be exhausted, but today she feels she could swim forever, motoring full speed at the water's surface. Hot, cold, pleasure, pain. She has no time to consider these sensations. One thought pulses: Go, go go. A syllable with every stroke. Her biceps and triceps, her shoulders and her back, her hamstrings and her quads – all pulse. Will they fail her? Can they finish? Something in her doubts this body. Rest. Surely she needs rest. Even on this good day, her muscles whisper at her: Enough. No more. She blocks these thoughts. She can die later, can rest when it's over. Today means everything. Her body buzzes with this knowledge. Only the next two minutes matter. One swimmer's head is at her waist, lane five, and another swimmer's head is at her feet, lane three. But today she will win. Today her body takes charge. Two lengths left and the others will try to pull ahead, but no matter how hard they pull, she will pull harder. She will win. In her last length one word fills her: Happening, it's happening.

GLOSSARY

mingling - mixing/combining
stroke – a swimming movement using the arms and legs
whisper – speak very quietly
buzz – a feeling of excitement

2 How do you know that Sadie badly wants to win? What does this tell you about what kind of person Sadie is?

3 What tense is the text in? What is the effect of this?

4 In what ways does the author create a feeling of energy and speed?

5 How does the text make us feel like we are in the water with Sadie?

6 What qualities do you need to be a successful sports person?

GET IT right!

Units 7&8

have to / don't have to

We always use the base form of the verb after *have to / don't have to*.

✓ *He has to **tidy** his room today.*

✗ *He has to ~~tidied~~ his room today.*

✗ *He has to ~~tidying~~ his room today.*

Remember that the negative of *have / has to* is *don't / doesn't have to*, NOT *haven't / hasn't to*.

✓ *You **don't have to** help me. I can do it.*

✗ *You ~~haven't to~~ help me. I can do it.*

1 Find six mistakes in the text. Correct them.

Helping at home

I have to do a lot of housework at home, but I'm OK about that. I have to tidying my room, but I haven't to vacuum the floor. My brother has to does that. We have to do the washing up, but we don't have do the washing. My dad does that once a week. I haven't to do the cooking – my mum likes cooking. She says it helps her to relax. Of course, I have to doing my homework every day after school. I'm not OK about that!

should and *must*

Don't use *to* after *should* or *must*!

✓ *Students **shouldn't take** their mobiles into lessons.*

✗ *Students shouldn't ~~to~~ take their mobiles into lessons.*

✓ *You **mustn't go** swimming there.*

✗ *You mustn't ~~to~~ go swimming there.*

Be careful when you write these words.

Don't forget the *t* in *mustn't*.

✓ *You **mustn't** do that! It's dangerous!*

✗ *You ~~musn't~~ do that! It's dangerous!*

Don't forget the *u* and the *l* in should.

✓ *You **should** listen to her!*

✗ *You ~~shold~~ listen to her!*

✗ *You ~~shoud~~ listen to her!*

2 Find the correct sentence! Then correct the incorrect sentences.

1 You shoud take some medicine for that headache.
2 You musn't speak to me like that!
3 We mustn't to arrive late. Charlotte will be really angry!
4 What should I take to school for lunch tomorrow?
5 Shold I tell him to come at ten o'clock?

Past continuous vs. past simple

We use the past continuous to talk about <u>background</u> actions in the past, and the past simple for actions which happened at <u>one moment</u> in the past.

✓ *I **was watching** television when the lights **went** out.*

✗ *I ~~watched~~ television when the lights went out.*

3 Complete the story with the past continuous or past simple of the verb in brackets.

The surprise!

It [1]… (happen) last Saturday while I [2]… (have) a party at my house. At 9 o'clock, we [3]… (dance) and having a fantastic time. Then, suddenly, the lights [4]… (go) out. I [5]… (close) my eyes and screamed! But when I [6]… (stop), I heard that all my friends [7]… (laugh). When I [8]… (open) my eyes, everybody was smiling at me. When my mum [9]… (arrive) with a cake and candles, I finally understood.

SAY IT right!

Strong and weak forms of *was* and *were*

1 Work in pairs and read the conversations. Say if the 'weak' or 'strong' form of *was* or *were* is used.

MAN: [1]<u>Was</u> Richard at the shops?
WOMAN: Yes, he [2]<u>was</u>.

WOMAN: [3]<u>Were</u> they eating at home?
MAN: No, they [4]<u>weren't</u>.

MAN: How [5]<u>was</u> the football match?
WOMAN: It [6]<u>was</u> great!

2 🔊 **2.30** Listen and check your answers. Then practise with your partner.

RULE: We can pronounce was /wəz/ or /wɒz/, and were /wə/ or /wɜː/. Spanish speakers often pronounce them all as strong.

test yourself

Units 7&8

VOCABULARY

1 Complete the sentences with the words in the list. There are two extra words.

calculator | sailing | remote control | coffee machine | does | headphones
volleyball | up | windsurfing | satnav | make | skiing

1 We're lost. We need a ... .
2 I have to ... my bed every morning before I go to school.
3 What a mess. Someone should do the washing- ... .
4 I love ... . I've got a small boat and I go every weekend.
5 What is 7% of 270? I need a ... .
6 I was playing ... when the ball hit me on the head.
7 Pass me the ... , please. I want to watch the news.
8 My mum was ... and she fell over in the snow three times!
9 Dad ... the cooking in my house.
10 I'm trying to work and your music is too loud. Can you wear ... ?

GRAMMAR

2 Complete the sentences with the past simple or past continuous form of the verbs.

see | walk | stop | eat | find | play

1 She ... her dog when I saw her.
2 I was tidying my room when I ... my favourite pen that I lost last week.
3 The docking station ... working while we were listening to music.
4 We started running when we ... the bus.
5 I ... my dinner when the phone rang.
6 We ... football when Mum called us for dinner.

3 Find and correct the mistake in each sentence.

1 My mum and my dad was playing in the sand with my sister.
2 You not have to go if you don't want to.
3 We mustn't run. The train doesn't go for an hour.
4 You must to be careful. It's very dangerous.
5 I played football when I broke my leg.
6 Yesterday the sports shop was sell them for only £15.

FUNCTIONAL LANGUAGE

4 Write the missing words.

1 A You ... have to eat it if you don't want to.
B Thanks, I don't ... like it.
2 A I can't come to your house. I've got lots of things to do.
B Like ... ?
A Well, I've got to help my dad ... the shopping, for a start.
3 A At ... I was a bit scared but ... a while I was OK.
4 A What ... you doing at nine o'clock?
B I was ... the washing-up.

MY SCORE

22–30

10–21

0–9

CAMBRIDGE EXAMS
Review Units 7 & 8
Go to page 147.

9 THE WONDERS OF THE WORLD

LEARNING OUTCOMES

FUNCTIONS: paying compliments; talking about the weather

GRAMMAR: comparative adjectives; superlative adjectives; *can / can't* for ability

VOCABULARY: geographical features; the weather; Phrases with *with*

Work in pairs. Look at the photo and answer these questions.

1 Where are these people and what are they doing?

2 Would you like to do what they are doing?

3 Which natural wonders of the world do you want to see?

An amazing place

READING

1 Look at the photos on these two pages. Which of the animals can you name in English?

2 Name other animals in English. Write them down.

3 Work in pairs. Look at the animals on your list. What countries do you think of?

Pandas come from China.

You find spiders all over the world.

4 Work in pairs. Look at the photos again and answer the questions.

1 What do the photos show?
2 Where do these people live?
3 What do you think they eat?
4 What dangers are there?
5 What do these people know a lot about?
6 What's interesting for tourists about this place?

5 3.02 Read and listen to the article on page 101. Are the statements T (True) or F (False)? Correct the false information.

1 The bush people get their water from the river.
2 When the San people are ill, they get medicine from a hospital.
3 The bush people teach children important things about living in the Kalahari.
4 The north of the Kalahari is wetter than the south.
5 There are more animals and plants in northern Kalahari.
6 A holiday in the Kalahari is never dangerous.

They eat wild animals, plants, berries, nuts and insects. They hunt with bows and arrows. There are lots of dangerous snakes, spiders and scorpions. There are lions, leopards, cheetahs and hyenas. It's one of southern Africa's hottest places, and there is often no water. Then they have to get their water from plants, for example from desert melons. When they are ill, there are no hospitals. The people have to get their medicine from plants too.

They are the San, the last people living in the Kalahari. The San people have another name –'bush people'. Their lifestyle is very simple, but they know more about animals and plants than most people do. The San people live in small groups of 25–50. They live in huts – little 'houses' that they make from wood and grass. There are no schools for the children. Children learn from the older people in the group. There are lots of things they have to learn so that they can live in a dangerous place like the Kalahari. In the evenings, the groups of people often sit around a fire and tell stories. Many of the stories are about animals and how to hunt them.

The Kalahari is a big area of bushland in southern Africa. It has got two parts. There is less rain in the southern part than there is in the northern part, so the south is drier. There are fewer plants and animals there, and it's a lot more difficult for people to live. But when it rains at the end of the summer, the land becomes greener and more beautiful. For a few weeks, there are millions of little flowers and even butterflies! But soon, the grass and the bushes get dry and turn brown. Then life becomes more difficult again for people and animals.

Every year, thousands of tourists from all over the world visit the Kalahari. They love driving around the bushland in open jeeps. They love watching the wild animals. Their guides are often San bushmen and the tourists love listening to their stories about the wonders of the Kalahari. The tourists stay in small huts called 'lodges'. They have comfortable beds and showers, but there is no electricity in the huts. When they go out of their hut, they have to be very careful. Sometimes there are lions or leopards around!

GET IT *right!*

A *tourist* is a person. The adjective to describe an area where tourists go is *touristy*.

✓ *The centre of Seville is quite **touristy**.*

✗ *The centre of Seville is quite ~~touristic~~.*

Touristic is not a word in English.

6 Work in pairs or small groups. Think about and answer these questions.

1 Would you like to go to the Kalahari? Why (not)?

2 Are you interested in wildlife? Why (not)?

I'd love to / I wouldn't like to ... because ...

I'm (not) interested in ...

I think it's too dangerous to ... / wonderful to ...

I love / hate taking photos.
watching ... / staying in ...

THINK *values*

Valuing our world

1 Read and choose the statements that show that the natural world is important.

1 Why should I want to go on a safari? There's a nice zoo in my city where I can see lots of animals.

2 I want to build a hotel for 800 people in the Kalahari Desert. We can make a lot of money like that.

3 It's great to learn about wild animals. It helps me to understand more about the world.

4 Who needs lions, leopards and hyenas? They're dangerous animals and that's it!

5 I watch a lot of nature programmes on TV. I support a project to save the tiger in India.

2 Compare your ideas in pairs.

Statement 1 shows that the natural world is not important for this person.

Why do you think that?

Because the person doesn't want to see wild animals in nature.

But maybe that's not true. Maybe he or she thinks flying to other places is not good for nature.

GRAMMAR

Comparative adjectives

1 Look at the article on page 101. Find examples of comparisons. Then complete the table on the right.

	adjectives	comparative form
short adjectives (one syllable)	small big hot	0 smaller (than) bigger (than) 1 ...
adjectives ending in consonant + *-y*	happy dry early	happier (than) 2 ... (than) 3 ... (than)
longer adjectives (two or more syllables)	attractive beautiful	4 ... (than) more beautiful (than)
irregular adjectives	bad good far	worse (than) 5 ... (than) farther / further (than)

2 Complete the sentences. Use the comparative form of the adjectives.

1 Africa is ... (big) than Europe, but ... (small) than Asia.
2 Be careful with the spiders in the Kalahari. They're ... (dangerous) than in Europe.
3 Cars these days are ... (good) quality than they were 30 years ago.
4 Sarah loves wildlife. For her, holidays in the Kalahari are ... (interesting) than going to the seaside.
5 My sister has got two children. Her son is nine. His sister is two years ... (young).
6 John is a musician. It's ... (easy) for him to learn a new instrument than it is for me.

Workbook page 82

GET IT right!

Correct the mistake:

Spain is hotter then England.

VOCABULARY

Geographical features

1 3.03 Match the words (1–10) to the features (A–J) in the picture. Then listen, check and repeat.

1 ocean | 2 hill | 3 mountain | 4 jungle | 5 river
6 desert | 7 lake | 8 beach | 9 island | 10 forest

2 Work in pairs. Ask your partner to close their book and then ask them about the picture.

What's A?

I think it's ... / I'm not sure if I can remember. Is it ... ? / Can you give me the first letter, please?

3 Work in pairs. Compare some of the places. Use the adjectives in the list to help you, or use other adjectives.

hot | big | dangerous | high | nice
difficult | beautiful | exciting

A mountain is higher than a hill.

Yes, and it's more difficult to climb a mountain.

Workbook page 85

LISTENING

1 Match the things in the list (1–4) with the photos (A–D).

1 vultures | 2 a lion and its kill
3 a spear | 4 an antelope

2 3.04 Listen to an interview with a bushman from the Kalahari. Choose the title that best sums up what he talks about.

1 Life in the Kalahari
2 Lions, vultures and antelopes
3 A difficult task for a young man
4 Big cats can't run fast when it's hot

3 3.04 Listen again. For questions 1–5, choose A, B or C.

1 Where was PK born?
  A in the Kalahari
  B in the Sahara
  C in Kenya
2 Before a young man can get married, he has to
  A do a task.
  B find a lion.
  C kill an antelope.
3 It's important for the future family that the young man
  A kills many lions.
  B likes the girl's father.
  C has courage.
4 What can show the bushman where the lion is eating?
  A antelopes
  B vultures
  C his future family
5 To take the kill away from the lion you have to
  A run faster than the lion can.
  B attack the lion with your spear.
  C be very quiet and surprise the lion.

GRAMMAR

can / can't for ability

1 Look at the examples. How do you say these sentences in your language?

1 A man **can** run even when it's very hot.
2 Lions **can't** do that.

2 Look at these sentences from the interview. Complete them with *can* or *can't*.

1 How ... you find a lion and its kill?
2 You ... get the kill from the lion at night.
3 How ... you take the meat away from the lion?

3 Complete the table.

Positive	I/you/we/they/he/she/it **can** run fast.
Negative	I/you/we/they/he/she/it [1]... (**cannot**) run fast.
Questions	[2]... I/you/we/they/he/she/it run fast?
Short answers	Yes, I/you/we/they/he/she/it **can**. No, I/you/we/they/he/she/it [3]... (**cannot**).

4 Make sentences with *can* and *can't*.

0 Simon + run fast / – swim fast
  Simon can run fast but he can't swim fast.
1 Matt + drive a car / – fly a plane
  Matt ...
2 Dogs + understand humans / – speak
  Dogs ...
3 I + write emails / – do maths on my laptop
  I ...
4 They + write stories / – spell well
  They ...

Workbook page 82

THINK *self-esteem*

Being brave is ...

Think about and answer these questions. Compare your ideas with a partner.

1 In what situations do people have to show courage?
2 When is it difficult to show courage?
3 Who could be a role model for you in situations where you need to show courage?

People have to show courage when they are in new situations.

It's difficult to show courage when you're scared.

READING

1 Read the article. Where's the world's driest place?

2 Read the article again. Answer the questions.

1 Which is hotter, El Aziziya or Death Valley?
2 What place holds the most weather records?
3 Why is it difficult to say where the world's best and worst weather is?

SPEAKING

Work in pairs. Discuss these questions.

1 Which of the facts did you know before?
2 Which of the facts were new to you?
3 Which of the places mentioned would you like to visit most? Why?
4 What's your answer to the question at the end of the article? Give your reasons.

WRITING

An email about a place

Imagine you want to tell a friend about the place in the article that you find most interesting. Write an email (100–125 words).

- Choose the place.
- In your email, say:
  - where the place is
  - what's special about the weather there
  - why you think it's interesting

PRONUNCIATION
Vowel sounds: /ɪ/ and /aɪ/
Go to page 151.

GRAMMAR

Superlative adjectives

1 Put the words in order to make sentences. Check your answers in the article.

1 world's / hottest / is / of / Death Valley / the / places / one
2 for / the / is / most fascinating / Antarctica / extreme / place / weather
3 coldest / the / place / world's / It's
4 the / Where / weather? / are / and / best / for / worst / places

Could you live there?

Death Valley, California

1 The hottest place on Earth

Death Valley is one of the world's hottest areas, but the place with the record for the highest temperature is El Aziziya in Libya. There, the temperature reached a record of 57.8°C in 1922. Death Valley's highest temperature on record is 56.7°C. That's not a lot cooler!

2 Antarctica – the place with the most weather records

Antarctica is the most fascinating place for extreme weather. It's the world's coldest place. And it's the wettest, but also the driest place. Are you surprised? Well, here are the facts. People cannot live in Antarctica all year round because it's too cold. In 1983 scientists recorded the lowest temperature ever: -89.4°C! It's also the wettest place on earth, but not because it's got the most rain or snow. It's the 'wettest' place because 98% of Antarctica is covered in ice. But it's also the driest place because it never rains there – it only snows! Antarctica holds another record too – there is a place there with the world's thickest ice; it's 2,555 m deep!

3 The world's best and worst weather

So where are the best and worst places in the world for weather? That's the most difficult question. What's good for one person may be bad for another. In 2012 an organisation named 'International Living' tried to answer this – their number 1 for the best weather was Italy, their number 2 was France, and Mexico was number 3! Where do you think your country would come?

GET IT *right!*
Which is right?
wether or *weather*

Italy
Antarctica

2 Copy the table. Complete the 'adjectives' column with the words in the list. Then complete the comparative and superlative forms.

~~low~~ | fascinating | happy | bad | hot

	adjectives	comparative form	superlative form
short adjectives (one syllable)	0 low high thick	lower 5 ... 6 ...	the lowest 14 ... 15 ...
short adjectives ending in one vowel + one consonant	1 ... wet	hotter 7 ...	16 ... 17 ...
adjectives ending in consonant + *-y*	dry 2 ...	8 ... happier	18 ... 19 ...
longer adjectives (two or more syllables)	3 ... difficult extreme	more fascinating 9 ... 10 ...	the most fascinating 20 ... 21 ...
irregular adjectives	4 ... good far	11 ... 12 ... 13 ...	the worst 22 ... 23 ...

3 Complete the sentences. Use the superlative form of the adjectives.

0 It's Cindy's birthday tomorrow. She's *the happiest* (happy) girl in class.
1 Brazil is ... (big) country in South America.
2 I had an awful headache this morning. I think I did ... (bad) test ever.
3 I think email is ... (good) way of contacting people.
4 We all live a long way from school, but Sam lives the ... (far).
5 She's great at Maths. She can solve ... (difficult) puzzles.

Workbook page 83

VOCABULARY

The weather

1 3.07 Match the words to the pictures. Listen and check.

freezing | sunny | rainy | humid | windy
wet | cloudy | dry | warm | foggy | cold | hot

2 Think about the different kinds of weather. Write reasons why you think they can be good.

a sunny day: We can ride our bikes.
a hot day: We can go swimming.
a rainy day: We can play computer games.

3 Work in pairs. Make dialogues with a partner.

What a nice day.
Yes, it's really warm. Let's ride our bikes.
Great idea.

Workbook page 85

PHOTOSTORY 5

THE COMPETITION

1 3.08 Look at the photos and answer the questions. Then read and listen and check your answers.

What competition is Mr Lane entering?

Why is Megan upset?

OLIVIA: Hi, guys. Where's Megan?

RYAN: She's not with us.

OLIVIA: That's strange. I'm sure she said three o'clock.

RYAN: Well, it's a nice ~~day~~. Maybe she went swimming?

LUKE: It's only quarter past now. She'll be here in a minute.

1

RYAN: Hi, Mr Lane. How are you?

MR LANE: I'm OK – a bit busy with this Prettiest Park Competition.

OLIVIA: Prettiest Park Competition? What's that?

MR LANE: It's a competition to choose the best park in the city.

2

MR LANE: We did really well last year. We came second.

RYAN: Oh! Well done!

LUKE: But this year you want to do better.

MR LANE: Of course. I want to show the judges that my park is the most beautiful one in the city.

LUKE: Well, good luck. I hope you win.

MR LANE: Thanks. It's a lot of work though, and I haven't got much time. And no one to help me, either.

3

MEGAN: Sorry I'm late.

OLIVIA: No problem. Are you all right?

MEGAN: Not really. I was at my granddad's new place. He's pretty upset about having to move. He really misses his garden.

OLIVIA: Does he like gardening, then?

MEGAN: Like it?! He loves it!

4

2 Work in pairs. Discuss what happens next in the story. Write down your ideas.

We think the four friends all go to see Megan's granddad's garden.

3 EP5 Watch to find out how the story continues.

4 Put the events in the right order.

b–1

a Megan's grandfather meets Mr Lane.
b Megan and Luke go and see her grandfather.
c They admire the garden.
d Megan's grandfather shows the trophy to Megan, Luke, Ryan and Olivia.
e Luke tells Megan's grandfather about the competition.
f Mr Lane and Megan's grandfather work in the park.

Phrases for fluency

1 Find the expressions 1–5 in the story. Who says them? How do you say them in your language?

0 ... in a minute. *Luke*
1 Well done! ...
2 ... , either. ...
3 No problem. ...
4 Not really. ...
5 ... , then? ...

2 Complete the conversations with the expressions in Exercise 1.

1 A I got 87% in the test, Dad.
B ... ! Did you study hard for it, ... ?
2 A Hi, James. I can't talk right now. Sorry. I'll phone you ... , OK?
B ... , Steve. Call me back when you can.
3 A Did you enjoy the film?
B No, ... I didn't like the book very much, ...

1

2

3

VOCABULARY

Phrases with *with*

1 Complete the sentences from the story with the phrases in the list.

busy with | to do with me | with us

1 Megan? She's not ... .
2 I'm a bit ... the competition.
3 What's this got ... ?

2 Match the parts of the sentences.

1 You kill the lion
2 It's a paradise
3 We don't offer you a hotel
4 Are you good
a with the biggest rooms.
b with your spear.
c with animals?
d with 200 different kinds of birds.

3 Complete the sentences with the phrases in Exercises 1 and 2.

0 He lives in a house *with* four bedrooms.
1 Sorry, I can't talk now, I'm ... my homework.
2 We went to the lake and some friends came ... .
3 I'm sorry you lost your book, but it hasn't got anything ... .
4 Have you got a problem with your cat? Talk to John – he's ... cats.

Workbook page 85

FUNCTIONS

Paying compliments

1 Put the words in order to make compliments.

1 a / garden / beautiful / What
2 wonderful / a / garden / It's
3 I / flowers / blue / those / love

2 Work in pairs. Use the photos to make compliments.

What a lovely picture!

Life skills

Helping our community

We all belong to communities – our family, our school, our town, our country – and there is always something everybody thinks should be better for that community. It's easy to do nothing and wait for other people to help. Helping our community isn't always easy, but it feels good.

1 Think about the photostory.

1 Imagine you are Mr Lane. Is winning the trophy the most important thing? What is?

2 Imagine you are Megan's grandfather. How do you feel about helping Mr Lane?

2 Read about the Under the Tree Foundation. What does it do?

3 Answer the questions about Jonathan.

1 What problem did Jonathan see?

2 What did he decide to do?

3 Why did he help?

4 What do you think of Jonathan's idea?

4 Work in pairs. Choose one of the communities below. On a piece of paper, write all the problems you can think of for people in that community. There is an example to help you start for each group.

Your country - *homeless people ...*

The world - *places with no clean water ...*

Your town/local area - *dog mess on the streets ...*

Your school - *the books in the classroom need organising ...*

your family - *the car is dirty ...*

5 Exchange your paper with another pair who wrote problems for a different community to yours and read the problems they thought of. Now write ideas for ways that you and your class can help with these problems.

6 Read the ideas of the classmates you changed papers with. What do you think of their ideas? Are there any you'd like to do?

Under the Tree Foundation

When he was 12, Jonathan Woods went Christmas shopping and had a great idea

He was buying toys to give to an organisation in his town. They gave the toys to young children whose parents didn't have enough money to buy Christmas presents. While he was looking for presents to buy, he had a thought. The organisation helped young children, but many children his age were probably in the same situation as the young children. Who was buying presents for them?

Jonathan decided to start an organisation to buy Christmas presents for older children. He called it the Under the Tree Foundation. He also asked an organisation working with older children and teenagers in his local area for advice on what to buy.

In 2007, Jonathan sent out letters to all his friends and family asking them to help Under the Tree. The response to these letters was fantastic. 25 older children received the presents they'd wanted for Christmas, and over 80 teenagers were invited to a pizza and movie night.

The next year, Under the Tree bought presents for over 50 children. The organisation still continues to help older children have a better Christmas.

Tips for helping your community

1 Identify what you are not happy about in your community and think of ways of improving it.

2 Always put the objectives of the community above your personal goals.

3 Don't be afraid to offer your own suggestions but listen and consider the opinions of others.

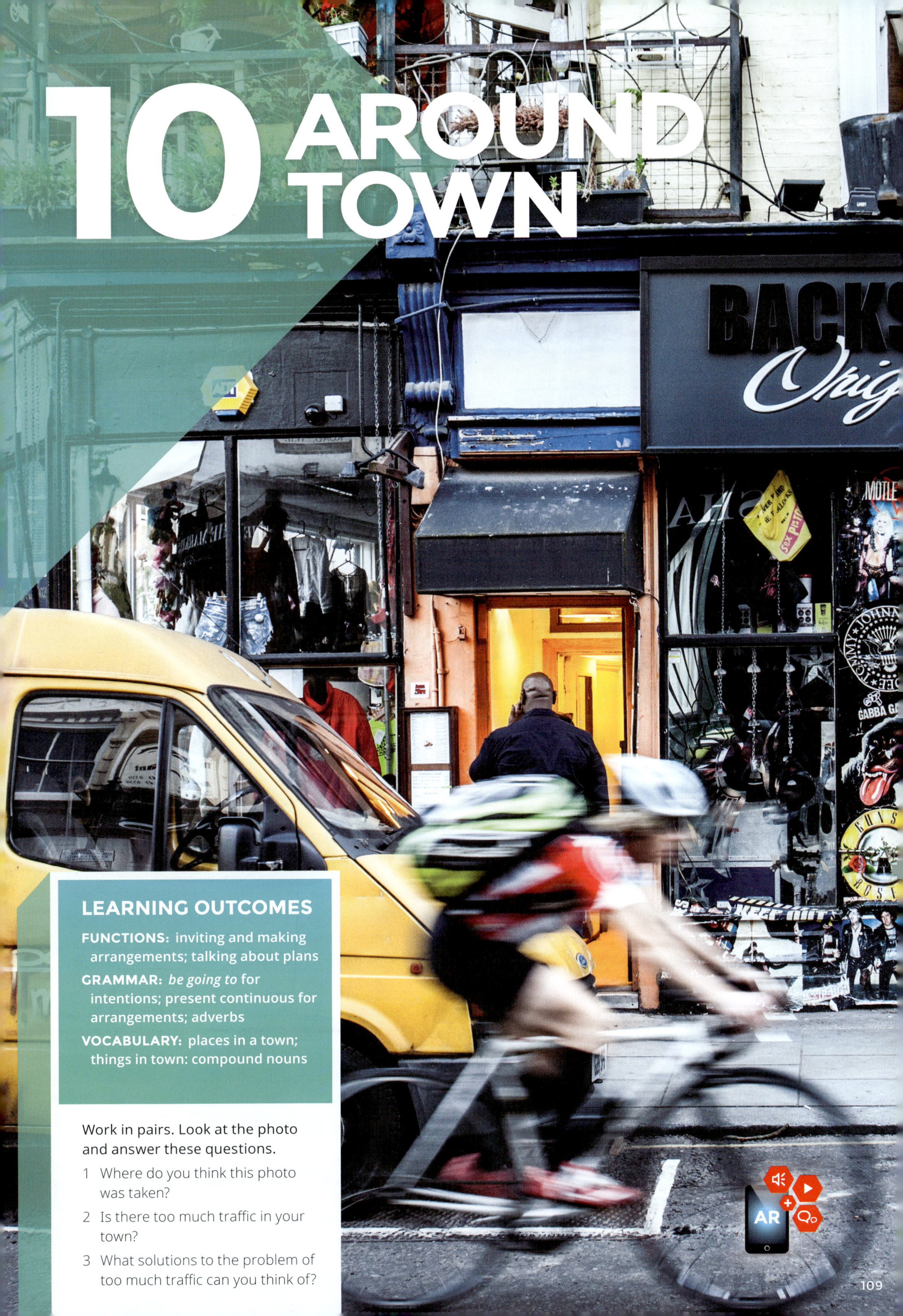

10 AROUND TOWN

LEARNING OUTCOMES

FUNCTIONS: inviting and making arrangements; talking about plans

GRAMMAR: *be going to* for intentions; present continuous for arrangements; adverbs

VOCABULARY: places in a town; things in town: compound nouns

Work in pairs. Look at the photo and answer these questions.

1 Where do you think this photo was taken?

2 Is there too much traffic in your town?

3 What solutions to the problem of too much traffic can you think of?

AR

READING

1 Look at the photos. In which one can you see these things?

1 a **harbour** full of boats
2 a **castle** made of ice
3 a really tall **skyscraper**

2 Work in pairs. Name more places in a town.

station, shop, museum

3 How important are these buildings for a town? Think about who each building is important for and why. Compare your ideas with another pair.

A hotel is important for tourists. They need a place to stay.

4 Work in pairs. Discuss the questions.

1 What is the population of your town?
2 Does your town have a festival each year?

5 **3.09** Read and listen to the blogs. Answer the questions.

1 Where are the writers living now?
2 Where are they going to live?
3 When are they moving?

6 Are the sentences 'Right' (A) or 'Wrong' (B)? If there is not enough information to answer 'Right' (A) or 'Wrong' (B), choose 'Doesn't say' (C).

1 Alice's mum's job is for a year and a half.
A Right B Wrong C Doesn't say
2 Alice is worried about getting bored in Dubai.
A Right B Wrong C Doesn't say
3 She is excited by the Arab culture.
A Right B Wrong C Doesn't say
4 It gets very cold in Yellowknife.
A Right B Wrong C Doesn't say
5 The Snowking Winter Festival takes place on ice.
A Right B Wrong C Doesn't say
6 Brian really likes sport.
A Right B Wrong C Doesn't say

Alice's World

Today – rain in London. Tomorrow – sun in Dubai! It's time to go. We're going to fly out tomorrow! I am soooo excited! OK, I'm a bit sad to say goodbye to my friends but we aren't going to be in Dubai too long. Mum's contract is only for 18 months. Actually, that's quite a long time but I'm certainly not going to get bored. There are loads of things to do in Dubai. Here's what I'm going to do:

- Go to the top of the Burj al Arab (you know – that building that looks like a ship's sail).
- Visit Port Jebel Ali – the largest man-made harbour in the world.
- Shop – there are zillions of shopping malls there. You can go skiing in one of them.
- Eat Middle Eastern food – I just love it.
- Get into khaliji music – it's amazing.
- Play some golf in the desert (yes, it's possible), and see some tennis at the Dubai tennis stadium.
- And go to school, of course. I'm going to go to the Dubai British School.

I think that's enough to keep me busy!

THINK values

Appreciating other cultures

1 Read and choose the things you do.

You are on an exchange trip in a new country for two weeks. Which of these things would you do?

- Make friends with the local children.
- Try and find children from your own country who are also on holiday there.
- Try and learn some of the language.
- Speak your own language (and hope people understand you).
- See if the TV shows programmes from your own country.
- Read the books you brought from home.
- Visit the museums.
- Listen to and buy some music by musicians in that country.

2 Work in pairs. Decide which of the things in Exercise 1 are good to help you find out more about a different culture. What other things can you think of that are also good to do?

The Life of Brian

Big news this week. We're moving! That's right, two months from now it's 'Goodbye Toronto' and 'Hello Yellowknife!'

For those of you who don't know, Yellowknife (population about 19,000) is right at the top of Canada so obviously it's pretty cold – minus 27°C in January! But it gets up to 17°C in the summer.

We're going because Dad's got a new job. He's going to work for a diamond company there.

Anyway the best thing about Yellowknife is every winter there's this really cool festival. It's called the Snowking Winter Festival. Basically, every year they build a really big ice castle on the frozen lake. Then they have loads of concerts and activities for children. They even show films on the walls of the castle. I'm definitely going to that. It's also a really good place to see the Northern Lights. I promise to take loads of photos and put them on my blog.

My sister and I are going to study at the Sir John Franklin High School. It's got a really good theatre so I'm going to do some acting there for sure. There's also a good sports centre too. It's going to be different but I'm sure I'm going to have a good time. And don't worry – I'm not going to stop writing my blog.

GRAMMAR

be going to for intentions

1 Complete the sentences from the blogs on page 111 with the correct form of the verb *be*. Use contractions when you can. Then choose the correct words to complete the rule.

0 I *'m* going to do some acting there for sure.
1 He ... going to work for a diamond company.
2 We ... going to be in Dubai too long.
3 My sister and I ... going to study at the High School.
4 I ... not going to stop writing my blog.

RULE: Use *be going to* to talk about our intentions for the [1]*future / present*.
Use the present tense of *be* + *going to* + [2]*base form / -ing* form of the verb.

2 Copy and complete the table.

Positive	Negative	Questions	Short answers
I'm (am) going to play	I'm not (am not) going to play	Am I going to play?	Yes, [5]... . No, I'm not.
you/we/they're (are) going to play	you/we/they [1]... (are not) going to play	[3]... you/we/they going to play?	Yes, you/we/they [6]... . No, you/we/they aren't.
he/she/it's (is) going to play	he/she/it [2]... (is not) going to play	[4]... he/she/it going to play?	Yes, he/she/it is. No, he/she/it [7]... .

3 Complete the future intentions with the correct form of the verbs in the list.

not watch | take | not fight
not borrow | do | eat

Some family plans – to make us happier!

0 I *'m not going to watch* so much TV.
1 My parents ... out more often.
2 We ... all ... more exercise.
3 My brother ... with me any more.
4 I ... the dog for a walk every day.
5 My sisters ... my clothes without asking any more.

4 Look at the table. Choose the things you are going to do.

tonight	this week	this year
do homework	play sport	write a blog
watch TV	visit relatives	have a holiday
tidy your room	play a computer game	learn something new

5 Work in pairs. Ask and answer questions about the activities in Exercise 4.

Are you going to watch TV tonight?
Yes, I am.
What are you going to watch?

Workbook page 90

VOCABULARY

Places in a town

1 Match the places in the town (1–8) with the people (A–H).

1 concert hall | 2 car park
3 shopping mall | 4 bus station
5 police station | 6 post office
7 football stadium | 8 sports centre

2 Work in pairs. Describe a place from Exercise 1 for your partner to guess.

You go here to buy clothes.

Workbook page 93

LISTENING

1 🔊 **3.10** Listen to Tom and Annie. Who is Tom going to the cinema with: Emily or Annie?

2 🔊 **3.10** Listen again and complete the sentences with places in a town.

1 Tom wants to take Annie to the … .
2 There's a new … in Bridge Street.
3 The restaurant is next to the … .
4 Annie is meeting Emily at the … .
5 Annie's relatives want to see the … .

3 🔊 **3.10** Listen again. Copy and complete Annie's diary.

Friday:	dinner with Dad
Saturday:	[1]… [2]…
Sunday:	[3]…

GRAMMAR

Present continuous for arrangements

1 Look at the examples. Choose the correct options. Then complete the rule with the words in the list.

1 What *are you doing / do you do* tonight?
2 I'*m having / have* dinner with my dad. We'*re going / go* to a restaurant.

present | future | arrangements

RULE: We can use the [1]… continuous to talk about [2]… for the [3]… .

2 Complete the sentences. Use the present continuous form of the verb.

0 I'm going (go) to Dan's party on Saturday.
1 Oliver … (not come) to my house this afternoon.
2 Sara and I … (do) our homework together after school.
3 We … (not visit) my grandparents on Sunday.
4 … your class … (go) on a trip next week?
5 My brother … (play) in the basketball final on Monday.

3 Complete the conversation. Use the present continuous form of the verbs in the list.

not do (x2) | go | buy | meet | do (x2) | play

KENNY: What [1]… you … this afternoon?
OLIVIA: Nothing. I [2]… anything.
KENNY: Paul and I [3]… football. Do you want to come?
OLIVIA: OK. Can I invite Tim? He [4]… anything either.
KENNY: Sure. And what about your brother? [5]… he … anything?
OLIVIA: Yes, he [6]… shopping with my mum. They [7]… his birthday present.
KENNY: OK. Well, we [8]… Jack, Adam, Lucy and Julia at the park at two.
OLIVIA: OK. See you at two, then.

Workbook page 90

FUNCTIONS

Inviting and making arrangements

1 Complete the sentences.

Inviting	[1]… … like to go the cinema with me? [2]… …want to go to the cinema with me?
Accepting	I'd [3]… to. That would be great.
Refusing	I'm sorry. I [4]… . I'm busy.

2 Work in pairs. Take turns to invite your partner to do these things.

watch DVD | go theatre | play tennis
go burger bar | come your house

3 Copy the table below. Think of three arrangements and put them in your diary.

Saturday	*Sunday*
morning:	morning:
afternoon:	afternoon:

4 Can you complete your diary? Walk around the classroom and:

1 invite people to do things with you.
2 find things to do when you're free.

Would you like to go to a football match with me on Saturday afternoon?

I'd love to.

READING

1 Look at the photos. What problem does each one show?

2 Read the letters page and match the problems (1–4) with the photos (A–D).

Our Town: What's wrong and what can we do about it?

1 Our town looks a mess and that's not good for tourism. I hate the litter in our streets. Why can't people put it in the bins? It's not difficult. We need to educate people quickly. We need more litter bins and billboards saying 'Don't drop it – Bin it!' and things like that.
We also need to punish people who drop litter. I think they should spend a day picking it up.
Charlie, 14

2 People always complain about the kids in our town. They don't like us hanging out in the shopping centre. They say they don't feel safe. But they're wrong. We never cause trouble. We only meet up there because there's nowhere for us to go. It's not easy being a kid. We need more things for young people to do and more places for us to go. A youth club would be great. There are lots of empty buildings in our town centre. They could use one of them.
Mack, 15

3 The biggest problem in our town is the cars. There are too many cars on our roads and the drivers don't care about the pedestrians. They drive really fast. Some of them don't even stop at zebra crossings! I ride my bike everywhere and I just don't feel very safe, even when I'm in a cycle lane. We can stop this problem easily. Let's get more speed cameras to catch these fast drivers and then stop them from driving in our town.
Pauline, 15

4 People like to complain about the graffiti on the shops in the high street. They think it's ugly. I agree that a lot of it is. But if you look closely some of this art is really good. Some of these people paint really well. Why don't we use them to make the town more attractive? I think we should create graffiti walls where these artists can show off their art. Maybe this will stop the problem of them doing it illegally.
Paris, 13

GET IT *right!*

In British English we write
✓ ***centre*** with *-re* at the end
not
✗ ~~***center***~~ with *-er* which is American English.

3 Read the letters page again. Answer the questions.

1 What does Charlie think people who drop litter should do?
2 What does Mack think young people need in the town?
3 What does Pauline want to stop?
4 What does Paris think will help stop the graffiti problem?

train to THINK

Problem solving

1 Work in pairs. Read and discuss the problem.

The young people in your town aren't happy. They say there is nothing to do.

Make a list of suggestions to help solve this problem.

have a music festival
build a skateboard park

2 Think about your suggestions. What are the advantages and disadvantages of each one?

Suggestions	🙂	☹
music festival	*young people love music / fun*	*noisy / make a mess /expensive*

3 Decide which suggestion you think is the best. Compare your ideas with the rest of the class.

We think a musical festival is the best idea because all young people love music. It's also a lot of fun.

GRAMMAR

Adverbs

1 Copy these sentences from the letters page on page 114. Underline the adjectives and circle the adverbs.

0 They drive really fast.
1 We can stop this problem easily.
2 It's not easy being young.
3 Let's get more speed cameras to catch these fast drivers.
4 We need to educate people quickly.
5 Some of this art is really good.
6 Some of these people paint really well.

2 Complete the rule.

RULE: To form adverbs:

- add [1]... to regular adjectives (e.g. *quick* → *quickly*).
- delete the 'y' and add [2]... to adjectives ending in -y.

Some adjectives have irregular adverb forms.
e.g. *fast* → *fast* *good* → [3]...

Adverbs usually come immediately after the object of the verb or the verb (if there is no object).
He plays tennis well. NOT *~~He plays well tennis~~*.

3 Complete the sentences. Choose the correct words and write them in the correct form.

0 His car was really *fast*. He won the race *easily*. (easy / fast)
1 Her French is very ... . She speaks really ... . (good / fluent)
2 It's not ... . You need to do it very ... . (careful / easy)
3 We need to walk ... . I don't want to be ... . (late / quick)
4 I did my homework ... . I was really ... . (tired / bad)
5 He drives really ... . I get quite ... in the car with him. (scared / dangerous)

Workbook page 91

GET IT right!

Correct the following sentences:

He was playing good.
I play tennis bad.

VOCABULARY

Things in town: compound nouns

1 Choose a word from A and a word from B to make things you can find in a town. Look at the letters on page 114 to help you.

A zebra | youth | speed | graffiti | cycle | litter | bill | high

B wall | street | camera | bin | lane | crossing | board | club

2 Complete the sentences with the words in Exercise 1.

0 Slow down. There's a *speed camera* just ahead.
1 I really like that ... advertising the new Italian restaurant in town.
2 Don't drop your paper on the floor. There's a ... behind you.
3 Don't try and cross the road here – there's a ... just down there.
4 We live in a flat above one of the shops in the ... .
5 The new ... is really popular. Loads of people are painting on it.
6 I ride my bike to school. There's a ... from outside my house all the way there.
7 We go to the ... every Friday night. I usually play table tennis and chat with my friends there.

Workbook page 93

PRONUNCIATION

Voiced /ð/ and unvoiced /θ/ consonants
Go to page 151.

Culture

1 Look at the photos. What do you think a ghost town is?

2 Read the article quickly. Where are these towns?

3 🔊 **3.13** Read the article again and listen. Say if the sentences are T (true) or F (false).

1 Kolmanskop was once a very rich town.
2 The UFO buildings are a popular tourist attraction in Taipei.
3 Fordlândia became a problem because there was nowhere for the factory workers to live.
4 The Ford family sold Fordlândia for $20 million.
5 They closed Centralia because of an accident.
6 It still isn't safe to visit Centralia today.

Ghost Towns around the World

We build towns for people to live in. But what happens when they don't want to live in them any longer? All over the world there are ghost towns, towns where people don't live any more. Here are a few.

In 1908, many Germans arrived in Luderitz in the southern African country of Namibia. They wanted to look for diamonds and they found a lot. With the money from the diamonds they built the town of Kolmanskop. It had lots of beautiful buildings, a hospital, a school, and even a theatre. But when there weren't any more diamonds, they left the town. These days the only things that visitors to Kolmanskop see are empty buildings and a lot of sand.

In 1978, a building company started building a holiday resort in the Sanzhi District of New Taipei City. For the next two years they built a lot of round buildings. They didn't look like normal houses, but more like spaceships. People called them the 'UFO houses'. In 1980, they stopped building the houses because there wasn't enough money and for 28 years the resort was a ghost town. However, no one can visit this city today because in 2008 they demolished all the buildings. All we can see now are photos of these strange looking houses.

In Northern Brazil, there is the ghost town of Fordlândia. In 1928, Henry Ford – famous for his cars – decided to build a big factory there to make car tyres. He also built houses for the workers and their families. Unfortunately, the weather in the area wasn't good for growing the trees they needed to make tyres. Ford tried to make the city a success but it was difficult. In 1945, his grandson Henry Ford II sold Fordlândia. The company lost $20 million. The empty buildings of the town are still there today.

About 70 years ago, Centralia was a busy town in Pennsylvania, USA. It had five hotels, seven churches and 19 big stores. In 1962, a fire started under the town at an old mine. They spent millions of dollars trying to stop it but that didn't work. It became too dangerous to live there and everyone had to leave the town. These days a sign across the road to the town tells people to 'stay out'. The fire is still burning today.

4 There are six highlighted words in the article. Match the words with these meanings.

0 very expensive stones *diamonds*
1 destroyed
2 a company that makes houses
3 a small holiday village or town
4 you find a lot of it on beaches and in the desert
5 holes in the ground from where substances such as coal, metal and salt are removed

5 Work in pairs. Discuss.

1 Imagine you are going to make a film set in one of these towns. Think about:

What kind of film is it? (horror, love, science fiction?)

What's the story about briefly? (It's about a ...)

Who is going to star in your film? (It's going to star my favourite actors ...)

2 Present your ideas to the group and vote on the best idea.

WRITING

An informal email

1 Read the email. Answer the questions.

1 Where is Emily going to spend her summer holidays?
2 What is she going to do there?

Hi Luke,

[1] How are you? I hope you're not studying too hard. Don't worry, there are only two more weeks of school. Anyway, I'm writing because I've got some really cool news. You won't believe it. Mum and Dad are taking me to Sydney for the summer. Sydney, Australia! I can't wait.

[2] So I did some research on the Internet. It looks like a really amazing place. Of course, there's the famous harbour with the bridge and the Opera House but there are so many other great things to do there. I'm definitely going to hang out on Bondi Beach. And guess what? Mum's going to buy me some surfing lessons. I'm going to be a surfer! We're going to be there for the whole of August. It's winter there but I think the Australian winter is hotter than our summer. So that's it – my big news. What do you think?

[3] By the way, Dad says we're going to be in Bangor next weekend. Is there any chance we can meet up? Let me know.

Love

Emily

2 Find these expressions in the email. Use them to answer the questions below.

Guess what? | You won't believe it.
I can't wait. | By the way, ... | Anyway, ...

1 Which two expressions do we use to change topic?
2 Which two expressions do we use to introduce some surprising news?
3 Which expression means 'I'm really excited'?

3 Look at paragraphs 1 and 2 of Emily's email. Match the functions (a–d) with the paragraphs.

Paragraph 1: ... and ...

Paragraph 2: ... and ...

a Describe the city
b Give news
c Ask how your friend is
d Talk about your plans

4 What is the function of paragraph 3?

5 Which paragraph answers these questions?

a What famous buildings are there in Sydney?
b What's your news?
c How long are you going to stay in Sydney?
d What's the weather like in Sydney?
e What are you going to do in Sydney?
f Where are you going?

6 Imagine you are going to spend your next holiday in a famous city. Write an email (about 100–120 words) to your friend telling her the news.

- Use the questions in Exercise 5 to help you.
- Use some of the language in Exercise 2.

Literature

THE PHANTOM OF THE OPERA
BY GASTON LEROUX

Christine is a young opera singer in Paris. After her father dies, a mysterious voice speaks to her in her room in the opera house and gives her singing lessons.

1 Read the text and answer the following question. How does Christine feel about the voice she hears?

I had heard him for three months without seeing him. The first time I heard it, I thought that that adorable voice was singing in another room. I went out and looked everywhere... and I could not find the voice outside my room, whereas it went on steadily inside. And it not only sang, but it spoke to me and answered my questions, like a real man's voice, with this difference, that it was as beautiful as the voice of an angel. I had never got the Angel of Music whom my poor father had promised to send me as soon as he was dead. I really think that Mamma Valerius was a little bit to blame. I told her about it; and she at once said, 'It must be the Angel; at any rate, you can do no harm by asking him.' I did so; and the man's voice replied that, yes, it was the Angel's voice, the voice which I was expecting and which my father had promised me. I thought that it had finally come, and from that time onward, the voice and I became great friends. It asked permission to give me lessons every day. I agreed and never failed to keep the appointment which it gave me in my dressing-room. You have no idea, though you have heard the voice, of what those lessons were like. We were accompanied by a music which I do not know: it was behind the wall and wonderfully accurate. The voice seemed to understand mine exactly, to know precisely where my father had stopped teaching me. In a few weeks' time, I hardly knew myself when I sang. I was even frightened. I seemed to fear a sort of witchcraft behind it. My progress, by the voice's own order, was kept a secret.

2 Why do you think Christine can hear the voice but cannot see anyone?

3 Christine is speaking to someone in this passage. Do you think that Christine trusts the person she is speaking to? Find evidence to support your answer.

4 What do we learn about Christine's father? Do you think he loved her?

5 Why do you think the voice wants Christine to keep the lessons a secret? Do you think Christine is in danger?

6 How do you think the story will develop - what will happen to Christine and the voice?

GET IT right!

Units 9&10

Comparative adjectives

Remember that we form the comparative of one-syllable adjectives with *-er*. Don't use *more*!

✓ *His room is **smaller** than mine.*

✗ *His room is ~~more small~~ than mine.*

✗ *His room is ~~more smaller~~ than mine.*

1 Correct the sentence.

1 Lions can run more faster during the night.
2 The weather in the Kalahari is more dry than in Europe.
3 It's more hotter in the summer than in the winter.
4 People in the countryside are more friendlier than people in the city.

can / can't for ability

Don't use *to* or *-ing* after *can / can't*.

✓ *He can **swim**, but he can't **surf**.*

✗ *He can ~~swimming~~, but he can't ~~to~~ surf.*

2 Choose the correct answer. Do it quickly!

1 I love living by the sea. On sunny days, I can *going / go* to the beach.
2 On cold days, you can *do / to do* the shopping in the town centre.
3 We can *learn / to learn* a lot about wildlife from nature programmes.
4 You can't *drive / driving* a car if you're fifteen.
5 They can't *coming / come* to the party because they're on holiday.

be going to for intentions

Remember to use *am*, *is* or *are* with *going to*.

✓ ***He is going** to study all weekend.*

✗ *~~He going~~ to study all weekend.*

3 Work in pairs. Take turns to complete the sentences with *be going to* and the verb in brackets.

1 He ... (paint) his bedroom on Saturday.
2 I've bought a new chair. I ... (put) it near the TV.
3 We ... (visit) my cousin because he is ill.
4 They ... (go) to the sports centre by car.
5 We ... (watch) a film tonight.
6 Clara ... (not play) in the football match this weekend.

Present continuous for arrangements

We use the present continuous to talk about arrangements for the future. We don't use the present simple.

✓ *I'm **going** to visit my grandparents tomorrow.*

✗ *I ~~go~~ to visit my grandparents tomorrow.*

In present continuous questions put *am*, *is*, *are* <u>before</u> the person doing the action, NOT after.

✓ *What **are you** doing tomorrow?*

✗ *What ~~you are~~ doing tomorrow?*

4 Find six mistakes in the dialogue. Correct them.

LARA: Hi Sam, what you are doing on Saturday?
SAM: Well, in the morning, I play football in the park.
LARA: What are you doing in the afternoon?
SAM: I don't do anything. What are you doing?
LARA: I paint my bedroom.
SAM: Cool! What colour do you use?
LARA: I'm going to choose the colour when I go to the shop.
SAM: Which shop you are going to?
LARA: I go to the shop in the high street at 2 o'clock.
SAM: OK. I'll meet you there! I can help you to choose.

Practise the conversation with your partner.

SAY IT right!

/ð/ (<u>th</u>is) and /d/ (<u>d</u>iscuss)

1 🔊 **3.14** Listen and repeat the sounds and words.

/ð/ <u>th</u>is /d/ <u>d</u>iscuss

2 🔊 **3.15** Listen and choose which one you hear: A or B.

	A	B
1	there	dare
2	they	day
3	then	den
4	breathe	breed
5	than	Dan
6	these	D's

3 Work in pairs. Take turns to read out one of the words from each pair in Exercise 2. Which word does your partner say?

We pronounce /ð/ with our tongue and /d/ with our teeth. Spanish speakers often pronounce these two sounds in the same way.

test yourself Units 9&10

VOCABULARY

1 Complete the sentences with the words in the list. There are two extra words.

windy | zebra | lake | hall | mountains | bin
island | lanes | cloudy | sunny | station | house

1 It's very ... today. You can't see the sun at all.
2 We live on a small ... . There is sea all around us.
3 Mum and Dad are going to the concert ... tonight. They're very excited.
4 It's one of the highest ... in the world and it took the climbers three days to get to the top.
5 It's so ... that my hat just blew off my head.
6 Don't try and cross the road here. There's a ... crossing just up there.
7 It's easy to get about town on a bike because there are cycle ... everywhere.
8 I lost my wallet in the city centre. I went to the police ... but they didn't have it.
9 Put your rubbish in the litter ... over there.
10 We went fishing on the ... but we didn't catch anything.

GRAMMAR

2 Put the words in order to make sentences.

1 going / She's / nine / to / me / at / phone
2 Monday / We're / morning / on / leaving
3 homework / carefully / her / did / very / She
4 keys / I / I / remember / my / where / can't / left
5 the / It's / day / hottest / of / year / the
6 than / It's / mine / car / expensive / a / more

3 Find and correct the mistake in each sentence.

1 I speak badly French.
2 This is the more popular sport in the world; everybody likes it.
3 I had a lot of presents. But the one most I liked was a blue watch from my mother.
4 She plays tennis very good.
5 He's ten and he still can't to ride a bike.
6 We are to meeting him at nine o'clock.

FUNCTIONAL LANGUAGE

4 Write the missing words.

1 A ... a horrible day!
B Yes, ... stay inside and watch TV.
2 A What are you ... later?
B Nothing. Why?
A ... you want to go skateboarding with me?
3 A ... you like to come to my house for dinner on Friday?
B I'd ... to. Thanks.
4 A ... what?
B What?
A Mum's taking me to Disneyland Paris this summer. I ... wait!

MY SCORE

22–30

10–21

0–9

CAMBRIDGE EXAMS
Review Units 9 & 10
Go to page 148.

11 FUTURE BODIES

LEARNING OUTCOMES

FUNCTIONS: sympathising; making predictions

GRAMMAR: *will / won't* for future predictions; first conditional; time clauses with *when / as soon as*

VOCABULARY: parts of the body; *when* and *if*; expressions with *do*

Work in pairs. Look at the photo. Discuss these questions:

1 What do you think this robot is doing?
2 Do you think robots will be normal in homes in the future?
3 How will robots replace humans?

READING

1 Match the parts of body labelled in the picture (A–L) with the words in the list (1–12).

1 arm | 2 leg | 3 mouth | 4 muscle | 5 finger
6 foot | 7 ear | 8 eye | 9 toe | 10 hair
11 bone | 12 thumb

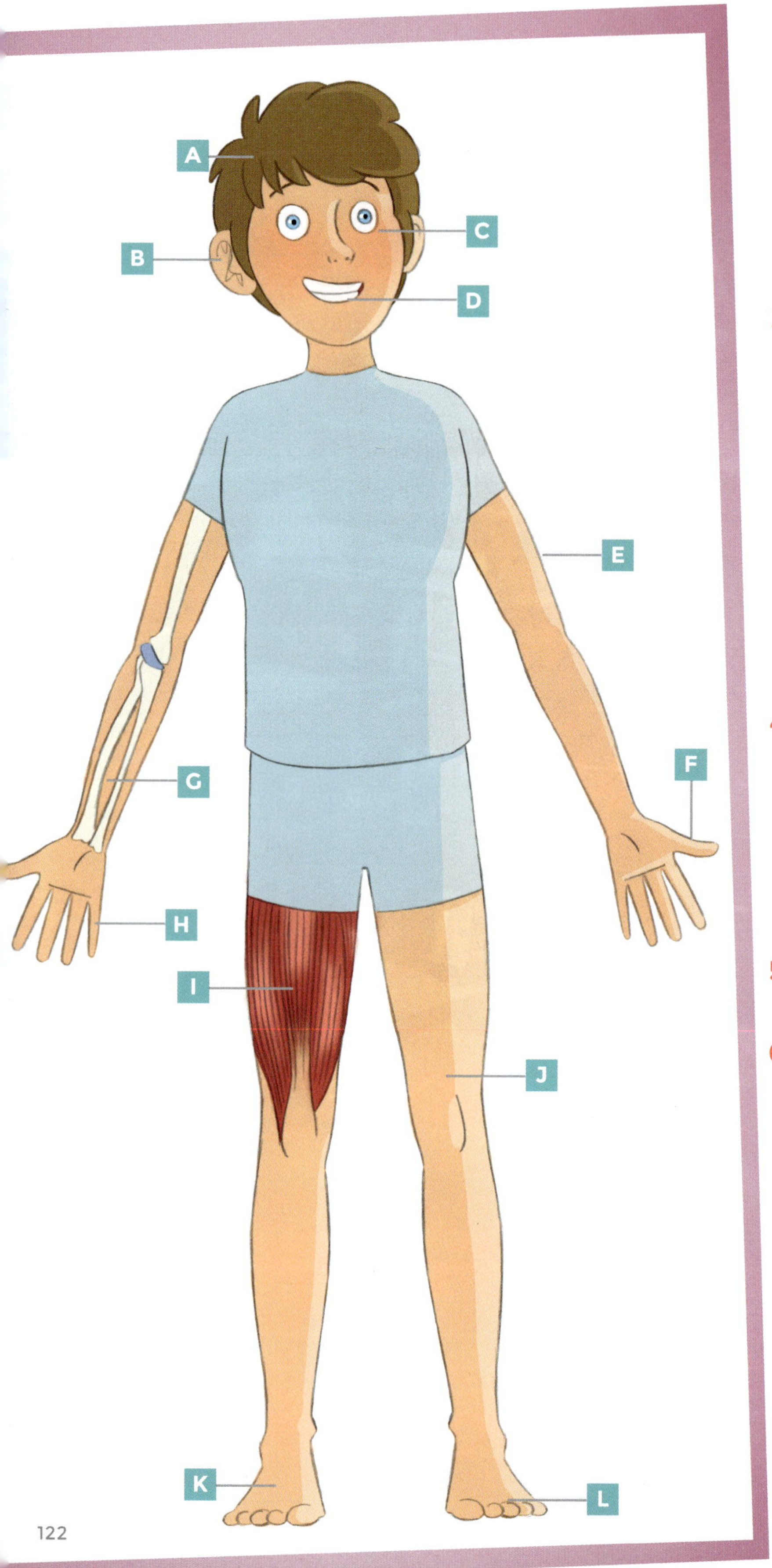

2 Copy the table and write the words from Exercise 1 in the correct column.

Body	Face
arm	*mouth*

GET IT *right!*

Remember for the digits at the end of our feet, we say

✓ *toes*

not

✗ ~~*feet fingers*~~

3 Work in pairs. Discuss the questions.

Which parts of the body do you use when you:

- read a book?
- make a phone call?
- play football?
- eat a meal?
- watch television?
- walk to school?

When you read a book you use your hands and your eyes.

4 Look at the picture on page 123 and the title. What do you think the article will be about? Choose one of the following.

1 What we want to look like in the future.
2 What the human body will be like in the future.
3 How we can change our bodies if we want.

5 3.17 Read and listen to the article and check your ideas.

6 Read the article again and answer the questions.

1 What is the most important reason why our bodies will change in the future?
2 Why will people be taller?
3 Why will people get weaker?
4 What will happen to eyes and fingers?
5 Why will we have one less toe?
6 Why won't people have so much hair on their bodies?

Changing bodies

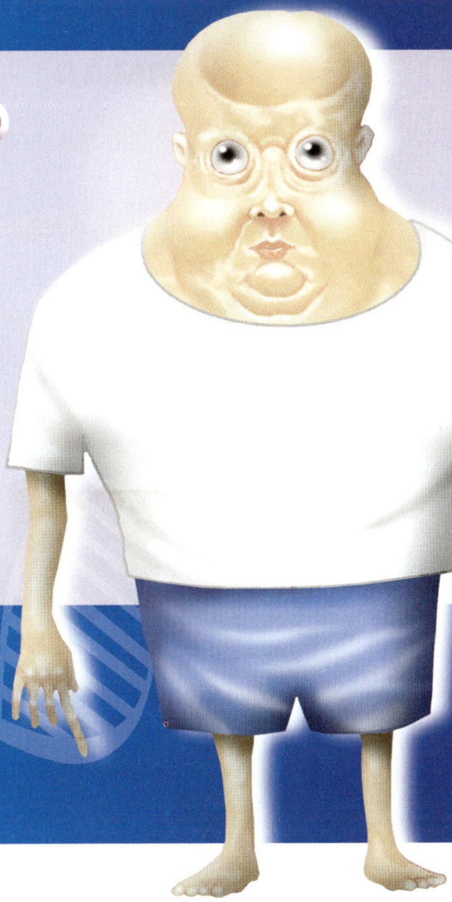

A long time ago, people were very different from the way we are now. For example, if you find a really old house somewhere, you'll see that the doors are usually much lower than they are today. Why? Because hundreds of years ago, people were shorter. Over time, the human body changes to adapt to a new way of life.

Can we expect the human body to change in the future? For sure. And the main reason is that we have more and more technology, and it is changing how we live.

What kind of changes can we expect? Well, no one can be 100 per cent sure, but here are some possibilities.

1. Let's start with the example above. Humans are now ten centimetres taller than 150 years ago. So, in the future, people will probably be even taller. Most of us now have much better food than people in the past – and so we grow more.
2. We'll get weaker in more than one way. The most important way is that our muscles will not be as strong as now because we won't do a lot of physical work.
3. We are already using our feet less, and our hands more (think about computers and tablets and so on.) So we can expect that our legs will get shorter and our feet smaller, and at the same time, our fingers will get longer. And our fingers and our eyes will both get better, because they'll have to do more work together.
4. Now, what about the mouth? It'll get smaller, perhaps, because technological improvements will mean that we don't need to talk so much – and also because our teeth will get smaller (so mouths don't need to be so big to keep them in).
5. Here's a good one – it's very possible that people will have four toes, not five. The little toe really isn't needed any more (people who lose them don't miss them) so it will probably disappear some time in the future.
6. And last but not least – people won't have as much hair on their bodies as now, as we don't need it to keep ourselves warm any more.

Will all these things happen? And if so, when? These are questions that no one can answer for sure.

GET IT right!

Be careful with the spelling of *thing*. We *think* with our heads, but we talk about a *thing* or *things* around us.

THINK values

Exercise and health

1 Read the sentences. Give each one a number from 1 to 5 (1 = doesn't give a lot of importance to health and 5 = gives a lot of importance to health).

- You should do regular exercise to make sure your muscles are strong.
- It's OK to spend a lot of time sitting in front of the television.
- A wonderful thing to do is go for long walks in the fresh air.
- Using a computer and writing text messages gives your hands and arms exercise.
- You don't have to do sport to be healthy and keep fit.
- It's a good idea to do a lot of simple exercise (for example, use the stairs and don't take the lift).

2 Work in small groups. Talk about health and exercise.

1 Together, decide the number that the group is going to give to each of the sentences in Exercise 1.

2 Together, decide on and write another sentence that shows how the group feels about health and exercise.

3 Compare your ideas with other groups.

GRAMMAR

will / won't for future predictions

1 Look at the sentences from the article on page 123. Complete with *will / 'll / won't*. Then complete the rule.

1 Our fingers ... get longer.

2 They ... have to do more work together.

3 Our muscles ... be as strong as now, because we ... do a lot of physical work.

> **RULE:** Use [1]... (*will*) or [2]... (*will not*) + base form of the verb to make predictions about the future.

2 Complete the table.

Positive	Negative
I/you/we/they/he/she/it [1]... (will) come	I/you/we/they/he/she/it [2]... (will not) come

Questions	Short answers
[3]... I/you/we/they/he/she/it come?	Yes, I/you/we/they/he/she/it [4]... . No, I/you/we/they/he/she/it [5]... (will not).

3 Complete the conversation. Use 'll, will or won't and a verb from the list.

~~get~~ | stay | go | see | give | be | help

ALICE: Oh, Mark, it's the French test tomorrow! I hate French. I'm sure I [0]*won't get* the answers right!

MARK: Don't worry, you [1]... fine! You got a good result in your last test.

ALICE: Yes, but this is more difficult. I really don't feel well. Maybe I [2]... to school tomorrow. I [3]... in bed all day.

MARK: That [4]... you. The teacher [5]... you the test on Wednesday.

ALICE: You're right. But what can I do?

MARK: Look, why don't I come round to your place this afternoon after school? We can do some French together. You [6]... that it's not so difficult.

ALICE: Oh, thanks, Mark.

4 Work in pairs. Act out the conversation in Exercise 3.

Workbook page 100

PRONUNCIATION
The /h/ consonant sound
Go to page 151.

VOCABULARY

Parts of the body

1 Match the words (1–10) with the photos (A–J).

1 ankle | 2 back | 3 elbow | 4 knees
5 lips | 6 neck | 7 shoulder | 8 stomach
9 throat | 10 tongue

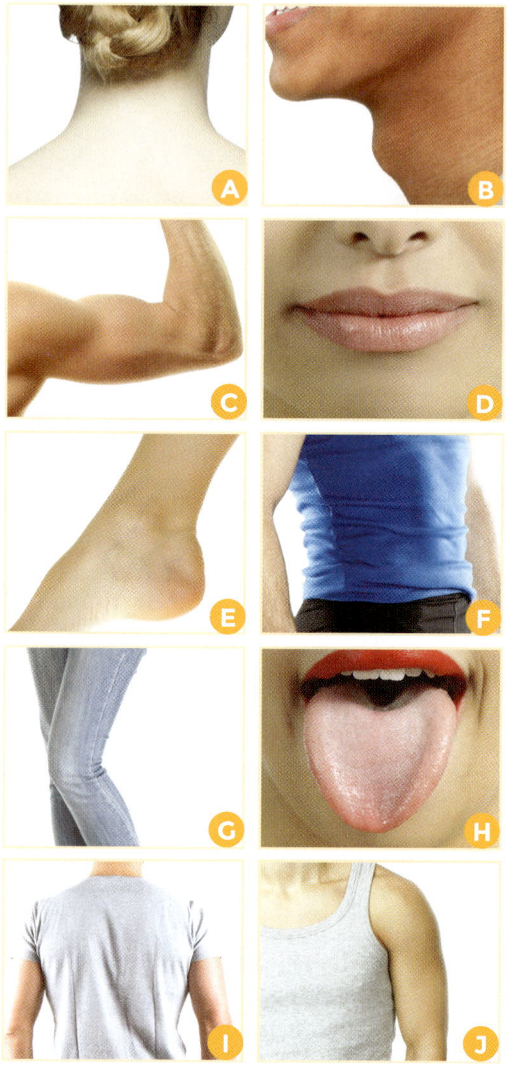

2 3.20 Listen and match the speakers (1, 2 and 3) with the pictures (A–C).

Workbook page 102

A

B

C

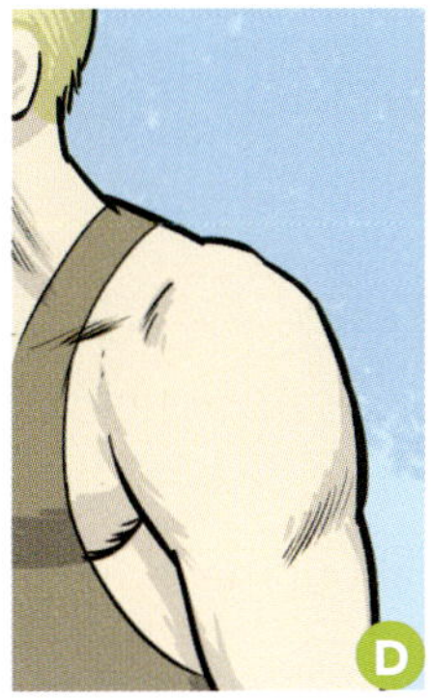
D

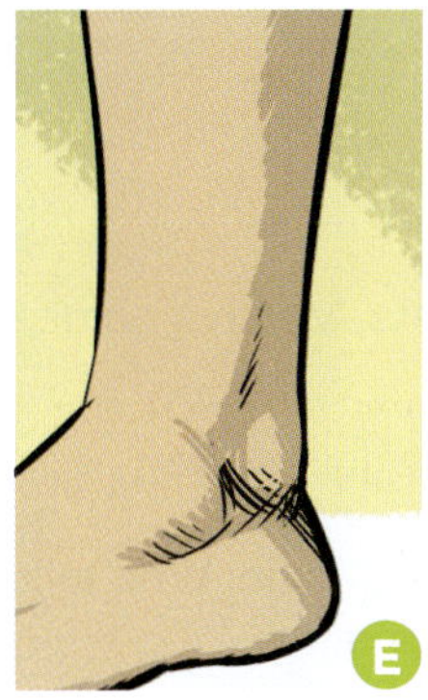
E

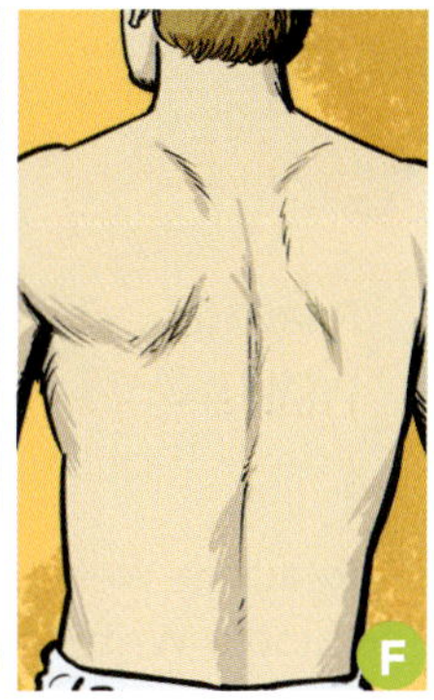
F

LISTENING

1 Look at the pictures A–C. Answer these questions for each one.

1 Who are the two people?

2 Where are the two people?

2 **3.21** Listen to three conversations. Match the pictures with the conversations. Copy and complete the table. Write A, B or C in the 'Speakers' column and D, E or F in the 'Problem' column.

	Speakers (A, B, or C)	**Problem (D, E, or F)**
Conversation 1		
Conversation 2		
Conversation 3		

3 **3.21** Listen again. In your notebook, mark the statements T (true) or F (false).

1 Katie hurt her shoulder while she was watching skateboarding.

2 When Katie fell, it wasn't a bad fall.

3 David's ankle hurts all the time.

4 David's mother wants to take him to the doctor.

5 Sam didn't tell his parents about his back.

6 Molly wants to take Sam to see the doctor at school.

4 Who said these things? Match the sentences with the speakers.

1 Are you all right? a the doctor

2 Does it hurt? b David's mother

3 What's the matter? c Sam

4 It hurts a bit. d Molly

5 My shoulder hurts. e David

6 I've got backache. f Katie

SPEAKING

Work in pairs. Choose one of the pictures above (A, B or C) in Exercise 2. Role play the conversation.

1 Decide who will be each person in the picture.

2 Choose a different part of the body from the conversation you heard for your picture (example: for Picture A, choose 'head' not 'back').

3 Have a conversation.

4 Now choose another picture. Change roles.

THINK *self-esteem*

Getting help

1 Read and choose the sentences that are true for you.

1 I don't like going to the doctor and so I don't go.

2 If I have a problem, I don't like telling other people about it.

3 If I don't feel well, I tell someone.

4 I don't want other people to worry about me.

5 It's OK to get help from people around you.

6 It's important to go to the doctor if you often have the same health problem.

2 Compare your ideas in class.

3 Who can you talk to about these problems?

1 a headache

2 a problem at school

3 difficult homework

4 a problem with a friend

GET IT *right*

To talk about a part of your body we use **my** not **the**.

✓ *My head hurts*

not

✗ ~~*The head hurts*~~.

Look!

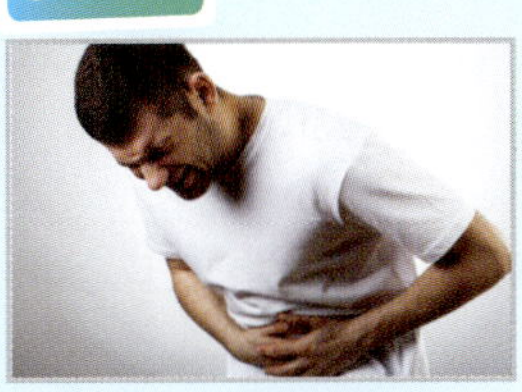
stomach ache

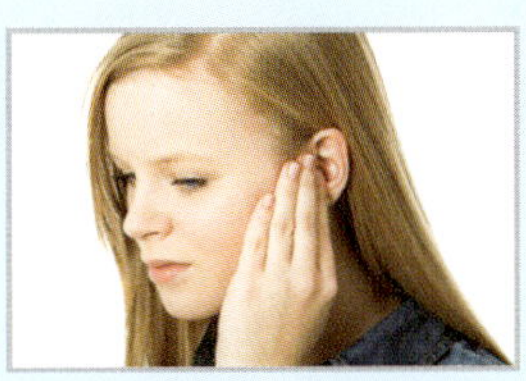
ear ache

headache

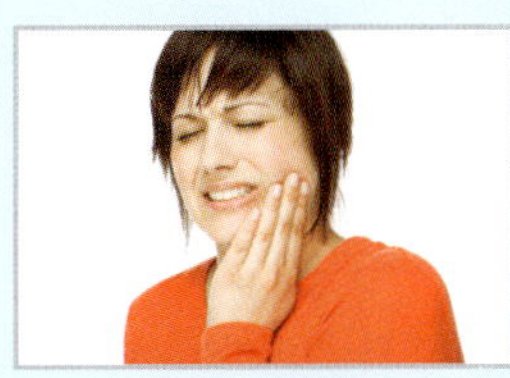
toothache

READING

1 Read the webchats. Match a name to each picture (A–E).

Arlene Pete Susie Julia Mike

2 Read the webchats again. Who talks about these things? Write the names.

1 eyes
2 a vegetable
3 dangerous things
4 making faces
5 making a noise

3 Do you know any more 'crazy' things that adults say to children? Tell the class.

A

B

C

D

E

Crazy things that parents say to their kids

Arlene
Now I'm eighteen, I can look back at all those happy days when I was a kid at home! And I remember the things that my mum and dad said to me again and again. For example: when my sister and I were making a noise, my father always said, 'If I have to come over there, you won't be happy to see me!' lol. Did your parents ever say things like that to you?

LIKE • COMMENT • SHARE

Pete
Oh of course! My little brother and me, we loved TV and we sat and watched it for hours every day. And my mum always looked at us and said, 'If you watch TV all the time, you'll get square eyes.' Well, we watched a lot of TV and our eyes are still normal. haha!

Susie
You reminded me, Pete. My dad always said, 'If you sit too close to the TV, you'll go blind.' But he had another favourite too (I think he was always worried about our eyes, for some reason) – he said, 'If you eat all your carrots, you'll see in the dark.' I really like carrots – I ate them when I was a kid and I eat them now – but I still can't see in the dark!

Julia
I always liked doing dangerous things – you know, climbing trees and things. And my dad said, 'If you fall you'll break your leg.' And he always added, 'And when you break your leg, don't come running to me for help!' I didn't understand the joke for years!

Mike
Nice one, Julia! OK here's another one, and I think every child in the world hears this. If I was angry or upset, I always made a face, and my mum said, 'If you go on making that face, the wind will change and your face will stay like that forever!' That's the only one I remember – but as soon as I think of others, I'll send them to you!

GRAMMAR

First conditional

1 Match the parts of the sentences. Check your answers in the webchats. Then complete the rule and the table. Choose the correct words.

1 If you eat all your carrots,
2 If I have to come over there,
3 If you fall,

a you won't be happy to see me.
b you'll break your leg.
c you'll see in the dark.

RULE: Use the first conditional to talk about [1]*possible /certain* events and their [2]*present / future* results.

If clause	Result clause
If + present simple,	[3]… *('ll)* / [4]… *(won't)* + base form

It is possible to put the result clause first:
If you fall, you'll hurt yourself. OR
You'll hurt yourself if you fall.

2 Put the words in order to make sentences.

0 see Jane, / If / tell / I / I'll / her

If I see Jane, I'll tell her.

1 my parents / I'm / will / If / late, / be angry

2 I / bring it / I'll / to school tomorrow / If / remember,

3 you'll / Jake / come / If / you / meet / to the party,

4 rain tomorrow / if / the / it / doesn't / We'll / to / beach / go

5 the concert / if / tonight / I / don't / I / won't / feel better / go / to

3 Complete the first conditional sentences with the correct form of the verbs.

0 If Kate *gives* (give) me some help, I *'ll finish* (finish) my homework in an hour.

1 You ... (not meet) anyone if you ... (not go out).

2 I ... (come) to your party if my mum ... (say) I can.

3 If Ken ... (not want) his ice cream, I ... (eat) it.

4 Susan ... (be) angry if she ... (hear) about this.

5 If we ... (buy) hamburgers, we ... (not have) enough money for the film.

4 Work in pairs. Student A: Go to page 159. Student B: Go to page 160. Ask and answer the questions.

Workbook page 101

Time clauses with *when / as soon as*

5 Read the two sentences and answer the questions. Then complete the rule with *will* and *present simple*.

When we get to school, I'll take you to see the nurse.

As soon as I think of other examples, I'll tell you.

1 What is the difference between *when* and *as soon as*?

RULE: In sentences about the future, we use the ¹... form after ***if*** or ***when*** or ***as soon as***, and ²... + base form of the verb in the main clause.

2 Do get and *think* refer to the present or future?

6 Complete the sentences. Use the verbs in the list.

finish (x2) | get (x2) | arrive

1 As soon as I ... my exam results, I'll phone you.

2 When I ... home, I'll check my messages.

3 The party will start as soon as my friend ... with the music!

4 When the game ... we'll go and have a pizza.

5 I'll lend you the book as soon as I ... reading it.

Workbook page 101

VOCABULARY

when and *if*

1 Match sentences 1 and 2 with the explanations.

1 **When I see Martin**, I'll give him your message.

2 **If I see Martin**, I'll give him your message.

a It is possible that I will meet Martin.

b I know that I will meet Martin.

2 Complete the sentences with *if* or *when*.

0 I can't talk to you now. I'll phone you *when* I get home.

1 A What are you doing tomorrow?

B ... there's a good film on, I'll probably go to the cinema.

2 I'm not sure if I want to go to the party tonight. But ... I decide to go, I'll phone you.

3 It's too hot to go for a walk now. Let's go out in the evening, ... it's cooler.

4 You can watch some TV ... you finish your homework, and not before!

5 It's the football final tonight. I'll be very happy ... my team wins.

Workbook page 102

LISTENING AND WRITING

A phone message

1 Which of these things do you NOT need to write down if you take a phone message?

1 the name of the caller

2 the telephone number of the person who takes the message

3 the name of the person who the message is for

4 the telephone number of the caller

5 what the caller wants

2 3.22 Listen to a telephone conversation. Copy and complete the message.

Message from: ¹...

For: ²...

Message: she needs ³... .

Please ⁴...

Number to call: ⁵...

PHOTOSTORY 6

THE PHONE CALL

1 3.23 Read and listen to the photostory and answer the questions.

Why is Megan's father stressed?

Who phones Megan while she's in the park?

OLIVIA: Aw, look!

LUKE: Looks like they're having a good time.

WOMAN: Jason?! You stop that. Do you hear me? Stop it!

RYAN: What did you say, Luke?

OLIVIA: Well, we all know what that's like – your parents, shouting at you.

1

MEGAN: Oh, don't, please! The last couple of days ...

RYAN: What?

MEGAN: Oh, my dad. He's really stressed. He's got a big business meeting he has to attend, out of town tomorrow and Friday.

LUKE: Something important?

2

MEGAN: I suppose so. I don't know.

RYAN: Well, I think you should know. I mean, he's your father, right? Family and stuff.

MEGAN: Yeah, yeah. Whatever. But I know one thing: he shouts at me all the time. Everything I do is wrong.

OLIVIA: Poor you.

WOMAN: Jason! I told you – don't do that! If I have to go over there ...

MEGAN: Just like that. Another few years and I can leave home! I can't wait!

3

OLIVIA: Just think, Megan. You'll be a mother too one day. Then you'll remember this.

RYAN: That's right. And when we're parents, we'll be just the same as our parents. Wait and see.

MEGAN:Hello? Oh, hello, Dad. What is it? I'm in the park.

LUKE: Tell you what, though. If our parents weren't ...

MEGAN:Shh!! Dad, say that again. What? The hospital? Mum?

4

2 Work in pairs. Discuss what happens next in the story. Write down your ideas.

Perhaps Megan has to go to the hospital.

3 **EP6** Watch to find out how the story continues.

4 Answer the questions.

1 What happened to Megan's mother?
2 When will her mother go home?
3 What is the problem for Megan's father?
4 Why can Megan help without going to school?
5 What does Megan say to the others is 'the good thing'?
6 What does Luke mean when he says: 'It's all ups and downs'?

Phrases for fluency

1 Find the expressions 1–6 in the story. Who says them? Match them to the definitions a–f.

1 I suppose so.	a What I want to say is ...
2 I mean, ...	b I really don't care.
3 Whatever.	c Here's what I think ...
4 I can't wait.	d I think that's possibly true.
5 Wait and see.	e You'll know in the future.
6 Tell you what ...	f I hope it happens very soon.

2 Complete the conversations. Use the expressions 1–6 in Exercise 1.

1 A I'm going to see the new Ryan Gosling film on Saturday! ... !
B ... – we could go together. ... , if that's OK with you.

2 A What are you going to give me for my birthday?
B ... . It's a surprise!

3 A You look so funny in that yelllow shirt.
B ... , Alex.

4 A Can I go out tonight, Dad?
B ... . But don't be late back, OK?

VOCABULARY

Expressions with *do*

1 Complete the sentences from the video.

1 She was doing some ... upstairs.
2 I can do the ... and everything.
3 Thanks. She's doing ... , though.

2 Complete the sentences with a word from the list.

ice cream | homework | cooking | well

1 Joe's upstairs – he's doing his ... .
2 Did you do ... in your exam?
3 They do great ... at the new café.
4 Mum has a rest on Sundays and we all do the ... .

3 Complete the questions. Then ask and answer with a partner.

1 ... you ... a lot of exercise?
2 Where ... you ... your homework?
3 ... you ... OK with your schoolwork these days?
4 Who ... the cleaning in your house?

Workbook page 102

FUNCTIONS

Sympathising

1 Complete the extracts from the story with the phrases in the list.

Poor you. | That's a shame.
I'm sorry to hear that. | poor thing.

1 MEGAN: But I know one thing: he shouts at me all the time. Everything I do is wrong.
OLIVIA: ... .

2 MEGAN: Oh, ... Well, she'll be home tomorrow.
DAD: That's right. Then a few days at home.

3 RYAN: ... , Megan.
OLIVIA: Me too.
MEGAN: Thanks. She's doing OK, though.

4 MEGAN: But it means I can't go out with you guys on Friday.
RYAN: ... .

2 Read the situations. What can you say in each one?

1 You meet a friend. You know that your friend lost something important yesterday.

Poor you!

2 You hear that Alex broke his arm last weekend. You meet Alex's brother.

3 Your neighbour says: 'I feel terrible today – I think I'm ill.'

Life skills

Dealing with negative feelings

We all have negative feelings sometimes, and it's easy to do or say bad things when we feel like this. Learning what to do when we have negative feelings helps us not make situations worse, or hurt other people and their feelings.

1 Think about the photostory.

1 Imagine you are Megan's dad. How do you feel at the start of the story? Why?

2 How is Megan's dad behaving?

3 Imagine you are Megan at the start of the story. How do you feel?

2 Read James's story. Why were his parents angry with him?

My brother, Alex, and I are good friends most of the time. He's only a year older than me, so we like a lot of the same things and share a lot of friends. Sometimes, though, like most brothers, we fight and it can get quite bad.

Fights often start when we're playing computer games. We both like to win, especially when our friends are with us.

Two months ago, we had a really big fight. I was nervous because I had a violin exam the next week and so I was practising for an hour or two every day. When I practise, I have to wear my glasses. I wear them for any type of reading or computer work, so it's not strange for Alex to see me wearing them.

Anyway, one day, Alex started calling me 'four-eyes.' At first, I just didn't listen, but after two days, it started to annoy me and I told him to stop. He started laughing and dancing and singing 'Four-eyes! Four-eyes!' I was so angry and wanted him to stop, so I picked up a book that was on the table and threw it at him.

As soon as the book hit Alex in the face, I knew it was bad.

Alex and Mum spent six hours at the hospital. Alex's nose was broken. He didn't speak to me for a week, but Mum and Dad had a lot to say to me.

3 Work in pairs. Discuss these questions.

1 What did Alex do to James?

2 How did James feel?

3 What did James do?

4 How did James feel after this?

4 James threw the book because he was angry with his brother. Which of these actions do you think James should do when he feels angry with his brother in the future?

shout | cry | count to 100 | drink water
go for a walk/run | throw something bigger
go to his bedroom and sit quietly
speak to his mum or dad

Can you think of more ideas of good actions when you're angry?

5 Can you think of five other things that make people angry?

6 In small groups, act out one of the situations you thought of in Exercise 5. The first time, the person who is angry reacts in a bad way. The second time, the angry person should react in a good way.

Tips for negative feelings

1 Don't react to a bad situation when you are angry about it. Take a break and think calmly about how to react.

2 Talk to others. It can help to get a different perspective from a friend.

3 If you react badly, learn from it. Think about how you can react differently next time.

12 TRAVELLERS' TALES

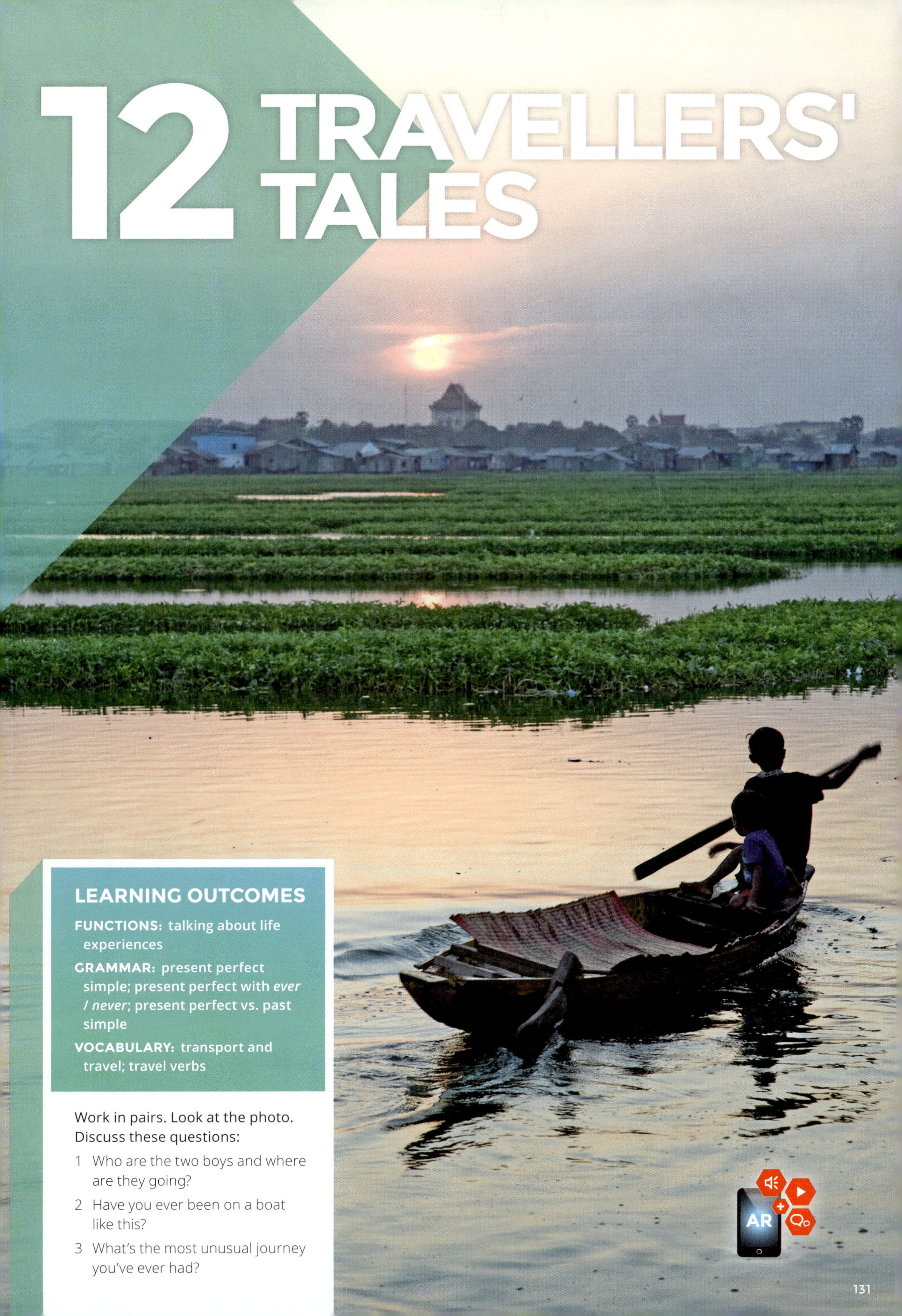

LEARNING OUTCOMES

FUNCTIONS: talking about life experiences

GRAMMAR: present perfect simple; present perfect with *ever / never*; present perfect vs. past simple

VOCABULARY: transport and travel; travel verbs

Work in pairs. Look at the photo. Discuss these questions:

1 Who are the two boys and where are they going?

2 Have you ever been on a boat like this?

3 What's the most unusual journey you've ever had?

UNIT 12

READING

1 Match the words (1–6) with the photos (A–F).

1 bicycle | 2 bus | 3 boat | 4 car
5 plane | 6 train

2 Name other kinds of transport in English.

3 Work in pairs. Ask and answer the questions.

How do you travel ...

- to school?
- to the cinema?
- to the shops?
- when you go on holiday?

I usually go by bike.

Sometimes I take the bus. Sometimes I walk.

Sometimes I walk, but sometimes my dad drives.

GET IT *right!*

Remember: to talk about a future arrangement to travel somewhere, we use present continuous.

✓ ***I'm travelling** there by car*

not

✗ ***~~I travel~~** there by car.*

4 Work in pairs or small groups. Read about these people. For each one, say how you think they could travel.

1 A British family – wife, husband and two children – want to go to the USA on holiday.
2 A student living in London wants to go to Paris.
3 A businesswoman who works in a city is going to a meeting on the other side of the city.
4 Three teenagers in a city want to go to a party at a house that is five kilometres away.

5 Think about the ways of travelling in Exercises 1 and 2. Which one(s) is (are):

- cheap?
- dangerous?
- expensive?
- boring?
- exciting?
- your favourite?
- an adventure?
- your least favourite?

6 Look at the photos and the title of the blog on page 133. What do you think the blog is about? Choose one of the following.

1 Someone who travels to many different places.
2 Different ways to travel.
3 Different places to travel to in the world.

7 **3.24** Read and listen to the blog and check your ideas.

8 Read the blog again. Correct the information in these sentences.

1 Nora Dunn wanted to travel the world until she got old.
2 Nora gets her money from some rich friends.
3 Sometimes she writes home to ask for some money.
4 She does the same job everywhere she goes.
5 She travelled by boat to the Caribbean.
6 She has appeared on television in every country she's visited.
7 Life is always easy for her when she travels.
8 She has a website to tell people how to spend a lot of money travelling.

Ted's Travel Blog

home about news contact

The non-stop traveller

Hello to all my readers. This week, I've decided to write about travel. Perhaps, like me, you've always thought that travelling is something for rich people. Well, now I think I've been wrong all this time. Why? Well, I've discovered Nora Dunn.

Nora is one of a new kind of traveller – a professional world traveller. She travels all the time. Nora is from Toronto, Canada and until she was 30, she had a business there. But then she made a big decision. Her dream was to travel the world – and to do it before she got old! So she sold her business and got rid of her belongings. And off she went.

Nora hasn't got rich parents or anyone who gives her money. And she doesn't have a high-paying job. But she's learned how to travel without spending lots of money.

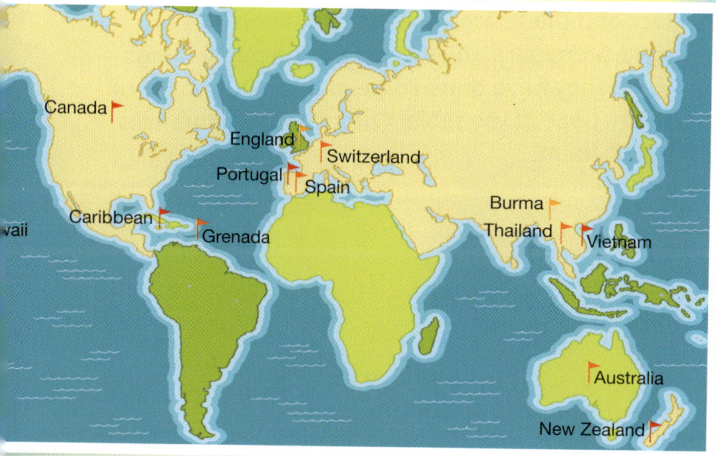

Nora goes to a place and stays there for some time. She works to earn enough money to have a good time and to save a bit, then she moves on to another place.

She prefers simple forms of transport like trains or buses, but of course there are times when planes are a necessity. And she writes from wherever she is, which earns her some money too. She's done a lot of different jobs, including working in hotels and in restaurants. And she's learned things like cooking and meditation.

So where has Nora been? Well, everywhere! She's been to all five continents and she's travelled to over thirty countries. All in six years! She's taken a train across Canada and she's travelled by train from Portugal to Vietnam – an incredible journey. She's lived on a boat in the Caribbean and she's worked for her accommodation in Hawaii, Australia, New Zealand, Spain, England, Grenada and Switzerland, and a number of other places too. And she's been on television shows in three countries. She's had a lot of fantastic adventures, and she hasn't stopped finding new things!

Some of her experiences have not been easy ones. In 2008 she helped people in Thailand and Burma after a cyclone hit their countries. And in 2009 she helped to fight forest fires in Australia.

So, she's seen a lot so far. She's learned that full-time travel doesn't have to be expensive, and she knows now that there are plenty of ways to do it – so many ways, in fact, that she's started a website to tell other people about them. It's theprofessionalhobo.com. I've seen lots of travel sites, and this is one of the best. Have a look. Perhaps you'll be the next 'world traveller'?

See you next week.

THINK values

Travel broadens the mind

1 Read what people said about Nora Dunn. Match the comments (1–4) with the values (a–d).

1 She's seen so many different countries, so I think she probably understands all kinds of people.
2 She's probably a better person now, because she's learned so many things.
3 I think it's wonderful, what she did in Burma with the cyclone and in Australia with the fire.
4 I think it's great that she's living her life without thinking about money all the time.

a helping other people
b self-improvement
c not worrying about money
d learning about other cultures

2 How important are the values in Exercise 1 for you? Put them in order from 1–4. Compare your ideas in class. Say why you think the values are important or not.

GRAMMAR

Present perfect simple

1 Complete the sentences from the blog on page 133. Then complete the rule.

1 Perhaps, like me, you ... always ... that travelling is something for rich people.
2 Now, I think I ... wrong all this time.
3 She ... a lot of different jobs.
4 So where ... Nora ... ?
5 Some of her experiences ... easy ones.

RULE: Use the present perfect to talk about actions that happened some time in your life up to now.
Form the present perfect with the present simple form of ... + past participle.

2 Find other examples of the present perfect in the blog on page 133.

3 Complete the table.

Positive	Negative	Questions	Short answers
I/you/we/they 've (1 ...) worked	I/you/we/they haven't (have not) worked	4 ... I/you/we/they worked?	Yes, I/you/we/they 6 ... . No, I/you/we/they haven't.
he/she/it 's (2 ...) worked	he/she/it hasn't (3 ...) worked	5 ... he/she/it worked?	Yes, he/she/it has. No, he/she/it 7 ... .

4 Copy and complete the list with the past participle forms. Use the irregular verbs list on page 128 of the Workbook to help you.

base form	past participle	base form	past participle
0 be	*been*	6 speak	...
1 do	...	7 eat	...
2 go	...	8 take	...
3 see	...	9 fly	...
4 write	...	10 swim	...
5 meet	...	11 win	...

GET IT *right!*

1 *She **has gone** to New York.* = She is not here now – she is in New York.
2 *She **has been** to New York.* = She went to New York and came back (at some time in the past).

5 Jack and Diane are 25 years old. When they were teenagers, they wanted to do many things – and they have done some of them but not all of them. Look at the table. Complete the sentences about them.

	learn French	visit Paris	write a book	work in the USA	make a lot of money
Diane	✓	✗	✓	✓	✗
Jack	✓	✓	✗	✗	✗

0 Jack and Diane *have learned* French.
1 Diane ... Paris.
2 Diane ... a book.
3 Jack ... Paris.
4 Jack ... in the USA.
5 They ... a lot of money.

6 Look at the information about Sue and Harry. Write sentences about them.

	visit another country	fly in a plane	swim in the sea	touch a snake	take a driving test
Sue	✓	✗	✗	✗	✓
Harry	✓	✓	✗	✓	✗

7 Work in pairs. Say things about yourself and people you know.
Remember: don't say when in the past.

My mother has lived in Africa.
I've won two tennis competitions.

Workbook page 108

LISTENING

1 3.25 Steve Anderson is at his old school giving a talk about his travels. Listen to the end of Steve's talk. Mark the statements T (true) or F (false).

1 He wants to get married and start a family.
2 When he was younger, he didn't like staying at home.
3 He's going to stop travelling soon.

2 3.26 Now the children ask Steve questions. Listen and match the events (1–3) with the places (a–c).

1 The most interesting place he's been to.
2 The place where he ate a cooked spider.
3 The place where he was ill.

a Africa b India c Mexico

3 3.26 Listen again and answer the questions.

1 Has he ever eaten snake?
2 Did he like the spider that he ate?
3 Has he had any accidents in a minibus or taxi?
4 What do tourists and travellers take with them?

GRAMMAR

Present perfect with *ever / never*

1 Complete the sentences with *ever* or *never* and complete the rule.

1 I've … eaten snake.
2 Have you … eaten anything really horrible?

RULE: When we use the present perfect to talk about experiences and we want to say:

- 'at no time in (my) life' we use the word [1]…
- 'at any time in (your) life' we use the word [2]…

The words *ever* and *never* usually come between *have* and the past participle.

2 Complete the mini dialogues with the words in the list.

been | yes | eaten | have
never | no | ever | played

1 A Have you … watched a silent film?
  B Yes, I … .
2 A Have you ever … to the Olympic games?
  B … , I've never been to them.
3 A Have you ever … tennis?
  B … , I have.
4 A Have you ever … a really hot curry?
  B No, I've … tried curry.

Workbook page 109

FUNCTIONS

Talking about life experiences

Work in pairs. Ask and answer the questions.

1 ever / see / a snake?
2 ever / eat / something horrible?
3 ever / be / on television?
4 ever / speak / to someone from the USA?
5 ever / win / a prize?
6 ever / be / to another country?

Have you ever seen a snake?

Yes I have. It was a python at the zoo.

No, I haven't.

GET IT *right*

Negative sentences in English only have one negative.

✓ *I have **never** eaten snake.*
✓ *I **haven't** eaten snake.*

not

✗ *I ~~haven't never~~ eaten snake.*

SPEAKING

Work in pairs. Think of a famous person. Ask about things that the famous person has done in their life, and imagine the answers. Use some of the verbs in the list.

travel | stay | play | win | eat | see | drive | write

Mr President – have you ever eaten fried spiders?

Yes, I have. I eat them all the time.

train to THINK

Exploring differences

1 Work in small groups. Look at the pairs of things. Answer the questions.

a What is the same? b What is different?

1 A car and a taxi
2 A train and a plane
3 A holiday and a journey
4 A tourist and a traveller

The same: a car and a taxi have wheels / doors / a driver.
Different: you drive your car but a taxi-driver drives the taxi. In a taxi, you have to pay.

2 Compare your ideas with others in the class.

PRONUNCIATION
Sentence stress
Go to page 151.

READING

1 Read the interview. Match the four questions (a–d) to the correct paragraphs (1–4).

a Have you ever had any famous passengers?
b Have passengers ever left anything in your taxi?
c What's the worst part of your job?
d When did you start?

THE TAXI DRIVER

Fiona McIntyre is a taxi driver in London. She tells us about her work and some of her experiences.

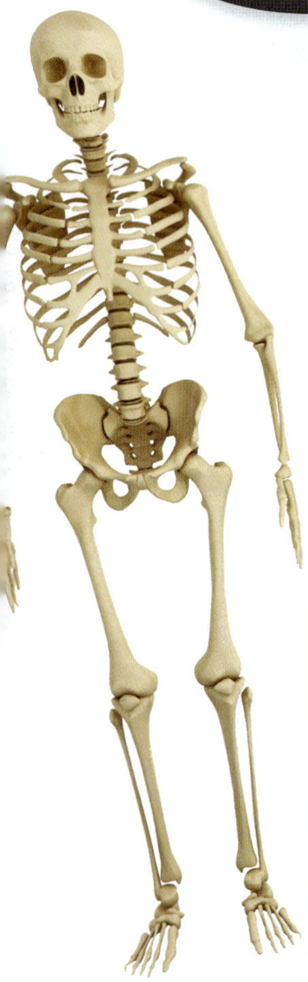

1 ...

I've been a taxi driver for about five years. Before that I was a bus driver in London, and I enjoyed it, but I wanted to be more independent so I changed and started driving my taxi.

2 ...

Oh yes. I've had film stars, politicians, you know, lots of famous people. About a year ago, a really famous actor got in my taxi. I took him to the airport. There was a lot of traffic and it took a long time to get there, so he missed his plane. It wasn't my fault but when he got out of the taxi, he said some things that weren't very polite! I said to him, 'Next time, take a bus!'

3 ...

Oh yes! People have left all kinds of things in here – a suitcase, a hat, mobile phones of course, even a dog once! Years ago, a woman left a pair of shoes on the back seat. And one time a passenger left his teeth here! Not real teeth, of course – false teeth. And people have asked me to do some strange jobs. Once a doctor stopped me outside a hospital and asked me to take a skeleton to another hospital. And I did. But I asked the doctor to pay first – the skeleton couldn't pay, after all!

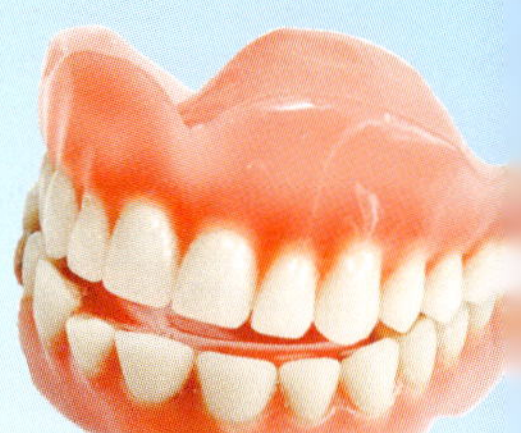

4 ...

Good question. I've always enjoyed being a taxi driver and I don't want to change. But of course, sometimes, it's not great. I don't like driving around without a passenger, but it's better than just waiting at the airport or at a railway station. I think that's the worst part – waiting.

2 Look at the photos. Say how each picture is connected to the article.

> There's a picture of a bus. She was a bus driver before she became a taxi driver.

3 Read the interview again and answer the questions.

1 Why did she stop being a bus driver?
2 Why was the famous actor angry when he got out of the taxi?
3 Why did she ask the doctor to pay first when she took the skeleton?
4 What two things does she not like about her job?

4 Work in two groups. Group A: you are bus drivers. Group B: you are flight attendants. In your group, think of answers to these questions.

1 When did you start your job?
2 Tell us about an accident you've had.
3 Tell us about a funny moment you've had.
4 Do you like your job or do you want to change?

5 Work in pairs – one student from Group A with one student from Group B. Ask and answer the questions.

6 Decide whose answers were best: the bus driver's or the flight attendant's.

GRAMMAR

Present perfect vs. past simple

1 Complete the things Fiona said in the article on page 136. Complete the rule with the names of the tenses.

1 I ... film stars, politicians, you know, lots of famous people.
2 A year ago, a really famous actor ... in my taxi.
3 People ... all kinds of things.
4 One time, a passenger ... a pair of false teeth.
5 People ... me to do some strange jobs.
6 Once, a doctor ... me outside a hospital and ... me to take a skeleton to another hospital.

> **RULE:** Use the [1]... to talk about situations or actions at a particular time in the past.
> Use the [2]... to talk about situationsor actions in the past, when we don't say when they happened.

2 Find more examples of verbs in the past simple and present perfect in the article on page 136.

3 Choose the correct forms.

My name's Michael Edwards and I'm 26. [1]*I've been / I was* very lucky in my life because I have a good job and I travel a lot for work. [2]*I've lived / I lived* in three different countries: Thailand, India and Singapore. [3]*I've lived / I lived* in Singapore from 2012 to 2014. I live in Thailand now.

[4]*I've got / I got* married two years ago. My wife and I travel a lot together and [5]*we've seen / we saw* some wonderful places. Last year [6]*we've seen / we saw* the Taj Mahal in India.

[7]*I've done / I did* some crazy things in my life but the craziest was last month – [8]*I've gone / I went* by minibus all the way to the north of Thailand. [9]*It's been / It was* really scary!

Workbook page 109

VOCABULARY

Transport and travel

1 3.29 Match the words with the photos. Listen and check.

0 – a minibus

a minibus | a helicopter | a tram
a motorbike | a scooter | an underground train

Travel verbs

2 Complete the sentences with the correct form of the verbs in the list.

miss | fly | catch | take | ride | drive

0 I had to walk home because I missed the bus.
1 I ran very fast but I didn't ... the train.
2 I have never ... in a helicopter.
3 My brother's got a motorbike and now he's learning to ... it.
4 We got in the car and we ... to France.
5 The rain was terrible so we ... a taxi.

3 Work in pairs. Ask each other questions. Use the verbs in Exercise 2 and the forms of transport you can see on this page and page 132.

Have you ever flown in a helicopter?

No, I haven't. Have you ever taken a tram?

Yes, I took a tram in Lisbon when I was on holiday.

Workbook page 111

Culture

1 Look at the photos and answer the questions. Then say what you think the article is going to be about.
Where can you see
- a student riding to school on a donkey?
- children walking to school along some rail tracks?

2 🔊 **3.30** Read and listen to the article and say which country each photo is from.

Hard journeys for schoolchildren

'How do you get to school?' This question often gets an answer like 'By bus' or 'I walk' or 'My parents take me by car'. But not always – there are children in many different parts of the world who, every day, have to go on a difficult journey in order to get to their lessons. They travel for kilometres on foot, or by boat, bicycle, donkey or train. They cross deserts, mountains, rivers, snow and ice: for example, the children of the Iñupiat community in Alaska go to school and then come back when it is dark, in extremely cold temperatures. And they are not the only ones – kids in many countries do this and more.

These children in Indonesia have to cross a bridge ten metres above a dangerous river to get to their class on time. (The bridge fell down in 2001 after very heavy rain.) Then they walk many more kilometres through the forest to their school in Banten village.

A pupil at Gulu Village Primary School, China, rides a donkey as his grandfather walks beside him. Gulu is a mountain village in a national park. The school is far away from the village. It is halfway up a mountain, so it takes five hours to climb from the bottom of the mountain to the school. The children have a dangerous journey: the path is only 45 centimetres wide in some places.

In Sri Lanka, some children have to cross a piece of wood between two walls of an old castle every morning. Their teacher watches them carefully. But in Sri Lanka, many girls don't go to school – they have to go to work or get married young. So girls are happy to take a risk in order to get to school.

Six-year old Fabricio Oliveira gets on his donkey every morning to ride with his friends for over an hour through a desert region in the very dry Sertão area of north-east Brazil. Their school is in Extrema. It's a tiny village – only very few people live there.

These children live in poor houses on Chetla Road in Delhi, India. Their homes are near the busy and dangerous railway lines that go to Alipur station. Every morning they walk along the tracks to get to their school, forty minutes away.

So one question we can ask is: why do the children do this? Because their parents make them do it? The answer, in many cases, is no – it's because for them going to school means a better future: They hope to get a job and money, so they can help their families and their neighbours. And this is why rivers, deserts or danger won't stop them on their way to school.

A

B

C

GET IT right!

Journey and *trip* are both nouns. *Travel* is usually used as a verb in English.

✓ *They **travel** for kilometres on foot.*

✓ *have a 30-minute **trip** / **journey** to school.*

✗ *have a 30-minute ~~**travel**~~ to school.*

3 Read the article again. What difficulties do children in these places face to get to school?

1 The children of the Iñupiat community in Alaska.
2 The children who go to the school in Banten, Indonesia.
3 The children who go to the Gulu Village Primary School, China.
4 The children who go to school in Galle, Sri Lanka.
5 Fabricio Oliveira in Brazil.
6 The children who live along The Chetla Road in Delhi, India.

4 There are eight highlighted words in the article. Match the words with these meanings.

0 from one side to the other *wide*
1 people living in houses near you
2 a trip
3 do something that can be dangerous
4 a group of houses usually in the countryside
5 the things that trains move on
6 very, very small
7 not late

5 Which journey is the one you would least like to have to do? Compare with others in the class.

WRITING

Someone I admire

1 Read Mariana's essay about 'Someone I admire'. Answer the questions.

1 When and where was her uncle Tim born?
2 Where does he live now, and when did he move there?
3 How does he travel in his work?
4 What does he want to do in the future?
5 Why does Mariana admire her uncle?

2 Find examples in the essay of the word *in* with these things.

1 a year 3 a city
2 a month 4 a country

3 Look at the four paragraphs of Mariana's essay about her uncle. Match the paragraphs with the contents.

Paragraph 1 a What he does, and how
Paragraph 2 b Why she admires him
Paragraph 3 c When and where he was born
Paragraph 4 d Why he does these things

4 Think of someone that you admire: a famous person; or someone you know in your own life; or someone you invent.

For the person, think about:

- facts about their life (when they were born, etc.)
- what they do, where and how, when they started
- what they want to do in the future
- why you admire them

5 Write an essay called 'Someone I admire' in about 150 words. Use the example essay and language above to help you.

Someone I admire

(1) My uncle Tim is a really great guy. He was born in England in 1980, in a city called Halifax, but now he lives and works in Cambodia. He went to Cambodia in 2014.

(2) My uncle is a doctor and he worked at a hospital in Manchester for a few years. But in 2014 he decided to go and work in small villages in Cambodia because he heard that they needed doctors. He travels from village to village to help people. He has a small motorbike that he uses. Sometimes, though, he goes in a very small plane because the roads aren't good enough.

(3) Uncle Tim says that he wants to stay there because there is a lot of work to do. He has also met a girl there – he told me in an email that they are getting married in July next year. Uncle Tim hopes that he can help to teach Cambodian people to become doctors in the future. He has learned a lot of the language – that can't be easy!

(4) I said before that he's a great guy. Why do I think that? Well, because he is helping other people and is happy doing that, and because he has learned a lot about another culture.

Literature

FROM A RAILWAY CARRIAGE
BY ROBERT LOUIS STEVENSON

When this poem was written train travel was very new. There were no cars and people used horses and carts. The speed of the train was something incredible.

1 Read the poem and answer the following question. What sounds do you hear as you read the poem?

Faster than fairies, faster than witches,
Bridges and houses, hedges and ditches;
And charging along like troops in a battle
All through the meadows the horses and cattle:
All of the sights of the hill and the plain
Fly as thick as driving rain;
And ever again, in the wink of an eye,
Painted stations whistle by.

Here is a child who clambers and scrambles,
All by himself and gathering brambles;
Here is a tramp who stands and gazes;
And here is the green for stringing the daisies!
Here is a cart runaway in the road
Lumping along with man and load;
And here is a mill, and there is a river:
Each a glimpse and gone forever!

2 Look at each pair of lines (1&2, 3&4 etc.) What is the effect of the way the words in each pair end?

3 Why do you think the writer compares the train to fairies and witches?

4 How do the things seen from the window create a feeling of speed?

5 What do you think the people outside think and feel as they see the train go by?

6 What do you think makes a journey exciting? The speed? The view? The company? The destination?

GET IT right!

Units 11&12

Present simple and *will*

We generally don't use the present simple tense to indicate future events. Don't use the present simple where *will* + base is required.

✓ *I **will** meet you at 6pm.*

✗ *~~I meet you~~ at 6pm.*

1 Work in pairs. Take turns to choose the correct answer. Do it quickly!

1 This evening we *meet / will* meet at my house at 9 o'clock.
2 How do you *get / will you* get to their house tomorrow?
3 I normally *go / will go* shopping on Saturdays.
4 The teacher *gives / will give* you his phone number this afternoon.
5 I don't *take / won't take* the bus on Sundays.
6 It usually *takes / will take* fifteen minutes to get to school.
7 What *do you / will you* bring to the party?

Present perfect simple

Don't use the present perfect when you want to talk about things that happened at a specific time in the past.

✓ *A year ago, I **met** a famous actor.*

✗ *A year ago, I ~~have~~ met a famous actor.*

2 Find five mistakes in the text. Correct them.

My travels

My parents work for international companies, so I have travelled a lot. When I was six, I have been to the USA for six months. Then, when I was eight, I lived in Spain for two years. When I was there I have visited Portugal and France too. I always loved France! Last year I have been on a school trip there - Paris is fantastic! My favourite place has been The Louvre.

Been and *gone*

Remember that the verb *go* has two past participles: *been* and *gone*.

been = to go and come back
gone = go and not come back yet

✓ *She's **been** to Jake's house five times this week.*

✓ *I'm sorry. He's not in. He's **gone** to Jake's house.*

✗ *She's ~~gone~~ to that shop five times this week!*

3 Work in pairs. Complete the sentences with ***been*** or ***gone***. Do it quickly!

1 So, you're back! Where have you ...? It's 10 o'clock!
2 Your brother has ... to football practice so he can't help with your homework.
3 My parents have ... to Liverpool to visit my sister at university three times.
4 Have you ever ... to Legoland?
5 Where has she ...? She was here a minute ago.
6 I've never ... to a live concert. Have you?

SAY IT right!

The /h/ consonant sound

1 Work in pairs. Take turns to practise saying these tongue twisters:

Horrible Harry hates his hairy hands.
He has a happy hamster.
Holly and Hannah have History homework.

2 🔊 **3.31** Listen, check and repeat.

RULE: In English the /h/ sound is always soft. Spanish speakers often pronounce it as hard.

test yourself

Units 11&12

VOCABULARY

1 Complete the sentences with the words in the list. There are two extra words.

neck | trams | ride | scooter | helicopter | tongue | caught | back
stomach ache | missed | lip | flew

1 He's really rich. He goes to work by ... and he lands on the roof of his office building.
2 I've got a ... . I think it was something I ate.
3 We ... the last train home, so we slept in the station.
4 Open your mouth. I want to take a look at your ... .
5 I can't ... a motorbike and I don't want to learn how to. I think they're dangerous.
6 I fell and cut my mouth and made my top ... bleed.
7 My dad rides his ... to work. It's quicker than going by car and a lot cheaper.
8 We ... over the mountains in a small plane. The views were fantastic!
9 I always sleep on my ... .
10 Many cities are now using ... to get people to and from work.

GRAMMAR

2 Put the words in order to make sentences.

1 phone / I'll / home / you / get / soon / as / I / as
2 taxi / I / train, / miss / If / the / take / a / I'll
3 ever / Have / Europe / you / been / to / ?
4 seen / She's / sea / never / the
5 different / five / lived / countries / in / They've
6 grandchildren / be / easy / for / won't / our / Life

3 Find and correct the mistake in each sentence.

1 She's played football yesterday.
2 If we will be late, the teacher will be angry.
3 I have ever broken an arm or a leg.
4 I've never gone to America.
5 She has took a lot of photos on holiday.
6 One day in the future people will living on the moon.

FUNCTIONAL LANGUAGE

4 Write the missing words.

1 A What's the ... ?
B My leg ... a lot.
2 A I've ... a headache.
B I'm sorry to ... that. Can I get you an aspirin?
3 A Have you ... been to Canada?
B No, I ... .
4 A Do you think it ... rain tomorrow?
B I don't know. I'm not ... .

CAMBRIDGE EXAMS
Review Units 11 & 12
Go to page 149.

MY SCORE

22–30
10–21
0–9

EXTRA MATERIALS

CONTENT

CAMBRIDGE EXAMS: KEY

Units 1&2

READING AND WRITING

PART 3: Multiple-choice replies

Workbook page 17

1 Complete the five conversations. Choose the correct answer A, B or C.

0 C

0 What are you doing?
A I play computer games.
B I'm a doctor.
(C) I'm trying to find my school bag.

1 How often are you late for school?
A on Mondays
B about once a month
C at ten o'clock

2 Does your brother go to your school?
A Yes, he does go.
B Yes, he goes.
C Yes, he does.

3 What do you think of my new haircut?
A It looks really good.
B It's looking really good.
C It sounds great.

4 Do you like doing puzzles?
A Yes, I like.
B Three times a week.
C No, I can't stand them.

5 Do you live in a big town?
A No, we aren't.
B Yes, we do.
C No, you don't.

PART 6: Word completion

Workbook page 43

2 Read the descriptions of clothes. What is the word for each one? The first letter is already there. There is one dash for each other letter in the word.

0 You can wear this over your shirt when you go out.
jacket
1 Wear these shoes to play sport. t - - - - - - -
2 Put this on if it's cold. j - - - - -
3 Some boys wear trousers to school, other boys wear these. s - - - - -
4 You wear this around the top of your trousers. b - - -
5 A lot of teenagers wear these. j - - - -

LISTENING

PART 1: Multiple-choice pictures

Workbook page 25

3 1.31 You will hear five short conversations. There is one question for each conversation. For each question, choose the right answer (A, B or C).

0 B

0 What are the girls talking about?

1 When does Oliver play tennis?

2 Where is Brian?

3 What is Molly's hobby?

4 How much is the red jumper?

READING AND WRITING

PART 2: Multiple-choice sentence completion

Workbook page 61

1 Read the sentences about a trip to a café. Choose the best word (A, B or C) for each space.

0	99% in my maths test! Mum is really A.	(A) proud	B scared	C upset
1	She takes me and my little ... to the café for an ice cream.	A uncle	B aunt	C sister
2	I eat ... of ice cream.	A many	B any	C a lot
3	My mum doesn't want her ice cream, so I eat ... too.	A her	B mine	C hers
4	And then I drink ... cola.	A not enough	B too many	C too much
5	I ... feel very well, so we go home.	A not	B don't	C am not

PART 3: Dialogue matching

Workbook page 35

2 Complete the conversation. What does Anita say to the waiter? For questions 1–5, choose the correct letter A–H.

WAITER: Can I help you?
ANITA: (0) G
WAITER: Of course, here you are.
(5 minutes later)
WAITER: OK, so what can I get you?
ANITA: (1) ...
WAITER: Of course. Would you like a starter?
ANITA: (2) ...
WAITER: And what would you like to drink?
ANITA: (3) ...
WAITER: And would you like a dessert?
ANITA: (4) ...
WAITER: OK, so that's a cheese omelette and strawberry ice cream.
(20 minutes later)
ANITA: (5) ...
WAITER: Of course. I'll be back soon.

A How much is it?
B An orange juice, please.
C I'd like a cheese omelette, please.
D And the orange juice.
E Can I have the bill?
F No, thanks. Just the omelette.
G I'd like to see the menu, please.
H Yes, please. Can I have some strawberry ice cream?

LISTENING

PART 3: Three-option multiple-choice

Workbook page 43

3 1.46 Listen to Jackie talking to Oliver about her family. For each question, choose the right answer (A, B or C).

0	The party was last	(A) Friday evening.	B Saturday evening.	C Friday afternoon.
1	The party was for Oliver's	A brother.	B dad.	C uncle.
2	Oliver's uncle is	A 20.	B 34.	C 44.
3	Oliver's aunt is called	A Anna.	B Carla.	C Ruth.
4	Mike is Oliver's	A brother.	B dad.	C cousin.
5	Oliver has got	A two sisters.	B one sister.	C one sister and one brother.

Units 5&6

READING AND WRITING

PART 5: Multiple-choice cloze

Workbook page 53

1 Read the article about a strange house. Choose the best word (A, B or C) for each space.

I **(0)** … on holiday with my family in California a few years **(1)** … , when Dad saw an advert for 'The Craziest House in the World' in the local paper. We decided to visit it, but on the way there we got lost. Dad **(2)** … want to ask anyone for directions, but after half an hour Mum told him to stop. We found a really **(3)** … man on a street in the town. He **(4)** … us a map for free! And ten minutes later, we were at the house.

From the outside, it just looked **(5)** … a normal big house. When we went inside we saw how **(6)** … it was. The house has 40 bedrooms, three lifts, 47 fireplaces and 467 doors!

It was the project of a rich American woman called Sarah Winchester. They **(7)** … building it in 1884 and they only stopped in 1922 when Sarah died. She never drew any plans but every time she got **(8)** … with the house, she just called the builders to come and build some more rooms for her.

0	A am	(B) was	C were
1	A last	B before	C ago
2	A doesn't	B did	C didn't
3	A helpful	B jealous	C confident
4	A give	B gave	C giving
5	A like	B at	C for
6	A amazed	B relaxing	C amazing
7	A start	B started	C starting
8	A bored	B boring	C interesting

PART 6: Word completion

Workbook page 43

2 Complete the words.

0 You usually keep your clothes in this.
wardrobe

1 You can keep your books on this. s …

2 You use this to look at yourself. m …

3 Someone who knows a lot of things is this.
i …

4 Someone who always shares their things is this. g …

5 Someone who is relaxed and doesn't worry much is this. e … - …

PART 3: Dialogue matching

Workbook page 45

3 Complete the conversation between two friends. What does Nick say to Sue? For questions 1–5, match the correct letter A–H in each space.

0 – E

SUE: It's Adam's birthday next week.
NICK: (0) …
SUE: I think that's a great idea. But what?
NICK: (1) …
SUE: I don't think that's a good idea. He doesn't like reading.
NICK: (2) …
SUE: He downloads all his music. He hasn't even got a CD player.
NICK: (3) …
SUE: I'm not so sure. It's difficult to buy clothes for him.
NICK: (4) …
SUE: Let's invite him to the cinema. He loves films.
NICK: (5) …
SUE: Great. I'll get three tickets.

A OK. Have you got any ideas?
B We could get him a CD. He loves music.
C Why don't we ask his dad?
D Let's do that.
E Why?
F Why don't we get him a present?
G How about buying him a book?
H That's true. How about a T-shirt?

LISTENING

PART 2: Matching

Workbook page 61

4 2.15 Listen to Jen telling Mark about her room. Who gave her each of the pieces of furniture? For questions 1–5, match a letter A–H.

0 – E

PRESENT	PEOPLE
0 armchair	A Dad
1 sofa	B Uncle Tim
2 curtains	C Aunt Abi
3 carpet	D brother
4 desk	E Grandpa
5 lamp	F Uncle Simon
	G Mark
	H Mum

READING AND WRITING

PART 1: Matching

Workbook page 71

1 Which notice (A–H) says this (1–5)? Write the letters A–H.

0 Adults only. C
1 You don't have to pay if you're eight.
2 You shouldn't leave your car here.
3 The shop closes in the afternoon.
4 You should call for more information.
5 You mustn't swim here.

PART 3: Multiple-choice replies

Workbook page 17

2 Complete five conversations. Choose the correct answer A, B or C.

0 It's not cold today.
A You mustn't wear shorts.
B You must wear a jacket.
(C) You don't have to wear a jumper.

1 It's very dark. I can't see anything.
A You need some headphones.
B Here's a torch for you.
C I've got a docking station, if you want.

2 I've got a headache.
A You should go to bed for half an hour.
B You should watch TV.
C You shouldn't get some rest.

3 Let's go sailing tomorrow.
A I can't. I haven't got a bike.
B OK, I've got a ball.
C Sorry, I don't like water.

4 Where were you at 3 pm?
A I am watching TV.
B I walked in the park.
C I was playing basketball.

5 Do you want to go to the cinema?
A No, I have to.
B Sorry. I've got to tidy up.
C Yes, I must.

LISTENING

PART 4: Note taking

Workbook page 79

3 2.31 You will hear a woman asking for information about a football match. Listen and complete each question.

Football match

Day of game:	0 Sunday
Game starts:	1 ...
Family ticket:	2 £ ...
Food:	3 Hot drinks and ...
Buy tickets at:	4 Club shop in ... Street

Units 9&10

READING AND WRITING

PART 2: Multiple-choice sentence completion

Workbook page 61

1 Read the sentences about holiday plans. Choose the best word (A, B or C) for each space.

0 On Monday we're ... to Rio de Janeiro.
A to fly (B) flying C fly

1 It's one of the ... beautiful cities in the world.
A most B more C less

2 The weather there is lovely. It's usually hot and very ... .
A freezing B foggy C sunny

3 We're ... to visit my uncle and his family in Brazil.
A going B go C to go

4 I'm also a bit scared because I ... speak Portuguese.
A can B not C can't

5 Mum says I shouldn't worry, because my cousins all speak English very ... .
A well B good C badly

PART 7: Open cloze

Workbook page 89

2 Complete the text about Llandudno. Write ONE word for each space.

My name (0) is Hugo and I would like to tell you about the town where I live. It's (1) … the north of Wales and it's called Llandudno. That's probably (2) … unusual name for you, because it's a Welsh name. Here in Wales, we have our own language. I (3) … born here and so I speak Welsh really (4) … .

Llandudno is (5) … most beautiful town in Wales. Well, that's what I think. It's by the sea and we have lots of beaches. They're (6) … sandy but have lots (7) … small stones on them. You (8) … swim in the sea if you want to, but it's quite cold most of the year.

There are lots of things to do in Llandudno. There (9) … parks and there's a small mountain where you can take a chair lift to a café at the top. There's a really good concert hall and lots of great bands play here. There's (10) … a youth club that I go to every Friday night with my friends.

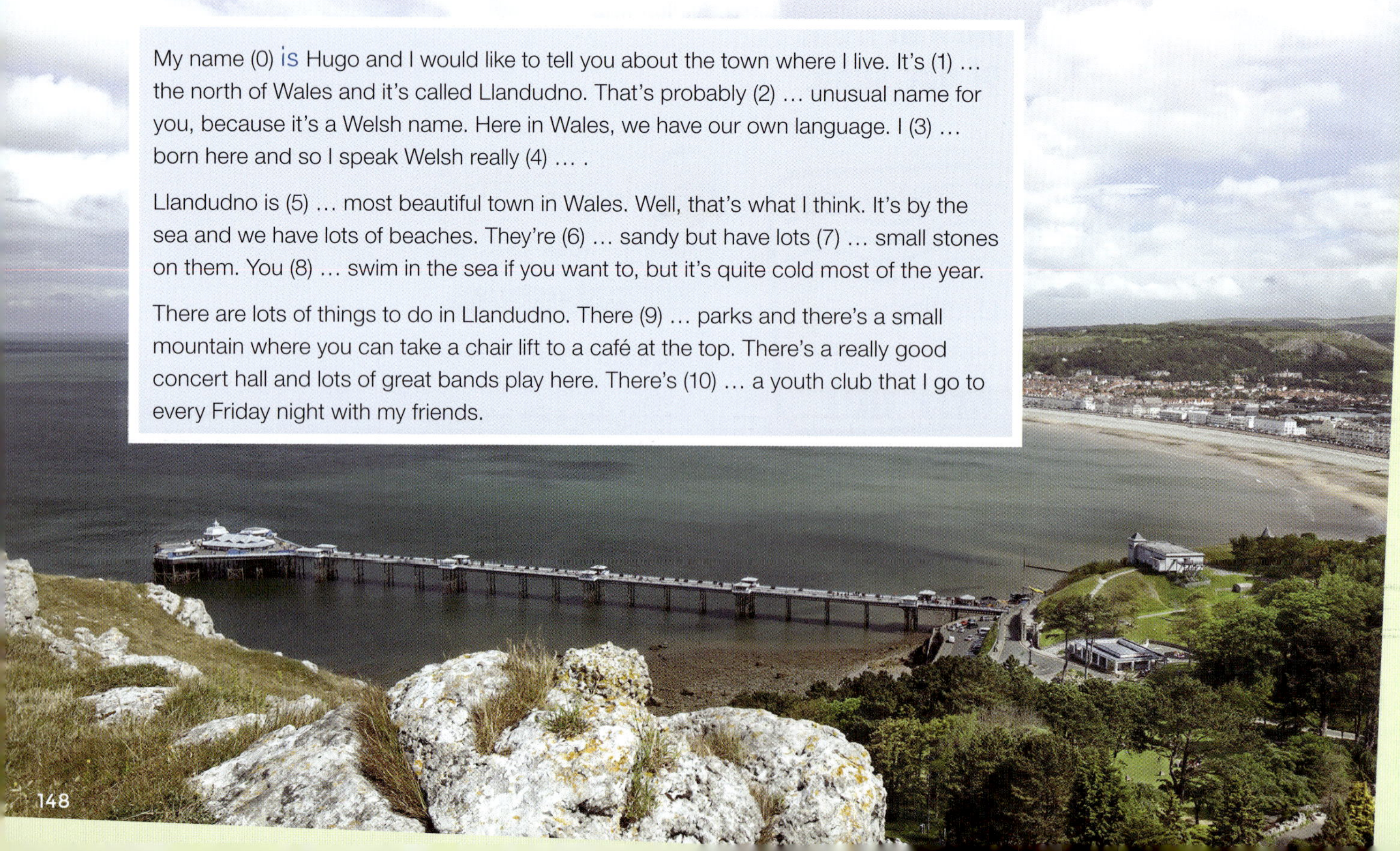

LISTENING

PART 5: Note completion

Workbook page 79

3 3.16 You will hear some information about a shopping centre. Listen and complete each question.

white river
SHOPPING CENTRE

- There are over (0) 300 shops.
- There are restaurants and a (1) ... on the fifth floor.
- Parking costs (2) £... every hour.
- Buses leave for the city centre every (3) ... .
- Shops close at 5.30 pm every day except (4) ... .

READING AND WRITING

PART 5: Multiple-choice cloze

Workbook page 53

1 Read the travel blog. Choose the best word (A, B or C) for each space.

I love (0) *travelling*. I spend all my holidays visiting other countries. I never stay at home. So far I've (1)… to 56 different countries and this year, if I (2)… the money, I'll visit three more: Cambodia, Vietnam and Laos. It's a part of Asia I've (3)… been to so I'm really excited about this trip. I want to make the whole journey without (4)… a plane. I plan to get to Thailand by boat and then (5)… buses to visit these countries. On the way home, I'll travel (6)… train through China and India, and then through Europe. It (7)… be a short trip – it (8) … probably take about four months. I hope my boss doesn't mind me taking some time off work!

0 (A) travelling	B travel	C to travelling
1 A gone	B been	C went
2 A had	B will have	C have
3 A ever	B always	C never
4 A taking	B riding	C going
5 A travel	B miss	C take
6 A on	B by	C in
7 A isn't	B won't	C will
8 A will	B is	C can

VIETNAM LAOS CHINA INDIA

PART 8: Information transfer

Workbook page 107

2 Read the information about the school trip. Complete Gina's notes.

SCHOOL TRIP

Tate Art Museum Liverpool

Saturday 4th August

Train leaves at 10.15 am • Meet in station car park

£14 per person

School trip to the Tate Art Museum Liverpool

Date [1]…

Travelling by [2]…

Transport leaves at [3]…

Meet at the [4]…about 9.30 am

Cost [5]£…

Dear Gina,

Problems with the trains to Liverpool on Saturday. We will now be travelling by bus. It leaves half an hour earlier. Please now meet at bus station 15 minutes before bus leaves.

Everything else is the same.

Best

Mr O'Brien

LISTENING

PART 2: Matching

Workbook page 61

3 3.32 Listen to Jack talking to a friend about his transport project. How does each person get to school? For questions 1–5, write a letter (A–H) for each person.

0 Jack *f*	A bike
1 Olivia	B boat
2 Rashid	C taxi
3 Morris	D bus
4 Leslie	E car
5 Adam	F on foot
	G scooter
	H train

Pronunciation

Unit 1

/s/, /z/, /ɪz/ sounds

1 1.17 Listen to the sentences.

Gus makes cakes and sweets. He works hard and sleeps a lot.

James enjoys all kinds of games. He plays a lot of football with his friends.

Liz's job is fun. She washes and brushes horses and relaxes by riding them.

2 Say the words with the /s/, /z/ and /ɪz/ endings.

3 1.18 Listen and repeat. Then practise with a partner.

Unit 2

Contractions

1 1.26 Listen to the dialogue.

TOM: **Here's** your pizza, Jane.

JANE: **That's** not my pizza. I **don't** like cheese.

TOM: But Jane! **They've** all got cheese!

JANE: No they **haven't**. **There's** one without it.

TOM: **You're** right ... **it's** this one. Here you are.

2 Say the words in blue.

3 1.27 Listen and repeat. Then practise with a partner.

Unit 3

Vowel sounds /ɪ/ and /iː/

1 1.36 Listen to the tongue twisters.

Jill wishes she had fish and chips for dinner.

Pete's eating meat with cheese and peas.

Pete and Jill drink tea with milk.

2 Say the words with the short /ɪ/ sound. Say the words with the long /iː/ sound.

3 1.37 Listen and repeat. Then practise with a partner.

Unit 4

-er /ə/ at the end of words

1 1.42 Listen to the tongue twister.

Jennif**er**'s fath**er**'s a firefight**er**,

Oliv**er**'s moth**er**'s a trav**el** writ**er**,

Pet**er**'s sist**er**'s a lorry driv**er**;

And Amb**er**'s broth**er**'s a deep-sea div**er**.

2 Say the words with the weak -er sound (the schwa /ə/).

3 1.43 Listen and repeat. Then practise with a partner.

Unit 5

Regular past tense endings: /d/, /t/ and /ɪd/

1 2.04 Listen to the dialogue.

MUM: What happen**ed** in the kitchen, Jack? It's a mess!

JACK: I start**ed** to make a cake; then I decid**ed** to make a pizza. I cook**ed** all morning and clean**ed** all afternoon.

MUM: You clean**ed**? What did you clean?

JACK: My bedroom!

2 Say the past tense words with the /d/, /t/ and /ɪd/ endings.

3 2.05 Listen and repeat. Then practise with a partner.

Unit 6

Stressed syllables in words

1 2.11 Listen to the sentences.

Sarah's funny, cheerful and helpful.

Jonathan's generous, confident and talented.

Elizabeth's intelligent, adventurous and easy-going.

2 Say the two, three and four syllable words. Stress the words correctly.

3 2.12 Listen and repeat. Then practise with a partner.

Unit 7

Vowel sounds: /ʊ/ and /uː/

1 2.21 Listen to the dialogue.

LUKE: Let's look in this room, Sue.

SUE: Wow! It's got things from the moon in it.

LUKE: Look at these cool boots! I saw them in our science book.

SUE: We should take a photo for our school project, Luke.

2 Say the words with the short /ʊ/ vowel sound. Then say the words with the long /uː/ vowel sound.

3 2.22 Listen and repeat. Then practise with a partner.

Unit 8

Strong and weak forms of *was* and *were*

1 2.26 Listen to the dialogue.

GIRL: Was she shopping?

BOY: Yes, she was. She was shopping for socks.

GIRL: Were they doing their homework?

BOY: No, they weren't. They were learning to surf!

2 Say the words with the /ɒ/ sound. Now say the words with the /ɜː/ sound. When was and were aren't stressed, we use the /ə/ sound. It's the same as /ɜː/ but shorter.

3 2.27 Listen and repeat. Then practise with a partner.

Unit 9

Vowel sounds: /ɪ/ and /aɪ/

1 3.05 Listen to the dialogue.

JILL: I'd like to live in the wild. What about you, Mike?

MIKE: I prefer a city lifestyle. I don't like lions or tigers – or insects!

JILL: But living in the wild's much more exciting!

MIKE: Yes, Jill – and it's more frightening, too.

2 Say the words with the short /ɪ/ vowel sound. Then say the words with the long /aɪ/ vowel sound.

3 3.06 Listen and repeat. Then practise with a partner.

Unit 10

Voiced /ð/ and unvoiced /θ/ consonants

1 3.11 Listen to the dialogue.

BETH: Look – there's the theatre.

HARRY: That's not the right one, Beth.

BETH: Well, it says, 'The Fifth Avenue Theatre'.

HARRY: But we want the one on Third Street!

2 Say the words with the voiced /ð/. Then say the words with the unvoiced /θ/.

3 3.12 Listen and repeat. Then practise with a partner.

Unit 11

The /h/ consonant sound

1 3.18 Listen to the dialogue.

DR HARRIS: Who's next? Oh, hello Harry. How can I help you?

HARRY: Well, Dr Harris – my head's very hot!

DR HARRIS: Let me see ... does it hurt here?

HARRY: Yes, doctor! That feels horrible!

DR HARRIS: It's your hat, Harry. It's too small!

2 Say the words starting with the /h/ consonant sound.

3 3.19 Listen and repeat. Then practise with a partner.

Unit 12

Sentence stress

1 3.27 Listen to the stress in these sentences.

<u>Car</u> – <u>plane</u> – <u>bike</u> – <u>train</u>.

A <u>car</u>, a <u>plane</u>, a <u>bike</u>, a <u>train</u>.

A <u>car</u> and a <u>plane</u> and a <u>bike</u> and a <u>train</u>.

A <u>car</u> and then a <u>plane</u> and then a <u>bike</u> and then a <u>train</u>.

2 Which words are stressed in every sentence? What happens to the other words?

3 3.28 Listen and repeat. Then practise with a partner.

Grammar reference

Unit 1

Present simple

1 We use the present simple for actions that happen repeatedly or habitually.

*Paul often **goes** to the cinema.*

*We **have** dinner at 8.00 every evening.*

We also use the present simple for things that are always or normally true.

*The sun **comes up** in the east.*

*We **go** to a big school in London.*

2 With most subjects, the present simple is the same as the base form of the verb. However, with a third person singular subject (*he*, *she*, *it*), the verb has an *-s* ending.

*I **play** tennis on Saturdays.*

*She **plays** tennis on Saturdays.* (✗ *She ~~play~~ tennis …*)

If a verb ends with *-sh*, *-ch*, *-ss* or *-x*, we add *-es*.

*he watch**es**, she catch**es**, he miss**es**, she fix**es***

If a verb ends with consonant + *-y*, we change the *-y* to *-i* and add *-es*.

*she stud**ies**, he worr**ies***

If a verb ends with vowel + *-y*, then it is regular.

*play – play**s**, say – say**s**, buy – buy**s***

3 The negative of the present simple is formed with *don't* (*do not*) or *doesn't* (*does not*) + base form of the verb.

*I **don't like** carrots.* *She **doesn't like** carrots.*

(✗ *She ~~don't~~ like …*)

4 Present simple questions and short answers are formed with ***do*** or ***does***.

***Do** you **like** cats?* (✗ *~~You like cats?~~*) *Yes, I **do**. / No, I **don't**.*

***Does** Jo **live** here?* (✗ *¿Does Jo live here?*)

*Yes, she **does**. / No, she **doesn't**.*

like + -ing

1 After verbs which express likes and dislikes we often use verb + *-ing*.

*We **love watching** films at home.* (✗ *We love ~~watch~~ …*)

*My sister **enjoys reading** travel books.*

2 If a verb ends in *-e*, we drop the *-e* before adding *-ing*.

*live → liv**ing*** *ride → rid**ing***

If a short verb ends in consonant + vowel + consonant, we double the final consonant before adding *-ing*.

*get → ge**tting**, shop → sho**pping**, travel → trave**lling***

Unit 2

Present continuous

1 We use the present continuous for actions that are happening now or around the time of speaking.

*My friends and I **are playing** an online game at the moment.*

*It'**s raining** now.*

2 The present continuous is formed with the present simple of *be* + verb + *-ing*.

*I'**m listening** to music.* *I'**m not listening** to music.*

*You'**re walking** very fast!* *You **aren't walking** very fast.*

*Alison **is talking** to Jo.* *Alison **isn't talking** to Jo.*

3 The question is formed with the present simple of *be* + subject + verb + *-ing*. Short answers are formed using *Yes*/*No* + pronoun + the correct form of *be* (positive or negative).

***Is** Susanna **eating**?* (✗ *Susanna is ~~eating~~?*)

*Yes, she **is**. / No, she **isn't**.*

***Are** the boys **having** fun?* *Yes, they **are**. / No, they **aren't**.*

*What **are** you **doing**?* *Why **is** she **crying**?*

Sense verbs

Sense verbs of perception (*taste* / *smell* / *look* / *sound*) are not used in the present continuous when they are used to give an opinion. They are used in the present simple only.

*This hamburger **doesn't taste** very nice.*

*Mmm! The food **smells** fantastic!*

*These trousers **don't look** very good on me.*

*I don't know who the singer is, but she **sounds** wonderful.*

Present simple vs. present continuous

1 We use different time expressions with the present simple and the present continuous.

Present simple: *every day, on Mondays, at the weekend, usually, sometimes, often, never*

Present continuous: *today, right now, at the moment, tonight* (✗ *~~this night~~*)

*James **usually walks** to school but **today** he'**s taking** the bus.*

2 Some verbs aren't normally used in the continuous form. They are called *state verbs* or *stative verbs* because they talk about a state, not an action. Here are some common examples:

believe, know, understand, remember, want, need, mean, like, hate

*I **believe** you. He **knows** a lot about music.*

*Morgan **wants** to have dinner now.*

Unit 3

Countable and uncountable nouns

1 Nouns in English are **countable** or **uncountable**.

Countable nouns have both singular and plural forms, for example:

*bicycle → **bicycles**, school → **schools**, egg → **eggs**, question → **questions**, man → **men**, woman → **women**, child → **children**, person → **people** (✗ ~~mens~~, ~~womens~~, ~~childrens~~, ~~persons~~)*

But uncountable nouns do not have a plural form. They are always singular, for example:

food, music, money, rice, bread, information

2 **Countable nouns** can take singular or plural verbs.

*That **car is** Japanese. Those **cars are** Japanese.*

*That **woman works** with me. Those **women work** with my mum.*

Uncountable nouns always take singular verbs.

*This **food is** horrible. The **music is** too loud!*

a / an; some / any

1 With singular countable nouns, we can use *a / an* to talk about a specific thing or person.

*They've got **a car**. She's eating **an orange**.*

2 With plural countable nouns, we use *some* (positive) or *any* (negative).

*I want to buy **some apples**. We haven't got **any eggs**.*

3 With uncountable nouns, we don't use *a / an* – we use *some / any*, like plural countable nouns.

*Let's listen to **some music**.*

*I don't want **any food**.*

4 We use *some* to talk about an unspecified number or amount. We normally use *some* in positive sentences.

*He bought **some fruit** in town.*

We often use *some* in requests and offers.

*Can I have **some** orange juice, please?*

*Do you want **some** cheese?*

5 We use *any* to talk about an unspecified number or amount. We normally use *any* in negative sentences, and in questions.

*He did**n't** buy **any fruit**.*

*Is there **any fruit** in the kitchen?*

(How) much and *(how) many*; *a lot of / lots of*

1 We use *many* with plural countable nouns and *much* with uncountable nouns.

Countable	Uncountable
*She doesn't eat **many vegetables**.*	*He doesn't eat **much fruit**.*
***How many children** have they got?*	***How much time** have we got?*

2 We usually use *many* and *much* in negative sentences and questions.

*I don't go to **many concerts**.*

*How **many eggs** do you want?*

In positive sentences, we normally use *a lot of* or *lots of*. *A lot of / Lots of* can be used with plural countable nouns and with uncountable nouns.

*Chris has got **lots of** / **a lot of DVDs**.*

*You can get **lots of** / **a lot of information** on the Internet.*

too much / too many / not enough + noun

1 If we want to say that the number or amount of something is more than we like or want, we can use *too many* or *too much*. We use *too many* with plural countable nouns, and *too much* with uncountable nouns.

*There are **too many chairs** in the room.*

*There's **too much salt** in my food.*

2 We use *not enough* with plural countable nouns and with uncountable nouns to say that we think more **is / are** needed.

*There **aren't enough chairs** in the room.*

*There **isn't enough salt** in my food.*

too + adjective / (*not*) + adjective + *enough*

1 We use *too* + adjective to say that it's more than we like or want.

*This soup is **too hot**. The clothes are **too expensive**.*
(✗ ... too ~~much~~ expensive)

2 We use (*not*) + adjective + *enough* to say that something is less than we like or want.

*This bag **isn't big enough** to put everything in.*

Unit 4

Possessive adjectives

1 Here is the list of possessive adjectives:
Subject pronoun: *I, you, he, she, it, we, they*
Possessive adjectives: *my, your, his, her, its, our, their*

2 We use possessive adjectives to say who something belongs to.
*My name's Jack. Is he **your brother**? Look at **his hair**! **Her bike** is really expensive.*
*The DVD isn't in **its box**. They love **their cat**.*

Possessive pronouns

1 Here is the list of possessive pronouns:
Possessive adjective: *my, your, his, her, our, their*
Possessive pronoun: *mine, yours, his, hers, ours, theirs*

2 Possessive pronouns can take the place of possessive adjective + noun.
*Is this **your book** / **yours**? No, it isn't **my book** / **mine**.*
*I like her hair, but I don't like **his**.*

Whose

When we want to ask a question about who is the owner of something, we use the word *whose*. There are two possible constructions after *whose*.
Whose book is this? or *Whose is this book?*

Possessive *'s*

To talk about possession we can add *'s* to the end of a name / noun.
***Annie's** bike is really fantastic.*
*That's my **brother's** bedroom.*

If the name / noun ends in an *-s*, (for example, plural nouns), we add the apostrophe (') after the final *-s*.
*That's our **neighbours'** dog.*
*I don't like **James'** shirt.*

Past simple of *be* (*was / were*)

1 We use the past simple to talk about actions and events in the past.

2 The past simple of *be* is *was / wasn't* or *were / weren't*.
*I **was** at school yesterday. You **were** late yesterday.*
*My sister **wasn't** there.*
*The DVDs **weren't** very good.*

3 Questions with *was / were* are formed by putting the verb before the subject.
***Were** you at school yesterday?*
(✗ ~~Did you were at school~~ ...) *Was Maria with you?*

Unit 5

Past simple: regular verbs (positive and negative)

1 In the past simple, regular verbs have an *-ed* ending. The form is the same for all subjects.
*I **walked** to the park. You **played** well yesterday.*
*Carla **opened** the window.*

If a verb ends in *-e*, we add only *-d*.
*like → like**d** hate → hate**d** use → use**d***

If a verb ends with consonant + *-y*, we change the *-y* to *-i* and add *-ed*.
*study → stud**ied** try → tr**ied** marry → marr**ied***

If a short verb ends in consonant + vowel + consonant, we double the final consonant before adding *-ed*.
*stop → sto**pped** plan → pla**nned** travel → trave**lled***

If a short verb ends in consonant + vowel + *-y*, it is regular.
*play → play**ed** stay → stay**ed***

2 The past simple negative is formed with *didn't* (*did not*) + base form of the verb. The form is the same for all subjects:
*I / We / She **didn't enjoy** the film last night.*
(✗ I / We / She didn't ~~enjoyed~~ ...)

3 Past time expressions are often used with the past simple.
Yesterday, yesterday morning, last night, last week, a month ago, two years ago, on Sunday

Modifiers: *very, really, quite*

We use the words *very*, *really*, *quite* to say more about an adjective. The words *very* and *really* make an adjective stronger.
*The food was good – The food was **very** good.*
*The film was exciting – The film was **really** exciting.*

We often use *quite* to say 'a little bit'.
*The room was **quite small**.* (= not very small, but a bit small)
*The film was **quite long**.* (= not very long, but a bit long)

Unit 6

Past simple: irregular verbs

A lot of common verbs are irregular. This means that the past simple form is different – they don't have the usual *-ed* ending.
*go → **went**, see → **saw**, eat → **ate**, think → **thought***

The form of the past simple for these verbs is the same for all persons (I / you / he / she / it / we / they).

See Workbook page 128 for a list of irregular verbs.

The negative of irregular verbs is formed in the same way as regular verbs: *didn't* (*did not*) + base form of the verb.

*We **didn't enjoy** the concert.*
*I **didn't know** the answer to the question.*

Past simple: (regular and irregular verbs) questions and short answers

1 Past simple questions and short answers are formed with *did*. The form is the same for regular and irregular verbs.

__Did__ you __talk__ to Barbara this morning?

__Did__ you __see__ that great match last night?

2 Short answers are formed with *Yes / No* + pronoun + *did / didn't*.

Did you like the film?
(✗ ~~*You liked the film?*~~ / *Did you ~~liked~~ the film?*) ***Yes, I did.***

Did she phone you last night? ***No, she didn't.***

Double genitive

We use the double genitive to talk about one of many things that we have. We form it with noun + *of* + possessive pronoun (see Unit 4 above). We can also use noun + *of* + noun with possessive *'s*.

*He's **a friend of mine**. (I have many friends)*
*They are **neighbours of ours**. (we have many neighbours).*

Unit 7

should / shouldn't

1 When we want to say that something is a good idea (or is a bad idea), we can use *should* or *shouldn't*.

*I **should study** this weekend.* (I think it's a good idea.)
(✗ *I should ~~to~~ study ...*)

*They **shouldn't buy** that car.* (I think it's a bad idea.)

***Should we go** out tonight?* (Do you think this is a good idea?)

2 *Should* is a modal verb. We use *should / shouldn't* + base form of the verb, and the form is the same for all subjects. We don't use any form of *do* in the negative.

*I **should try** to study more.*

*I **shouldn't watch** TV tonight.*

*You **should listen to** different music.*

*You **shouldn't listen to** the same things all the time.*

3 Questions are formed with *should* + subject + base form of the verb. Again, we don't use any form of *do* in questions or short answers.

***Should** we **tell** her?*

*Yes, we **should**. / No, we **shouldn't**.*

***Should** I **ask** the teacher?*

*Yes, you **should**. / No, you **shouldn't**.*

have to / don't have to

1 We use *have to* to say that it is necessary or very important to do something.

*I'm late, I **have to go** now. We **have to be** at school at 8.30.*

With a third person singular subject (*he*, *she*, *it*), we use *has to*.

*Maggie is very ill – she **has to stay** in bed.*

*My dad **has to go to** York tomorrow for a meeting.*

2 We use the negative form *don't / doesn't have to* to say that it isn't necessary or important to do something.

*It's Sunday, so I **don't have to get up early**.*
(✗ *I ~~haven't~~ to ...*)

*She isn't late – she **doesn't have to hurry**.*

3 We form questions with *do* or *does*.

***Do** I **have to go** to the dentist?* (✗ ~~*Have I to*~~ *...?*)

***Does** he **have to go** home now?*

4 All forms of *have to* are followed by the base form of the verb.

mustn't vs. don't have to

1 We use *mustn't* to say that it is necessary or very important <u>not</u> to do something.

*You **mustn't be** late.* *I **mustn't forget** to phone Jenny.*

2 *Mustn't* has a different meaning from *don't / doesn't have to*.

*You **don't have to tell** your friends.* (= It isn't necessary for you to tell them, but you can if you want to.)

*You **mustn't tell** your friends.* (= Don't tell your friends – it's a secret!)

Unit 8

Past continuous

1 We use the past continuous to talk about actions in progress at a certain time in the past.

*In 2012, we **were living** in the USA.*

*At 4 o'clock yesterday afternoon, I **was sitting** in a Maths lesson.*

*Last night, the TV was on, but I **wasn't watching it**.*

2 The past continuous is formed with the past simple of *be* + verb + *-ing*.

I ***was reading*** *a book. I* ***wasn't enjoying*** *it.*

You ***were running*** *very fast! But you* ***weren't winning****!*

Jo ***was playing*** *computer games. She* ***wasn't studying****.*

3 The question is formed with the past simple of *be* + subject + verb + *-ing*. Short answers are formed with *Yes* / *No* + pronoun + *was* / *were* or *wasn't* / *weren't*.

Was *James* ***running****? (✗ ~~James was running?~~)*

Yes, he ***was****. / No, he* ***wasn't****.*

Were *your parents* ***having*** *lunch?*

Yes, they ***were****. / No, they* ***weren't****.*

What ***were*** *you* ***studying****?* *Why* ***was*** *she* ***crying****?*

Past continuous vs. past simple

1 When we talk about the past, we use the past simple for actions that happened at one particular time. We use the past continuous for background actions.

When Alex ***arrived****, I* ***was having*** *dinner.*

He ***was running*** *very fast and he* ***didn't see*** *the tree.*

Sorry, what ***did*** *you* ***say****? I* ***wasn't listening****.*

(✗ I ~~didn't listen~~.)

2 We often use *when* with the past simple, and *while* with the past continuous.

I was reading ***when*** *the phone* ***rang****.*

When *my parents* ***arrived****, we were having a party.*

I went into the classroom ***while*** *the teacher* ***was talking****.*

While *my father* ***was running****, he fell into a river.*

Unit 9

Comparative adjectives

1 When we want to compare two things, or two groups of things, we use a comparative form + *than*.

I'm ***older than*** *my brother.*

France is ***bigger than*** *Britain.*

Your computer is ***better than*** *mine.*

2 With short adjectives, we normally add *-er*.

*old → old****er*** *cheap → cheap****er*** *clever → clever****er***

(✗ more old, more cheap, more clever)

If the adjective ends in *-e*, we only add *-r*.

*nice → nice****r*** *safe → safe****r***

If the adjective ends with consonant + *-y*, we change the *-y* to *-i* and add *-er*.

*easy → eas****ier*** *early → earl****ier*** *happy → happ****ier***

If the adjective ends in a consonant + vowel + consonant, we double the final consonant and add *-er*.

*big → bi****gger*** *sad → sa****dder*** *thin → thi****nner***

3 With longer adjectives (more than two syllables), we don't change the adjective – we put *more* in front of it.

expensive → ***more*** *expensive*

difficult → ***more*** *difficult*

interesting → ***more*** *interesting*

4 Some adjectives are irregular – they have a different comparative form.

good → ***better*** *bad →* ***worse*** *far →* ***further***

Superlative adjectives

1 When we compare something with two or more other things, we use a superlative form with *the*.

Steve is ***the tallest*** *boy in our class.*

Brazil is ***the biggest*** *country in South America.*

2 With short adjectives, we normally add *-est*.

*tall → the tall****est*** *short → the short****est***

*old → the old****est*** *clean → the clean****est***

Spelling rules for the *-est* ending are the same as for the *-er* ending in the comparative form.

*nice → nic****est*** *happy → the happ****iest***

*safe → the saf****est*** *big → the bi****ggest***

*easy → the eas****iest*** *thin → the thi****nnest***

3 With longer adjectives (more than two syllables), we don't change the adjective – we put *the most* in front of it.

delicious → the ***most*** *delicious*

important → the ***most*** *important*

intelligent → the ***most*** *intelligent*

This is ***the most important*** *day of my life.*

It's ***the most expensive*** *shop in town.*

4 Some adjectives are irregular.

good → ***the best*** *bad →* ***the worst*** *far →* ***the furthest***

Saturday is ***the best*** *day of the week.*

My team is ***the worst*** *team in the world!*

can / can't (ability)

1 We use *can* / *can't* + the base form of the verb to talk about someone's ability to do something. The form of *can* / *can't* is the same for every person.

My father ***can lift*** *100 kg.* *My brother* ***can't swim****.*

I ***can swim*** *5 kilometres.* *She* ***can't spell****.*

He ***can write*** *in Chinese.*

I ***can't lift*** *heavy things.*

2 To make questions, we use *Can* + subject + base form of the verb. Short answers are formed with *Yes / No* + pronoun + *can* or *can't*.

*Can your sister **swim**?* (✗ ~~*Does your sister can swim.*~~)
*Yes, she **can**.*

*Can you **lift** 50 kilos?* *No, I **can't**.*

Unit 10

be going to for plans and intentions

1 We use *be going to* to talk about things we intend to do in the future.

*I'**m going to visit** my grandfather tomorrow.*

*My sister'**s going to study** German at university.*

2 The form is the present simple of *be* + *going to* + base form of the verb.

*I'**m going to stay** at home on Sunday.*
(✗ ~~*I going*~~ *to stay …*) *I'**m not going to go** out.*

*She'**s going to look** around the shops. She **isn't going to buy** anything.*

***Are** you **going to watch** the film?*
(✗ ~~*You going*~~ *to watch …*)

***Is** he **going to give** us homework tonight?*

Short answers are formed using *Yes / No* + pronoun + the correct form of *be* (positive or negative).

Present continuous for future arrangements

We can use the present continuous to talk about arrangements for the future.

*We'**re having** a party next weekend.* (It's organised.)

*I'**m meeting** my friends in the park tomorrow.* (I talked to my friends and we agreed to meet.)
(✗ ~~*I meet*~~ *my friends … /* ~~*I'll meet*~~ *my friends …*)

*Our parents **are going** on holiday in Spain next month.* (They have their airline tickets and hotel reservation.)

Adverbs

1 Adverbs usually go with verbs – they describe an action:

*We **walked** home **slowly**.* (✗ *We walked* ~~*slow*~~*.*)
*The train **arrived late**.*

***Drive carefully**!*

2 A lot of adverbs are formed by adjective + *-ly*.

quiet → *quiet**ly*** *bad* → *bad**ly*** *polite* → *polite**ly***

If the adjective ends in *-le*, we drop the *-e* and add *-y*.

terrible → *terrib**ly*** *comfortable* → *comfortab**ly***

If the adjective ends in consonant + *-y*, we change the *-y* to *-i* and add *-ly*.

easy → *eas**ily*** *happy* → *happ**ily*** *lucky* → *luck**ily***

3 Some adverbs are irregular – they don't have an *-ly* ending.

good → ***well*** *fast* → ***fast*** *hard* → ***hard***

early → ***early*** *late* → ***late***

*I played **well** last week.* *He worked **hard** all day.*
*She ran very **fast**.*

4 Adverbs usually come immediately after the verb, or, if the verb has an object, after the object.

*She **sings well**.* *She **plays the piano well**.*

Unit 11

will / won't for future predictions

1 We use *will* (*'ll*) and *won't* to make predictions about the future.

*When I'm older, I'**ll travel** round the world. I **won't stay** here!*

*I'm sure you'**ll pass** the test tomorrow. The questions **won't be** very difficult.*

*In the future, people **will take** holidays on Mars. But people **won't live** there.*

2 We use *will / won't* + base form of the verb, and the form is the same for all subjects. We don't use any form of *do* in the negative.

*You'**ll pass** the test.* *You **won't pass** the test.*

*He'**ll pass** the test.* *He **won't pass** the test.*

3 Questions are formed with *will* + subject + base form of the verb. Again, we don't use any form of *do* in questions or short answers.

***Will** Andrea **go** to university?*
(✗ ~~*Does Andrea will go*~~ *…?*)

*Yes, she **will**. / No, she **won't**.*

***Will** your friends **come** to the party?*

*Yes, they **will**. / No, they **won't**.*

First conditional

1 In conditional sentences there are two clauses, an *if* clause and a result clause. We use the first conditional when it is possible or likely that the situation in the *if* clause will happen in the future.

*If I **pass** the test, my parents **will be** happy.* (= It's possible that I will pass, but I'm not sure.)

*If it **doesn't rain**, we'**ll go** for a walk.* (= Perhaps it will rain, but I'm not sure.)

2 The *if* clause is formed with *If* + subject + present simple. The result clause is formed with subject + *will* + base form of the verb. There is a comma after the *if* clause.

*If we **have** time, we'**ll do** some shopping.*
(✗ *If we* ~~*will*~~ *have time …*)

*If you **don't start** your homework soon, you **won't finish** it tonight.*

3 We can change the order of the two clauses. In this case, there is no comma between the clauses.

*We'**ll do** some shopping if we **have** time.*

*You **won't finish** your homework if you **don't start** it tonight.*

Time clauses with *when / as soon as*

In sentences about the future, we use the present tense after *when* or *as soon as*, and the *will* future in the main clause. (The structure of these sentences is very like the structure of 1st conditional sentences.)

*When I'**m** 18, I'**ll go** to university.*
*I'**ll call** you as soon as I **get** there.*

Unit 12

Present perfect simple with *ever / never*

1 We often use the present perfect to talk about things from the beginning of our life until now.

*Sandro **has travelled** to a lot of different countries.* (= from when he was born until now)

*I **haven't met** your parents.* (= at any time in my life, from when I was born until now)

2 When we use the present perfect with this meaning, we often use *ever* (= *at any time in someone's life*) in questions, and *never* (= *not ever*) in sentences. *Ever* comes between the noun or pronoun and the past participle. *Never* comes immediately after *have / has*.

*Have you **ever** eaten Thai food?*

(✗ ~~You have~~ ever eaten …?)

*I've **never** been interested in cooking.*

*Has he **ever** won a prize in a competition?*

*She's **never** tried to learn another language.*

3 The present perfect is formed with the present tense of *have* + past participle of the main verb. For regular verbs, the past participle has the same -*ed* ending as the past simple. Irregular verbs have different past participles.

Regular verbs	Irregular verbs
*We've **stayed** in Athens three times.* (✗ *We've stay …*)	*We've **been** there three times.*
*Have they ever **climbed** a mountain?*	*Have they ever **flown** in a plane?*

See Workbook page 128 for the past participles of irregular verbs.

4 There is a difference between *been* and *gone*.

*I've **been** to the supermarket* = I went to the supermarket and now I am back again.

*They've **gone** to the supermarket* = they went to the supermarket and they are still there.

Present perfect vs. past simple

Both the **present perfect** and the **past simple** refer to the past. But we use the **past simple** to talk about situations or actions at a particular time in the past, and we use the **present perfect** to talk about situations or actions in the past, at an unspecified time between the past and now.

Past simple
*I **ate** sushi **two weeks ago**.*
*I **read** a Shakespeare play **last month**.*
*He **was** late for school **yesterday**.*
*We **didn't buy** anything in town **on Saturday**.*

Present perfect
*I'**ve eaten** sushi a lot of times.*
*I'**ve read** six Shakespeare plays.*
*He'**s been** late to school four times.*
*We **haven't bought** anything in town for a long time.*

Speaking activities

Student A

Unit 2, page 25

Student A

1 You are a customer in a sports shop. You like a pair of trainers.
You want a black pair.
You want to know the price.
You want to try them on.

2 You are an assistant in a clothes shop. Student B likes a sweatshirt. It's €36.95. You have green, blue or red.

Unit 5, page 63

Student A

You and your friend have got £200. You are at a flea market buying furniture for a new room for your youth club. These are the prices of the pieces of furniture:

- 2 armchairs £30
- cooker £20
- shelf £5
- table with 8 chairs £70
- desk and lamp £25
- sofa £75
- large carpet £70
- mirror £10
- wardrobe £30
- small carpet £30
- sofa £40
- 8 posters of film stars £5

You want to buy the 2 armchairs, the large carpet, the cooker and the posters.

You do not want to buy the shelf or the wardrobe.

You are uncertain about the table with the 8 chairs and the sofas.

Have a conversation and agree on what to buy.

Unit 7, page 85

Student A

You are a son or daughter. You are at home.

You want to see a friend.

You are phoning your mum or dad about it.

When your mum/dad tells you that you should do some housework, ask her/him what you have to do.

Also, tell your mum/dad that there are some things she/he shouldn't forget. When she/he asks you what things, say:

She/He ...

- should do the shopping
- shouldn't be late tonight (you want to watch a DVD together with her/him)
- mustn't forget to bring some chocolate biscuits!

The line is not very good so you have to ask your mum or dad several times to repeat what she/he has said.

Unit 11, page 127

Student A

Ask your questions and answer Student B's.

1 What will you do if it rains this weekend?
2 What will you do if the weather's nice?
3 How will you feel if your teacher gives you a lot of homework today?
4 What will you wear if you go out to a party this evening?
5 What film will you see if you go to the cinema this week?
6 What programme will you watch if you watch TV this evening?

Student B

Unit 2, page 25

Student B

1 You are an assistant in a sports shop. Student A likes a pair of trainers. They're €34.99. You only have brown or red (not black).

2 You are a customer in a clothes shop. You like a sweatshirt.

You want a green one.

You want to know the price.

You want to try it on.

Unit 5, page 63

Student B

You and your friend have got £200. You are at a flea market buying furniture for a new room for your youth club. These are the prices of the pieces of furniture:

- 2 armchairs £30
- cooker £20
- shelf £5
- table with 8 chairs £70
- desk and lamp £25
- sofa £75
- large carpet £70
- mirror £10
- wardrobe £30
- small carpet £30
- sofa £40
- 8 posters of film stars £5

You want to buy the table with the 8 chairs, the cooker, the large carpet, and one of the sofas.

You do not want to buy the 2 armchairs or the posters.

You are uncertain about the desk and the lamp.

Have a conversation and agree on what to buy.

Unit 7, page 85

Student B

You are a mum or dad. Your son/daughter is phoning you.

Make sure he/she knows that he/she has to do some housework before he/she can go out. When he/she asks you, say:

He/She ...

- has to tidy up his/her room
- should load the dishwasher
- mustn't forget to vacuum the floor

When your son or daughter tells you that there are things you shouldn't forget, ask them what things.

The line is not very good so you have to ask your son or daughter several times to repeat what he/she has said.

Unit 11, page 127

Student B

Ask your questions and answer Student A's.

1 What will you do if you stay at home this weekend?

2 What will you study if you go to university?

3 What will you buy if you go shopping this weekend?

4 How will you feel if your parents ask you to do a lot of housework this evening?

5 What video game will you play if you decide to play video games this evening?

6 Where will you go if you meet your friends tonight?